Praise for
Shakespeare and the Resistance

"A wonderful book and an important contribution to Shakespeare studies. It flows like a good novel and takes the reader into the argument with scholarship and infectious enthusiasm. The neglected poems have been illuminated by this important commentary."

> —Michael Scott, author of *Shakespeare: A Complete Introduction*; honorary senior provost of the University of Wales Trinity Saint David

"Compelling. . . . Written with lovely clarity and verve."

> —Emma J. Smith, professor of English, Oxford University

"Continuing her learned and provocative account of Shakespeare's religion and politics in *Shadowplay*, Clare Asquith turns her attention, in this beautifully written and informative book, to the enigmatic narrative poems and persuasively argues that Henry VIII's Act of Supremacy, the pillaging of the monasteries, and the cruel suppression of every suspected challenge to Tudor hegemony are all referred to in Shakespeare's enigmatic *Rape of Lucrece*. Shakespeare would have been as gripped by such events as Russian writers were gripped by the communist terror, and as unable as they to express his thoughts directly. If you love Shakespeare, England, and our Christian heritage you will want this book by your bedside and that of your guests. Buy the book now, and prepare yourself for long evenings of fertile argument."

> —Sir Roger Scruton, editor of *The Salisbury Review*

"Another distinguished achievement. . . . Among other things, an excellent narrative of the last poignant months of Essex and his importance to Shakespeare and the Earl of Southampton. Asquith leads the way in impressing on our culture the power of the Catholic presence in Shakespeare and in England."

> —Dennis Taylor, professor emeritus of English at Boston College; editor emeritus of *Religion and the Arts*

"You don't have to agree with all the bold conclusions of this insightful and enjoyable book to relish its vivid and persuasive argument that we can and should renew our enquiry into Shakespeare's complex and disguised responses, under strict censorship, to the fraught and dangerous cultural politics of post-Reformation England."

> —Sir Michael Boyd, artistic director of the Royal Shakespeare Company, Stratford-upon-Avon, 2003–2012

SHAKESPEARE
AND THE
RESISTANCE

Also by Clare Asquith

*Shadowplay: The Hidden Beliefs and Coded
Politics of William Shakespeare*

SHAKESPEARE
— AND THE —
RESISTANCE

THE EARL *of* SOUTHAMPTON,
THE ESSEX REBELLION, *and*
THE POEMS THAT CHALLENGED
TUDOR TYRANNY

CLARE ASQUITH

PUBLICAFFAIRS

New York

PublicAffairs
Hachette Book Group
1290 Avenue of the Americas, New York, NY 10104
www.publicaffairsbooks.com
@Public_Affairs

Printed in the United States of America

First Edition: August 2018

Published by PublicAffairs, an imprint of Perseus Books, LLC, a subsidiary of Hachette Book Group, Inc. The PublicAffairs name and logo is a trademark of the Hachette Book Group.

The Hachette Speakers Bureau provides a wide range of authors for speaking events. To find out more, go to www.hachettespeakersbureau.com or call (866) 376-6591.

The publisher is not responsible for websites (or their content) that are not owned by the publisher.

Print book interior design by Amy Quinn.

Library of Congress Cataloging-in-Publication Data

Names: Asquith, Clare, author.
Title: Shakespeare and the resistance: the Earl of Southampton, the Essex Rebellion, and the poems that challenged Tudor tyranny / Clare Asquith.
Description: First edition. | New York: PublicAffairs, June 2018. | Includes bibliographical references and index.
Identifiers: LCCN 2018019816| ISBN 9781568588124 (hardback) | ISBN 9781568588117 (ebook)
Subjects: LCSH: Shakespeare, William, 1564–1616—Political and social views. | Shakespeare, William, 1564–1616—Poetic works. | Shakespeare, William, 1564–1616. Venus and Adonis. | Shakespeare, William, 1564–1616. Rape of Lucrece. | Politics and literature—Great Britain—History—16th century. | Political poetry, English—History and criticism. | BISAC: HISTORY / Europe / Great Britain. | LITERARY CRITICISM / Shakespeare.
Classification: LCC PR3017 .A76 2018 | DDC 821/.3—dc23
LC record available at https://lccn.loc.gov/2018019816

ISBNs: 978-1-56858-812-4 (hardcover), 978-1-56858-811-7 (ebook)

LSC-C

10 9 8 7 6 5 4 3 2 1

For Raymond

CONTENTS

INTRODUCTION

THE PRACTICE OF detecting covert contemporary references and hidden political allusions in the works of Shakespeare has a long and derided history. The Victorian poet Algernon Swinburne joked that Romeo must be a hidden caricature of Elizabeth I's all-powerful minister, Lord Burghley, precisely because of the cunning dissimilarity.[1] Shakespeare's universality, the fact that he speaks to us all on a profound level, means that we resent any attempt by academic, social, nationalist, religious, or political groups to appropriate him, to label and therefore limit him. This has not stopped thousands from trying. He has been variously portrayed as an Italian, a covert homosexual, a Jesuit, Francis Bacon, Christopher Marlowe, the Earl of Oxford; he has been by turns a loyalist, a dissident, a Tudor apologist, an atheist, a Catholic, a Protestant, a Puritan, an elitist, a populist, a proto-Marxist, and the love-child of Elizabeth I.

The unenviable task of Shakespeare scholars is to preserve the integrity of the text in the face of this barrage. But two awkward elements stand in their way. One is Shakespeare's famously undocumented background, which has been fully exploited by biographical fantasists in particular. The other is the fact that his work lacks a contemporary context, compounding the sense that Shakespeare exists in a kind of historical vacuum. His plots, situated at other periods or in other countries, are taken almost entirely from books, not from contemporary events. Even the themes are difficult to relate to the accepted view of the age and country in which he lived, and of which he has become almost a symbol—England on the rise: buoyant, self-confident, the victor of the Spanish Armada, a newly independent nation launched on the path of expansion and empire by a canny and charismatic queen. Their extraordinary creative vigour apart, Shakespeare's plays and poems seem curiously detached from all this. His themes revolve around social and political division, usurpation, the destructive work of time, coercion, tyranny. One of his biographers, Peter Ackroyd, highlights what he sees as Shakespeare's main preoccupations: they include divided loyalty, exile, the murder of innocence, the unquiet conscience, the perils of oath-taking, disguise, and sympathy with failure.[2] Literary critics locate the genesis of this conflicted material either somewhere in his shadowy private life or in the source of his universality—his insight into human nature.

Over the past fifteen years, however, certain historians—some of them, like Peter Lake, cautiously deferential, others, like Curtis Breight, angrily incensed—have begun to invade the territory of Shakespeare scholarship. Initially this was to challenge the recent 'New Historicist' angle on the sixteenth century, which aimed to reassess the literature and drama by setting it in what was understood to be the cultural and intellectual context of the time. Normally the first step in studying the creative work of the past, this approach, especially in the case of the context-free Shakespeare, was long overdue. But the historicists found they had stumbled into a hornets' nest. Elizabeth's reign, the last years in particular, have been undergoing a lengthy and contentious process of reassessment. According to many current historians, the New Historicists were working on an outdated and misconceived version of the period. They had been given the wrong handbook.

Stephen Greenblatt's influential 1989 analysis of the plays, *Shakespearean Negotiations*, drew on a series of long-held assumptions about Elizabeth's reign.[3] Power lay with the queen: yet, in material terms, she was weak. She had no standing army, no bureaucracy, and no police force to speak of. She relied instead on theatrical display and rhetorical persuasion: and with such success that, though 'a weak and feeble woman', she retained power for almost fifty years—and commanded the devotion of her subjects throughout, which, as she often declared, 'I do esteem more than any treasure or riches'. This was an age, then, when theatricality was the source of power: a great starting point for Shakespeare scholars.

But late Tudor power is not seen this way anymore. Instead, the latest body of evidence indicates that Elizabeth presided over a highly successful police state. In the view of Curtis Breight, her weakness had from the start compelled her 'to make alliances with some of the most clever and ruthless men ever to control the English state, lawyerly humanists who knew how to weave plots and engineer harsh legislation'.[4] Scholars such as Breight paint a picture of a country kept in check by terror and by the deliberate fomenting of aggressive wars abroad. They have highlighted damning evidence of the corrupt political dominance of Lord Burghley (William Cecil) and his son Robert, and have revised the traditional image of their doomed opponent, the Earl of Essex. So brilliant was the propaganda machine under the Cecils that Essex has been seen ever since his fall as an inept victim of a struggle between court factions. Over the past twenty years, however, thanks to the work of scholars led by Paul Hammer and Alexandra Gajda, Essex has emerged as a political and intellectual heavyweight whose ideals and character mobilised all those who had become disgusted by the self-serving rule of what was then known as the *regnum Cecilianum*, the reign of the Cecils.[5] Power, it now appears, resided not in the dazzling spectacle of the queen, but in the iron fist of her ministers: and this means, say historians, that as far as Shakespeare goes, the historicists have got the story wrong. Elizabeth's men, as hitherto marginalised evidence demonstrates, were experts in the use of torture, intimidation, propaganda, and the use of agents provocateurs to create the 'mass paranoia' of a society ridden with informers.[6]

A further aspect of the opposition to the Cecils has also recently come under scrutiny: the huge and varied corpus of political writings by Elizabethan exiles, many of them senior academics from Oxford and Cambridge. In 1594, the Jesuit Robert Persons's *Conference About the Next Succession*, a controversial analysis of the English political system and the problems of succession, was circulated in England. Merely to possess it was treasonable. Often vilified but rarely read, it has recently been described as a 'great tract' by the historian Peter Lake—an attitude unthinkable even ten years ago, when these often lucid and well-informed works were dismissed by mainstream academics as mere Catholic propaganda.[7] Altogether, says Breight, 'it is necessary that someone yank the Elizabethan Myth from its traditionally privileged position and thereby help to counter some four centuries of what Christopher Haigh calls "reverential historiography"'.[8] But the myth has deep roots.

In 2016, Peter Lake published a study of Shakespeare's history plays interpreting them in the light of the newly rehabilitated opposition discourse. The long preface is diffident, even apologetic, attempting—in vain, as it turned out—to deflect the disdain of Shakespeare scholars. Yet what Lake unearths is, he

believes, of such importance that, as a historian, he has no hesi-
tation in regarding the plays as source material, as an insight into
the ways in which Shakespeare and his contemporaries 'actually
thought about "politics"'. 'If I noticed these parallels,' he asks,
'might not members of an Elizabethan audience have noticed
them as well?'[9]

There is a world of difference between reading in meanings and unearthing them. The new directions pioneered by
recent historians amount to a radical shift in the consensus on
what it was like to live in England at the turn of the seventeenth
century. It is becoming clear that successive generations have
bought into a diligently documented propaganda myth spun
around the Elizabethan state by leading ministers of the Crown.
Now crumbling, this myth has for centuries formed the foundation stone of an England which dated the birth of its empire and
the establishment of its national church back to the days of the
Tudors, and adopted Shakespeare as its national figurehead.

My own interest in this shift of historical perspective—and
its impact on sixteenth-century literature—began almost twenty
years ago. My ancestry includes multiple countercultural strands,
from French Huguenot immigrants to an early member of the
Irish Republican Brotherhood, who, after his imprisonment in
Dublin, became a journalist and campaigner for human rights
in New York. My father's great-grandfather, an artist and architect, was a close colleague of Cardinal John Henry Newman.
His son was the scholar John Hungerford Pollen, who almost
single-handedly researched, transcribed, and saved for posterity
the records of the Elizabethan exiles. Growing up, I was always
conscious that there was an alternative view of the Elizabethan
period, but never questioned the traditional version, which was
revitalised for my own generation by the ebullient Tudor apologist A. L. Rowse. However, living in Moscow in the 1980s, I

experienced at first hand the way art, cinema, and drama operate in a totalitarian state—ostensibly toeing the government line, but actually using covert references to give release to the frustrations of a silenced population. I returned to England at the point when the 'revisionist' history of the sixteenth century was beginning to seep into the mainstream, and it encouraged me to look again at the neglected Catholic records and the recent work of scholars such as Patrick Collinson and Michael Questier, who explore the way in which religious dissidents survived—or did not—under Elizabeth.[10]

In 2001, I published an article in the *Times Literary Supplement* proposing a contemporary religious context for Shakespeare's mysterious poem 'The Phoenix and the Turtle'.[11] It was developed two years later in the same journal by the lawyer and historian Patrick Martin and the distinguished legal philosopher John Finnis.[12] My 2005 book, *Shadowplay*, drew on the work of many other scholars to propose a continuous religious and political subtext underlying Shakespeare's work and seamlessly integrated with the universal meaning. It was welcomed by historians and others, including the artistic director of the Royal Shakespeare Company, Michael Boyd, who commissioned programme notes on his history play cycle along with a series of talks to the cast. But it was vehemently rejected by Shakespeare scholars, who portrayed it as merely another attempt to prove that he was a Catholic. For David Scott Kastan, the search for allegory in Shakespeare's work is simply a 'category error', and Alison Shell's *Shakespeare and Religion* firmly distances her own view of Shakespeare's work from 'would-be allegorists' like myself and G. Wilson Knight.[13] Shakespeare is, she says, 'highly attentive' to religious tradition, but his 'invariable practice' is to 'subordinate religious matter to the particular aesthetic demands of the work in hand'.[14] In other words, topical issues may be visible—and Alison Shell is one of the scholars most sensitive to their presence—but their purpose is merely to intensify the impact of what was intended to be, first and foremost, an aesthetic work of art.

In this book I examine a single event, the Essex Rebellion of 1601, which, like so many other events of the time, has been reassessed over the past twenty years in the light of new work in local county records and the British National Archive. It sets the latest version of the rebellion side by side with two works by Shakespeare which are now rarely read: his full-length narrative poems. The purpose is to demonstrate that the poems remain impenetrable without the historical context; and that once understood, they, in their turn, serve to illuminate the causes and the consequences of this dramatic turning point, one of the most momentous of Elizabeth's reign, and, until recently, one of the most consistently misread.

This approach confirms the latest assessments of the widespread appeal of Essex and his cause. It also seeks to persuade readers that the supposedly detached, apolitical Shakespeare had opinions and was deeply engaged. The focus on his neglected writings is intended to sidestep the traditional resistance to topical readings of his universal work. By highlighting political subtexts in the marginalised narrative poems, this book demonstrates that a readiness to detect a highly sophisticated contemporary subtext does not diminish our appreciation of Shakespeare's work; on the contrary, it can actually make sense of its many obscurities. This book challenges the view that Shakespeare always subordinated the topical to the universal, that he never referred directly to the events of his own time, and that if he had done so it would have made him in some way a lesser genius. Instead, *Shakespeare and the Resistance* argues that in certain works Shakespeare took universal characters and ideas and applied them quite deliberately to the political circumstances of his own time. He did this partly because his era was one in which overt criticism of the regime was dangerous and allegory a useful deflection. But more important to Shakespeare were the themes that characterised sixteenth-century Europe, a time of such bloody upheaval and national convulsion that nothing less than the soul of England, its historical and spiritual essence, was at risk. It required a writer of extraordinary genius to find a way to adequately depict the passions of those days. To do so, he drew on classical scenes, reworking them brilliantly to speak to his fellow men and women about the deep divisions that threatened to break the country apart.

CHAPTER ONE

THE PRISONER

HANGING IN THE collection at Boughton House in
Northamptonshire is a curious portrait of a young nobleman incarcerated in the Tower of London. It was painted around
the year 1603 by the distinguished court artist John de Critz,
and the subject is Henry Wriothesley, the thirty-year-old Earl
of Southampton. For a man condemned to indefinite imprisonment for treachery, he looks surprisingly at ease as he lounges at
a window, a cat at his elbow. The diamond panes and wooden
paneling suggest a comfortable cell suited to his rank. His black
clothes are trimmed with lace. Celebrated for his beauty, Wriothesley was depicted from an early age with long, often elaborately coiffed hair—a deliberate affectation in an era when men
normally wore their hair short. Here, the famous hair is spread
loosely over his collar. Always a dandy, he wears a single glove
with a striking design of large black ribbons on white cuffs: his
left hand is conspicuously extended, apparently to display his unusually long, delicate fingers. There is a ring on the little finger

and a bracelet of tiny red coral beads at his wrist. Next to him lies a book bearing his coat of arms.

To the top right is a cameo of the Tower of London, indicating where he is and why. He was a key player in an abortive plot against Elizabeth's regime in 1601, a rising widely viewed by later historians as an impulsive act of folly on the part of Elizabeth's onetime favourite Robert Devereux, Earl of Essex. The long hair, the jewellery, the gloves, the cat, all suggest the immaturity and love of display which many believe drew Southampton to the circle of the charismatic Essex, and which, cited at his trial, saved him from following his leader to the block. The apparent vanity behind this Tower portrait fits this traditional view of Southampton as a narcissist and a hothead, a man who could be dismissed by one of his contemporaries, Lady Bridget Manners, as too 'young, fantastical and easily carried away' to be taken seriously.[1] The commission of an elaborate painting of himself in the role of state prisoner appears to be just one more instance of his 'fantastical' tendency, which clearly went too far for some of his descendants. In a copy which once belonged to the Wriothesley family, the picture of the Tower in the top corner has been omitted, presumably to erase embarrassing evidence of the disgraceful episode.[2]

But back at the turn of the seventeenth century, such pictures were read differently. Early viewers of the portrait would have interpreted its oddities symbolically, and for them it would have carried a political message. To Essex's many highly placed sympathisers, the imprisoned Southampton was an emblem of courage and integrity. In a sombre, thoughtful poem, their protégé, the influential poet Samuel Daniel, expresses admiration and support. Southampton's stance during the rebellion and afterwards clearly took those who shared Bridget Manners's opinion of him by surprise. He was not, it turned out, the playboy they had all assumed. 'How could we know', asks Daniel, 'that thou coulds't have endured / With a reposed cheer, wrong and disgrace?'[3] Later generations may have viewed the young Southampton as misguided, but Daniel presents him as a model of constancy and virtue, comparing him with classical opponents of injustice, corruption, and tyranny.

Closer examination indicates that we are indeed looking at a man who saw himself as a prisoner of conscience. Under the picture of the Tower is inscribed 'In vinculis invictus'—'in chains, but undefeated': defiant words which suggest a man suffering for a cause. Moreover, the conditions, and the prisoner, are not as comfortable as they at first appear. The elegant folds around Southampton's left arm in fact form a sling, a reminder of the serious but unspecified illness he suffered in the Tower, which left him unable to raise his arms or walk, and which almost killed him. His right arm is swollen; he is leaning against the windowsill for support, rather than striking a pose. A crack in the window reveals bright daylight outside, showing up the patchy, greenish grime on the glass as well as on the wall behind his head. The hair, beard, and moustache are wispy and unkempt, and his eyes, gazing steadily at the viewer, are deep-set and hooded. The book bearing the Wriothesley coat of arms is turned upside down, a reminder that he had been stripped of his wealth, estate, and rank. In another symbolic touch, the book is also imprisoned—attached by a ribbon to a metal fixing just under the window ledge. The jewellery on the unnaturally white hand now takes on a new significance. Coral was the traditional protection against infection and poison. The black and gold mourning ring is a reminder of the fate of his leader, the Earl of Essex, who had been executed as a traitor within the walls of the Tower, a fate which for three years, as his enemies plotted against him, was a daily possibility for Southampton. And finally, as in earlier portraits of Southampton, there is an oblique but emphatic religious motif. The window, book, and cuff all carry images of the cross—there are eight of them in all on the left-hand side of the picture, while four cross-shaped arrow-slits have been superimposed on the image of the Tower walls.[4]

A picture of this quality could of course only have been commissioned after Southampton had recovered his freedom, money, and status. The painted calendar under the Tower ends in April 1603, the month Southampton was set free by Elizabeth's grateful successor, James I, whose claim to the throne of England had always been supported by the Essex circle. And this brings us to the most disconcerting feature of the picture— the black and white cat crouched at the window, its head alertly cocked and the claws only partially sheathed. There is no evidence that Southampton ever had such a pet while he was a prisoner. But for Southampton's contemporaries, the image of a business-like cat sitting between a prisoner and his cell window would have recalled the widely circulated tale of a man who did. Around a century earlier, the courtier Sir Henry Wyatt had also suffered imprisonment for supporting a disputed claim to the throne of England—that of James I's great-great-grandfather, Henry VII. Richard III had imprisoned Wyatt for refusing to withdraw his allegiance to Henry even under torture. According to family legend, he was saved from starvation when a cat he befriended brought pigeons to his cell, which were cooked by an obliging jailer. Afterwards, Sir Henry, who became one of the new king's leading councillors, 'would ever make much of cats'; the story itself was made much of by the Wyatt family, ever keen to proclaim their loyalty to the Tudor successors of Henry VII.[5]

Here, then, is one reason why Southampton can describe himself as 'invictus'. Mystifying to us, the carefully depicted cat, its black fur merging companionably with the black jacket of the prisoner, would have reminded the Stuart court of Southampton's early, costly adoption of the cause of King James by aligning it with the story of Henry Wyatt's equally costly allegiance to James's Tudor ancestor. The portrait begins to look less like a piece of vain self-publicity, and more like evidence of a sharp political mind at work. And this fits with what we know of Southampton. He continued to play his cards shrewdly during the Stuart reign, beginning as a court favourite and becoming a leading player in affairs of state, one of the few to retain his political integrity until his death some twenty years later.

Attempting to step back into the mindset of the original viewers of this picture not only deepens our enjoyment of the skill of the artist, but invites us to reconsider crucial aspects of the key events of the day. Evidently not everyone thought Southampton was a flighty playboy and the Earl of Essex an ambitious hothead. In fact, a wide circle of nobility and literati in both England and Scotland, including James VI, supported Essex until his fall. But when it came to open confrontation, almost all of them remained on the sidelines. Their caution is understandable. Essex's programme included policies considerably more dangerous than support for the Stuart succession. He was denounced at his trial for proposing religious toleration and for attacking the corruption of the leading politicians who engineered his downfall, and who continued to dominate the country after his execution. The nobleman and poet Fulke Greville burned his play about Antony and Cleopatra in case it was read as an allegory of Essex, while Samuel Daniel and other writers were closely interrogated and punished by the Privy Council for suspect references in their work.

Powerful figures in the Privy Council ensured that the reasons for Essex's immense popularity in the last decade of

Elizabeth's reign were comprehensively erased and forgotten. Instead they laid the groundwork for his later portrayal as an unstable lightweight who owed his advancement to the queen's attachment to him, overreached himself, and became the naïve victim of factional infighting at court. Accounts of the more disreputable episodes in his life were widely circulated at the time, and they have been repeated ever since in countless histories, films, and novels—the moment, for instance, when Essex reached for his sword when the queen slapped him, or the infamous incident when, spattered with mud, he burst into the queen's bedroom before she was dressed. Consistently overlooked are his military and political achievements, his charm of character, his personal code of honour, his huge popularity at court and in the country. Essex has been presented to us as an emotional and irresponsible court favourite whose intemperate actions were outmanoevred, happily for the country, by wiser and steadier counsellors close to the queen.

As for Southampton, he would have been forgotten by now, along with the rest of Essex's inner circle, were it not for a chance connection. He is the only person to whom William Shakespeare dedicated any of his literary works. These two long poems—*Venus and Adonis*, published in 1593, and *The Rape of Lucrece*, published one year later, in 1594—are barely read now. But on the strength of their dedications, particularly the warm and intimate preface to the second poem, expressing love 'without end' from a writer wholly 'devoted yours', he has been excitedly identified by many with the 'Mr W.H.' to whom the far racier sonnets are dedicated. As many of these are love poems addressed to a fair young man, and as Southampton as a young man cultivated a bisexual image, the assumption is that the link between the two men was romantic; that 'Mr W.H.' was code for Henry Wriothesley; and that the young and beautiful

Southampton was, as Shakespeare puts it in one of his sonnets, 'the master-mistress of my passion'.[6]

So Southampton survives in popular histories as Shakespeare's wilful, beloved young man, just as Essex survives as Elizabeth's beloved, unstable favourite—both of them glamorous appendages to the two greatest figures of the age. But de Critz's odd portrait, and Daniel's obscure, neglected poem, suggest that 'the world', as Daniel calls those fellow admirers, took a different view. And the more closely we examine these two works, the more surprising that view becomes. The epigraph to Daniel's poem is taken from Seneca, the classical writer who, along with Tacitus, was one of the favourite authors of the Essex circle.[7] Like the poem, the quotation praises fortitude in adversity. But for both Seneca and Tacitus, the adversity was very often of a particular kind—the oppression endured by victims of tyranny. The same disturbing suggestion underlies the Tower portrait. Richard III, a popular embodiment of tyranny, was supposed to have personally stretched Sir Henry Wyatt on the rack; his grandson added one of the instruments of torture that had been used on Sir Henry—a wrench known as a 'barnacle'— to the Wyatt coat of arms. Southampton was not tortured; in fact, considering he had been one of the leaders of a seditious rebellion, he was let off lightly. And very few historians have portrayed Elizabeth I, even in her later years, as a tyrant. So are the shadowy links with Richard III and Seneca's wicked rulers a step too far? Could the opponents of the late Elizabethan regime really cast themselves as enemies, not simply of injustice, but of tyranny?

This book will propose an answer to this question, which draws on the latest researches into Southampton and Essex, the nature and extent of their following, and the volatile political context in which authors like Greville, Daniel, and Shakespeare wrote their plays and poems. But it will also suggest that the most eloquent and penetrating witness to the true motivation behind the suppressed opposition to the Tudor regime is Shakespeare himself; that it is only now, as scholars begin to uncover the nature and extent of the late Elizabethan resistance, that we can begin to hear his testimony, and to appreciate its breadth and sophistication. But a further question remains. If this testimony does indeed exist, why has it been hidden for the past four hundred years?

It is a surprising fact that the scholarship surrounding the relationship between Shakespeare and Southampton, his one known patron, has been focused on the single 1609 edition of the sonnets, a work that was not actually dedicated to him. Meanwhile, the two works that were written explicitly for Southampton have been all but ignored. This is even more surprising given their runaway popularity at the time. These were the two works that made Shakespeare's name; indeed, they became a byword for literary success. 'Who loves not Adon's love, or Lucrece rape?' sigh the satirical authors of the Parnassus plays, a series of witty, topical skits written for the students of St John's College, Cambridge, some five years after the poems' publication.[8] The writers mock smitten fans like the fop Gullio, who cries, 'Let this duncified world esteem of Spenser and Chaucer, I'll worship sweet Mr. Shakespeare, and to honour him will lay his *Venus and Adonis* under my pillow.'

Had Shakespeare stopped at *Venus and Adonis*—the fashionable poem idolised by foppish rakes like Gullio, who, according to the Parnassus plays, used it as a romantic handbook—our image of Southampton as an irresponsible playboy would have remained much the same. It is just the kind of calling card Bridget Manners might have expected an aspiring poet to present to the effete young earl: a wittily perverse take on a familiar

classical tale, gently mocking the vain attempts of an overpowering, passion-driven Venus to seduce a pouting, reluctant young
Adonis. True, there are longueurs for modern readers: it contains
too many digressions, too many artificial, rhetorical arias on the
part of Venus, suited to Renaissance tastes, perhaps, but not to
ours. But though it is unclear exactly what the point of the poem
is, the playful, ironic, tender tone and saucy subject matter mean
that it occasionally makes it onto the school syllabus, and it has
been successfully staged as a puppet play in London and Stratford
by the Royal Shakespeare Company.

The title of *The Rape of Lucrece* suggests that it will be more
of the same—another sensuous, provocative take on a classical
motif. It, too, was a best seller, and was frequently mentioned by
contemporaries in the same admiring tones as *Venus and Adonis*.
Indeed, discriminating readers, such as the scholarly Gabriel
Harvey, rated it more highly, even going so far as to compare
it with Shakespeare's finest play. 'The younger sort take much
delight in Shakespeare's Venus and Adonis', he wrote, 'but his
Lucrece, and his tragedie of Hamlet, Prince of Denmark, have it
in them to please the wiser sort'.[9]

If *Venus and Adonis* is now largely forgotten, *The Rape of Lucrece* has sunk almost without trace. Long, slow-moving, ponder-
ous, more weighted than ever with irrelevance and digression,
it is a challenge even for modern editors, one of whom commented wearily that it was 'overstocked with words'.[10] In what
way would this sententious, moralising piece have appealed to
the supposedly frivolous Southampton? And yet, for Shakespeare, this was his great gift to his patron—the 'graver labour'
that would eclipse the 'unpolished lines' of the earlier poem.
Here was worthy evidence of the love 'without end' he professed for his patron. 'What I have done is yours', he wrote at
the beginning of this second poem: 'what I have to do is yours;

being part in all I have, devoted yours'. Given the profound seriousness with which Shakespeare undertook this work, and the praise it won from the 'wiser sort' among his contemporaries, why, for us, is this poem all but unreadable?

The answer, as with the Tower portrait, may just be that for centuries we have been looking at it the wrong way. In the past twenty years, historians have opened up a new perspective on the last years of Elizabeth's reign. Set side by side with *The Rape of Lucrece*, the fresh context enables us to approach this neglected work with new eyes, allowing the poem to emerge as the *Hamlet*-like masterpiece Shakespeare's contemporaries believed it to be. In the following pages we will plunge into the way these people saw their own past, their future, and the predicament of their country. The result will deepen our understanding of the motivation of all those who openly or secretly joined the growing tide of opposition focused on the Earl of Essex and his second-in-command, the Earl of Southampton. It will demonstrate that in the early 1590s, when he wrote these poems, Shakespeare was among them. And it will enable us to relive the dramatic events leading up to the 1601 rebellion, using Shakespeare's own prescient analysis as a guide.

CHAPTER TWO

SUICIDE OR MURDER?

Two of Rembrandt's most haunting masterpieces are of a woman in the act of committing suicide. They were painted in the early 1660s, towards the end of his life. The portraits are close up, top lit, and set against a dark background. We are shown in miraculous detail the pallor, the glimmer of sweat on the brow, the reddened eyes filled with tears, the gleaming pearls at the throat and ears, the richly brocaded gown, and the white shift underneath. In the first portrait, the woman's extended right hand grips a dagger and her lips are slightly parted— this is her moment of final decision. The palm and fingers of the left hand are spread out towards the viewer in an ambiguous gesture—restraint, perhaps. In the second portrait, the gown has slipped back to reveal blood streaming down from an unseen wound in her left side and beginning to cling to the white fabric that covers it. She is paler now, her forehead glistens, her head inclines gently to her left, and she is tugging feebly at a gold cord or chain, maybe to summon her husband and father to witness her death.

Rembrandt's contemporaries would have recognised her at once. Her tale had been retold and repainted hundreds of times over the past two thousand years. Shakespeare, Southampton, and Essex would have read it in the original as schoolboys. She is Lucretia, wife of Collatinus, victim of the lust and brutality of the wily Sextus Tarquinius, son of the last king of ancient Rome.

The story first appears around 20 BC; it is told in poetry by Ovid, and in prose by the historian Livy.[1] A fledgling Rome is besieging Ardea, capital of a neighbouring people, the Rutuli. Around the campfire the talk turns to faithless wives. An argument develops as to whose wife is the most constant; finally, late at night, some of the men gallop back to Rome to check on their women. Only Collatinus's wife is at home, virtuously spinning with her maids as she worries about her absent husband. Collatinus is triumphant—but for his wife, Lucretia, the test proves fatal. The party's leader, Tarquin, is the king's son. He returns secretly the next evening and rapes her. If she resists, he says, he will pin the rape on a slave and kill them both. In despair after the rape, Lucretia tells her husband and father what has happened and, ignoring their protests that she is innocent, draws a knife and kills herself. The witnesses swear a solemn oath to avenge her, and her fate becomes a rallying call for the oppressed Roman people. Led by her kinsman Lucius Junius Brutus, they rise up against the hated Tarquin kings, and the first Roman Republic is born.

Why was this story so popular? Shakespeare himself seems to have it constantly at the back of his mind. It reverberates through the themes and language of his great plays, and there are frequent passing allusions: the villain and the raped victim in *Titus Andronicus* are linked with Tarquin and Lucrece; Lucrece is twice connected with Olivia, the heroine of *Twelfth Night*; Maria in *Taming of the Shrew* will prove, Petruchio hopes, another Lucrece; Macbeth moves 'with Tarquin's ravishing strides' towards the murder of King Duncan (2.1.55); in *Cymbeline*, the prurient Iachimo, creeping into Imogen's bedchamber, remembers how Tarquin, too, 'did softly press the rushes, ere he waken'd / The chastity he wounded' (2.2.11–12).

Shakespeare's contemporaries seem obsessed by her too. Inn-signs, printers' emblems, jewels, household objects, woodcuts, engravings, and paintings all depicted Lucrece, who is recognisable by her dagger and her rich clothes—or lack of any clothes at all. In the sixteenth century, Lucas Cranach the Elder turned out dozens of sinuously naked Lucreces, elegantly posed as they toy delicately with daggers. Titian depicted the rape itself more than once, setting his bejeweled Lucrece against a magnificently swathed and curtained bed—Veronese, Tintoretto, Rubens, and many others did the same. Like Mars and Venus, the subject provided an ideal showcase for the artists' skills in rendering human anatomy, and the results were clearly winners with their patrons.

The story was simultaneously an erotic fable and a morality tale—Lucrece from the beginning was held up as a model of wifely chastity who dies to protect her husband's reputation. However sensuous the pictures, Lucrece's expression is always one of nobility, and the pearls she wears symbolise inviolable purity. Livy makes her a majestic Roman heroine, upright and statuesque; Ovid's Lucrece is more gently appealing, but equally noble: 'Though you forgive me, I cannot forgive myself', she says as she draws the knife. Later, Geoffrey Chaucer and John

Gower both include her in their poetic catalogues of virtuous women—Chaucer goes so far as to call her a saint.[2]

Some theologians condemned her as a suicide, but for others Lucrece became a scapegoat or sacrificial lamb, the innocent victim who takes on the crime of the transgressor as well as the criminal injury. Certain representations of her, Rembrandt's among them, include Christ-like references—outspread arms, a stab wound in the left side, an expression of tragic acceptance. Rembrandt's Lucrece, at once homely and beautiful, expresses this acute inner dilemma, which was well described by the celebrated poet, soldier, and courtier Philip Sidney, Shakespeare's near contemporary, who wrote of 'the constant though lamenting look of Lucretia, when she punished in herself another's fault'.[3]

As well as the ancient story's mild eroticism and moral edification, for almost everyone there was a third reason why the story of the rape exerted such a magnetic pull right through to the nineteenth century: this was a tale of political power. Lucrece was raped not just by a man, but by a prince, and her courageous stand did more than vindicate her chastity—it brought down an entire political system and heralded the first Roman Republic. Botticelli's static, stylised fifteenth-century Lucrece is puzzling until we realise the painting celebrates the civic and humanist virtues of republican Florence. Lucrece's decorously clothed body lies on a sarcophagus at the base of vertiginous pillars, arches, pediments, and colonnades. A dark marble column in the centre appears to spring from her body, so that it seems that it is out of her corpse that this serene, airy, neoclassical city has sprung. Theatrically grouped around her in stylised poses of anger and grief are the future republican rebels, led by a dark, lowering Brutus. Brutus's brandished sword, on which the oath to bring down the tyrannical Tarquins has just been sworn, points upwards to the top of the column, where stands another classic champion of the underdog, David, hand on hip, Goliath's head at his feet.

The Protestant Reformation in the first half of the sixteenth century set princes against the church, and people against princes, in a new and cataclysmic development that convulsed the whole of Europe. The precise balance of power between ruler and subject became the most incendiary issue of the age, above all in England, where Henry VIII's three children— Edward VI, Mary, and Elizabeth I—successively brought in new forms of religion, enforcing their choices with high-profile burnings and disembowellings.

With the breakup of Christendom, religious wars and rebellions flickered across the Western world, and central to most of them was the question of the role of the monarch. Should a national ruler take over the powers of the papacy, as Henry VIII did? Or should he resign spiritual matters to his country's religious leaders? Should he introduce a measure of toleration, as Frederick of Bohemia and Henri IV of France did? For Martin Luther, who was horrified at the bloodshed the Reformation had unleashed among the German peasants, the solution was simple: the religion of the prince should be the religion of his people. For his fellow reformers John Calvin and Huldrych Zwingli, in Geneva and Zurich, respectively, the answer was more complicated. In the ideal godly states they conceived, the temporal monarch had no say over individual conscience. In the Netherlands, the brutal Duke of Alva enforced Catholicism at the point of the sword on behalf of the Spanish king, Philip II; in Cornwall and Devon, under Edward VI, foreign mercenaries were used to suppress the widespread 'Prayer Book Rebellion'; and in the north of England, over eight hundred people were killed in savage reprisals after the 1569 'Northern Rising' against Elizabeth's Protestant settlement.

Massacres triggered by the religious issue occurred in Ireland, the Low Countries, Germany, and France. Agonised writers and polemicists grappled with the problem, often writing in exile or under pseudonyms to avoid reprisals. Right across the religious spectrum, from Robert Persons, the English Jesuit, to Hubert Languet, the French Huguenot, political theorists were advancing anti-absolutist and republican ideas that even included regicide. How should a subject react to tyranny? Was deposition ever justifiable? As for what form a republic should take, the debate was endless and inconclusive. Meanwhile, rulers continued to force their subjects to betray their consciences by forbidding them to practice the religion of their own choosing. And wherever this occurred, the persecuted and those who spoke and wrote on their behalf often cited two well-known heroines. One was the blood-curdling biblical figure of Judith, who, to protect the religion of her people, beheaded the tyrant Holofernes. The other was Lucrece. Along with her champion, Lucius Junius Brutus, she was regularly invoked as a figurehead of popular movements from the Reformation right through to the nineteenth century.

Martin Luther was among the first to cite her in this way. After the German Peasants' Revolt of 1524, ending in the brutal torture and massacre of over one hundred thousand peasants in south and central Germany, he commended the patience of Lucrece to his followers, though not her resistance. Like Lucrece, they should submit their cause to a higher power rather than running amok like 'mad dogs'.[4] Across the border in Switzerland, a young follower of Zwingli, Heinrich Bullinger, picked up her story but took a different view, vindicating the people's

stand against debauched and corrupt rulers, and stressing the solemn oath sworn by Brutus and his followers on Lucrece's death.
Bullinger, like Zwingli, saw such oaths as the vindication of
the power of the people, for they invoked the God of Christian Scriptures, not human law, as the ultimate authority.[5] So
from the first, Lucrece had a role at the heart of the Reformation
debate.

She was not just a symbol for reformers—Catholic princes,
too, pressed her into service. William IV of Bavaria commissioned the painter Jörg Breu the Elder to depict her story after
his rival, the Emperor Charles V, sacked Rome in 1527. Breu's
Lucrece represents the Holy City destroyed by tyrannical imperial power.[6] Meanwhile, religious and intellectual dissidents
found a role model in Lucius Junius Brutus, who before taking
his momentous oath adopted a pose of frivolity in order to avoid
suspicion. The French Protestant writer Hubert Languet, a great
friend of Philip Sidney, signed his widely read study of tyranny
with the suggestive pseudonym 'Junius Brutus'[7]. The precedent
of Lucrece was also invoked by the Dutch republic in 1666, by
the French revolutionaries in 1789, by Italian patriots in 1848,
and by Americans in the course of the War of Independence—
in fact, by any movement urging justified resistance against a
monarch's outrageous abuse of power.[8] The shocking execution
of Charles I in the course of the English Civil War made post-
Restoration England particularly sensitive on the subject: when
Nathaniel Lee staged his play *Lucius Junius Brutus* in London in
1680, it was banned at once for 'Scandalous Expressions and Reflections upon the Government'.

It's hardly surprising that the theme of Shakespeare's poem
was so popular: it outsold all his plays by the time of his death.
By 1616, it had run to six editions, the same number as Christopher Marlowe's sensational homoerotic poem *Hero and Leander*,

and almost as many as *Venus and Adonis*, surviving copies of which show they were read almost to shreds. By contrast, *Romeo and Juliet* went to four editions, and *Hamlet* to only three. The key to the popularity of Shakespeare's version of Lucrece, however, was not just his choice of story: it was the meaning he embedded within it.

CHAPTER THREE

A PROBLEM POEM

RESTRAINED YET INTENSE, measured yet anguished: of all the treatments of Lucrece's rape and suicide, Shakespeare's comes closest to Rembrandt's in its dark and brooding tone, its sense of deep and painful engagement. For both artists, an event which occurred around two thousand years earlier in ancient Rome seems to have some immediate, unexplained personal significance. 'O rash false heat, wrapped in repentant cold, / Thy hasty spring still blasts and ne'er grows old!' (48–49), laments Shakespeare, as if the consequences of the rape have some enduring impact on him or on his times.

And in his account, the consequences are catastrophic. In most versions of the story, society gains from Lucrece's death. In Shakespeare's, society falls apart. Halfway through the poem, Lucrece launches into a bitter tirade linking her downfall with every imaginable evil—social, spiritual, and moral. As in Rembrandt's portraits of her, the causes of her tragedy seem to spread beyond the act of a single man to the darker forces that permitted the rape to happen. The frantic Lucrece cites Time, Night, and Opportunity as the culprits, accusing Opportunity, for example, of being guilty: 'of murder and of theft', 'of perjury and subornation', 'of treason, forgery and shift', guilty, in fact, 'of all sins past and all that are to come, / From the creation to the general doom' (921–924).

These outcries are a long way from the lightly ironic tone of *Venus and Adonis*, published a year earlier, in 1593, and recall the promise Shakespeare made then that his next poem would be 'some graver labour' (12). 'Labour' seems to be the right word here. *Lucrece* is a play-length work, longer than *Comedy of Errors*, nearly as long as *Macbeth*. It is intensely emotional, complex, and highly worked. In fact, the use of language is so elaborate that some critics see the poem as a kind of rhetorical showpiece, a poetic sampler demonstrating just how much decoration a story can take in the hands of a master—part of the challenge being to swamp the tale itself with the layers of bravura rhetorical effects so admired by Renaissance readers, but alien territory to most of us. For such critics, the poem is essentially a game, a gorgeous sixteenth-century contrast to the plain, classical, soldierly account in the 'Argument', or prose summary, that Shakespeare gives us at the beginning of the poem.

But connoisseurs of rhetorical ingenuity—which Shakespeare's patrons certainly were—would have been alert to a 'graver' meaning behind all this display. *The Rape of Lucrece* does have an organic unity, though it is easier to overlook than the organic unity of his great plays. Like iron filings around a magnet, the poem's letters, syllables, rhymes, phrases, tropes, and stanzas are all aligned with a single powerful concept that lies at the core of the whole thing—the concept of *undoing*. The idea of cancelling out, uncreating, effacing, runs through the poem's linguistic structure; it is part of its literary DNA. Negative 'privative' terms are everywhere—the first three verses alone have 'trustless', 'lightless', 'unmatched', 'unlocked', 'priceless', and 'peerless'. And in the fourth there is a cascade of 'undoing' words—'decayed', 'done', 'cancelled', 'expired'—all of them revolving round an image of happiness dissolving like dew in the sun. Throughout, sounds and meanings cleverly undo each other in a characteristic echo pattern. At her death, Lucrece 'sheathed in her *harmless* breast / A *harmful* knife, that thence her soul *unsheathed*' (1723–1724), hoping that she 'with blood had *stained* her *stained* excuse' (1316) (emphasis mine). The poem is built intellectually, as well as emotionally, on the concept of something quintessentially negative. At its climax, even the idea of undoing is undone, when Lucrece pleads with Time to *undo* the moment of her own undoing at Tarquin's hands.

Underlining the deep seriousness of this theme is the slow, majestic pace of the 'rhyme royal' in which the poem is written. Invented by Chaucer, these seven-line stanzas had become by Shakespeare's day a hackneyed medium for pedestrian narrative verse; the reading public was accustomed to page after undistinguished page of its predictable flow in popular anthologies. But Shakespeare injected new life into it. At the back of his mind, perhaps, was the example of Thomas Wyatt, grandson of the cat-loving Henry, whose famous rhyme-royal poem 'They flee from me that sometime did me seek', written probably about his secret love affair with Anne Boleyn, is an astonishing piece of impassioned lyrical utterance. Like Wyatt, Shakespeare continually disrupts the smooth verse form with queries, exclamations, abrupt halts, and sudden grammatical breaks within lines and between couplets. The medium becomes almost as flexible as the iambic pentameter of the plays—by turns conversational, surprising, reflective, momentous, or impassioned. But there is a great difference. Shakespeare deploys a whole battery of deliberately eye-catching poetic effects—alliteration, antitheses, chiasmus, anaphora—to highlight the tension between the natural rhythm of speech and what becomes, in his hands, the heavy, pulsing drumbeat of the verse. The effect is one of onward movement weighed down by agitated thought, by ideas constantly qualified or reconsidered, by saying and then unsaying, doing and undoing.

This should all add up to a rich and intricate poem in which deep emotion and rhetorical energy fuse in a many-faceted portrayal of loss. Yet for modern readers it does nothing of the kind. Scholars generally struggle to get a grip on it, to find some unifying theme. So much of the subject matter seems to us superfluous. What, much of the time, is Shakespeare talking about? Whole pages seem almost perversely random and off the point. The first few verses are typical—by turns momentous, prolix, and irrelevant. After a brilliant opening verse composed of a single sentence, in which the lust-driven Tarquin sweeps towards his prey, Shakespeare seems to put down his pen, sit back, and muse for the next five verses on a conundrum that does not even appear in any other version of the Lucrece story. Was Lucrece's husband, Collatine, he wonders, the real originator of the whole tragic episode? This irrelevant question is explored in great detail, none of which is picked up later in the poem. And this early pause reminds readers that Shakespeare has invented a puzzling twist. His Tarquin is originally inflamed with lust not by the sight of Lucrece's beauty, but by Collatine's boastful account of Lucrece's beauty. Why?

The sense of being irritatingly derailed becomes more pronounced as the long poem unfolds; along with the dense, complex wordplay, it makes *Lucrece* an exhausting journey for a modern reader. Just as with Collatine's possible guilt for a fault that the author has invented for no obvious reason, Shakespeare subjects every move of the other two protagonists to the same kind of microscopic examination, regularly mulling over the might-have-beens and what-ifs of each action, until the rapist and his victim pixillate and fragment. Then he zooms in and focuses on inexplicable corners of the screen.

No sooner has the poem picked up pace after the exploration of Collatine's boast than we stall again with a slow-motion panorama of Lucrece's face. Even by the standards of the day, in which the conventional 'blazon' of a woman's face had become a literary cliché (hair like gold, cheeks like roses, eyes like suns), this passage plumbs new depths. Poor Lucrece's face has nothing to do with personality, or even attractiveness—instead it is a chivalric device, or 'shield', a complex heraldic battleground between the qualities of beauty (red) and virtue (white), which Shakespeare imagines as two universal forces forever in conflict. He finds their intricate relative claims so absorbing that Lucrece, as a character, let alone a woman, is altogether forgotten.

Meanwhile, the speculations, hypotheses, and deviations mount up, culminating in a vast digression at the climax of the poem—the point just after Lucrece has summoned Collatine to hear her story and witness her suicide. This is the moment Rembrandt explored to such effect, and Shakespeare, too, gives us harrowing human moments. The passage itself begins with a moving scenario which is, again, entirely Shakespeare's invention—it does not appear in any other version of the story. Desperate for distraction from her own grief, Lucrece turns to a painting hanging in her house of the fall of Troy, and loses herself in the sorrows of Priam's widow, Hecuba. But by the time we reach Hecuba, we have almost forgotten about Lucrece. Shakespeare has examined everything else in the picture first, none of which appears to bear any relation to Lucrece's crisis. Not for the first time, she is left in suspended animation while the narrator turns his mind to other matters.

This virtuoso rhetorical exercise in ekphrasis—the poetic description of a work of art—has been seen as Shakespeare's bid to outdo similar passages in poems by rivals like Christopher Marlowe and Samuel Daniel. But here again is that failure to hit the spot, so unusual in Shakespeare, yet almost the trademark of this poem. In Daniel's 'Rosamond', the tale of another victim of royal lust, the pictures on the decorated casket Rosamond studies closely mirror her own situation. The downfall of the city of Troy, however, has no obvious connection with the downfall of Lucrece, yet it is Troy, not the weeping Hecuba, that fills the foreground.

Twelve verses are given over to aesthetic analysis by the narrator-turned-art-critic. He assesses the painter's treatment of Ajax, Ulysses, Nestor, the Greek crowd scenes, and the Trojan defenders. The more irrelevant the detail, the more time Shakespeare seems prepared to give it. An engaging piece of observation about the 'sad' eyes of the Trojan defenders peering through loop-holes in the city walls 'with little lust' might be appreciated from a companion in an art gallery, but it is a long way from the predicament of Lucrece. And indeed, much of this passage is addressed directly to us by the admiring narrator, who seems eager to point out every aspect of the artist's skill.

At last, his lens having travelled slowly across the whole vista of the siege and fall of Troy, Shakespeare turns to Lucrece encountering the figure of Hecuba. She almost tears the painting as she identifies with the old woman's grief, before turning to attack the figure of Sinon, the Greek warrior who enabled the Greeks to infiltrate the wooden horse into Troy by persuading the Trojans it was a gift. If artful irrelevance was indeed the purpose of the passage, as some critics maintain, then this is the point where even the most persistent modern reader parts company with the poem's original audience.

As she scratches madly at the painted image of Sinon, Lucrece is acting like a real human being—but not for long. Critics have noticed how often she is described as an inanimate object: a landscape, an icon, a material possession, a city, an island. And the landscape of her personality is densely packed with conflicting elements, like the red beauty and white virtue quarrelling in her cheeks. Her many attributes interact uneasily with each other and continually remind us of a divided, argumentative community. Heart, hand, soul, mind, body, are all at odds. Lucrece continues to be portrayed as a country rather than a woman through to the end: even her corpse 'like a late-sacked Island vastly stood / Bare and unpeopled in this fearful flood' (1740–1741).

So this poem fails on three of the levels that are traditionally part of the story of Lucrece. Apart from Tarquin's stealthy approach to her bedchamber, Shakespeare's wordy version is so far from erotic that the rape itself is barely mentioned; as a human drama, it fails to arouse our sympathy, and often, even our attention; and there is no serious engagement in the age-old debate about the morality of Lucrece's rape and suicide. But one more level remains, and, as we have seen already, for hundreds of years it would have been the first level people would have looked for when they read the title. Is this a political poem? Is Shakespeare, like many others before him, retelling the story in terms of contemporary events?

So much we have puzzled over would make sense if he was: the strangely geopoliticised characters who break down into societies, objects, maps, islands, lands, and armies; inner thoughts that take the form of advisors, messengers, or soldiers; motives that are observed, discussed, and assessed like rival political agendas; the fierce indictment of the forces of social disintegration; and, most of all, the narrator's tone, passionately engaged, grieving, exploratory, analytical, preoccupied more with concepts than with individuals. The image of the dead Lucrece as 'a late-sack'd island' brings the story close to home. As one editor notes: 'For dwellers in the island of Britain . . . it might have held a particular horror.'[1]

But there is a problem here. *The Rape of Lucrece* was published in 1594. Elizabeth's England had not been sacked, and her reign was not a period of social collapse—if anything, the reverse. It had not endured the kind of outrage that drove German, Dutch, and later French and American subjects to raise the republican banner and invoke the precedent of Judith or Lucrece. Of course, after years of religious upheaval, there were disgruntled minority groups. The bitter grievances of England's persecuted Catholics were matched by those of the Puritan reformers, who had been cheated by the Elizabethan religious compromise of the full reformation they had hoped for, and who disrupted Parliament and fulminated against 'the tyranny of the clergy of England'.[2] The most formidable dissidents were a sizeable group of the old nobility, who were increasingly sidelined and disenfranchised by the rising generation of lawyers and merchants who formed Elizabeth's hard-core supporters. Here there was angry talk of the succession, regime change, or a coup to remove her key advisors. But their complaint was of weak government: the unstable, vulnerable Richard II was closer to their view of the queen than the arrogant Roman Tarquins.[3]

So in spite of some recent efforts to align the poem with the prevailing political issues, and in spite of many persuasive allusions, their presence seems at most incomplete and fleeting. This poem does not plead the cause of a particular social group:

instead it plunges us into a nightmare vision of a dizzying social landslide, a momentous geopolitical event, the destruction of an entire society or the ruin of a culture fatally vulnerable to tyrannical aggression.

And yet, if we take Shakespeare's many digressions and additions seriously, England itself, in some form, seems a strikingly apt fit for Lucrece. In the matter of the history and heraldry of England, Shakespeare is by now pretty much an acknowledged expert. His own country is the central character in the history plays that made his name as a young dramatist, two of which (*Richard II* and *Richard III*) outsold all his other plays by the time of his death. In the multi-drama historical saga that began with his first great hit, the trilogy *Henry VI*, England is invoked repeatedly in terms of profound affection, even reverence. Her heraldic colours of red and white are in such constant motion throughout his work that the quirk was often commented on at the time. Here Richard II, describing the coming conflict, imagines England's countenance, remarkably like Lucrece's, as both a flower and a blood-stained conflict zone:

> Ten thousand bloody crowns of mothers' sons
> Shall ill become the flower of England's face,
> Change the complexion of her maid-pale peace
> To scarlet indignation and bedew
> Her pastures' grass with faithful English blood.
> (3.3.96–100)

Though wordplay on the red and white in a mistress's face is part and parcel of the Petrarchan poetic tradition of the day, the colours are never abstract for Shakespeare, and often they evoke peculiarly English oppositions and conflicts. Ever present in the minds of his generation were the bloody memories of the civil wars of the previous century between the great houses of York, symbolised by the white rose, and Lancaster, symbolised by the red. Real red and white roses are actually plucked on stage at the beginning of Shakespeare's history cycle, and at the end of the last play, *Richard III*, they form the mingled red and white Tudor rose, which symbolised the resolution of the conflict. The dramatic reunion of red and white also has a strong religious dimension; the future Henry VII, Elizabeth's grandfather, announces the healing of a bloodied, self-harming England in spiritual terms: 'As we have ta'en the sacrament, / We will unite the white rose and the red' (5.5.18–19).

The Tudor image of warring red and white held in tension merges in these plays with an older national symbol—the flag of St George. The crusader's device of the red cross on a white background was actually taken over from England's traditional enemy, the French, sometime in the early Middle Ages: before that, England fought under a white cross. Here, too, then, red and white have a shifting, changeable past. And occasionally, Shakespeare's reds and whites deliberately call to mind a third political opposition, inescapable for his own readers, for whom it had become a pressing and often frightening reality. This was the vexed relationship between the traditional religion and the religion of the reformers. Particularly in his poems, Shakespeare will expand in elaborate detail on the conflict between red beauty (connected with the ornamental, scarlet attributes of the traditional religion) and white virtue (evoking the whitewashed walls and plain print of the reformers)—two qualities that were originally intertwined in England's spiritual life, until they were torn apart by the Reformation.[4]

Lucrece's first appearance is puzzling if we expect her to be a personality, but she becomes a convincing reality if we try reading the poem as though she were another Shakespearean evocation of the numinous spirit of England, marked by inner conflicts held in precarious equipoise. Unpacking the long passage that introduces us to Lucrece is not meant to be simple. St George's cross is there; so is the red and white Tudor rose; so are the endemic disputes over the 'sovereignty' of red beauty and white virtue, hinting at the long and fraught relationship between Rome and an England often in the vanguard of reform. The whole passage is reverent, lyrical, yet firmly embedded in the practical language of heraldry. It ends with what could be seen as a summary of the essence of England, a 'silent war of lilies and of roses', on the eve of the Reformation:

> This heraldry in Lucrece' face was seen,
> Argued by Beauty's red and Virtue's white;
> Of either's colour was the other queen,
> Proving from world's minority their right;
> Yet their ambition makes them still to fight,
>   The sov'reignty of either being so great
>   That oft they interchange each other's seat.
>   (64–70)

If Lucrece in some way embodies England, it will not be the first time Shakespeare has personified the soul of the country. England is briefly and movingly identified with a small boy in *King John*, written at about the same time as *The Rape of Lucrece*. John is a usurper, and the boy, Arthur, is England's rightful heir: imprisoned by John, he dies under mysterious circumstances. An elegiac monologue for the fallen boy describes England's soul departing from a body that becomes food for squabbling predators. The passage strongly recalls the apocalyptic fallout after Lucrece's rape and death:

> The life, the right and truth of all this realm
> Is fled to heaven! And England now is left . . .
>   . . . and vast confusion waits
> As doth a raven on a sick-fall'n beast,
> The imminent decay of wrested pomp.
>   (4.3.143 ff.)

Striking though these parallels are between Shakespeare's treatment of Lucrece and his treatment of England, it is not surprising that few critics have pursued them. If Lucrece represents Elizabeth's England, then who is Tarquin? Why is Collatine's pride in his wife implicated so unusually in her rape? What, indeed, would the rape itself represent? Other questions arise, such as how to interpret the strange trio Lucrece invokes after the rape, Night, Opportunity, and Time, and why shame is the main motif of the poem, mentioned no less than thirty-three times. To sum up, what possible historical event can match this tragic scenario: the brutal infliction of some terrible indignity on England, an indignity for which the victim blames herself, with effects that do not diminish with time, which stir up deep emotion and regret in the narrator, and which require searching and detailed analysis in order to be truly understood?

Only within the past twenty years have historians and antiquarians begun to retrieve a neglected tradition of critique, outrage, and lament at an occurrence that was seen for centuries in precisely these terms—a self-inflicted wound, a national rape, instigated by one of England's own monarchs, which wrecked the social, moral, and religious fibre of the country so thoroughly that it took four hundred years for the damage to be repaired and the memory to fade of what was lost. The often distinguished voices we are going to hear from are not those of minority groups. This is not the protest of the disenfranchised and excluded. Some of them belong to people who are synonymous with what it is to be English. They are almost all loyal, mainstream, Protestant subjects. Their protests started in 1534, when the cataclysm began, and in their language and imagery they echo, sometimes word for word, Shakespeare's *Rape of Lucrece*.

Chapter Four

RAPE

'WHAT FOLLOWS IS calculated to make us shudder with horror, to make our very bowels heave with loathing, to make us turn our eyes from the paper and resolve to read no further. . . . From first to last, we have to contemplate nothing that is not of a kind to fill us with horror and disgust.'[1]

So wrote the radical reformer William Cobbett in the mid-1820s, and so he continues, for chapter after thunderous chapter, in one of the most exhilarating pieces of political polemic in the English language. Cobbett was a bluff, energetic journalist and campaigner and a thorn in the side of the establishment. His personal integrity, unflinching principles, and trenchant style led the historian A. J. P. Taylor to describe him as the second-greatest Englishman who had ever lived (Samuel Johnson being the first).[2] In Cobbett's lifetime, the book in which this passage appeared was far and away his most popular work, even outselling—according to him—the Bible.

So what was it that Cobbett considered almost too repulsive

to set down on paper, this event 'engendered in lust and brought forth in hypocrisy and perfidy', ushered in by 'the infamy of silent submission', which 'devastated and plundered the country', and which 'laid the sure foundation for that pauperism, that disgraceful immorality, that fearful prevalence of crimes of all sorts, which now so strongly mark the character of this nation, which was formerly the land of virtue and plenty'?[3]

The answer is a socioeconomic upheaval which has been called 'one of the most revolutionary events in English history', a transfer of land second only to the Norman Conquest: the dissolution of England's monasteries and takeover of the church's estate by Elizabeth I's father, Henry VIII.[4] The scale and speed of this takeover continues to awe scholars. Between 1536 and 1540, four million acres donated by nobility and laymen over hundreds of years to English religious communities, great and small, were inventoried, claimed, and appropriated by the Crown, the houses dissolved, their occupants pensioned off if the surrender was 'voluntary', and punished if it was not. The heist amounted to 16 per cent of rural England and included ancient buildings packed with valuable books as well as silver, gold, jewellery, stained glass, sculpture, paintings, lead from the roofs, and metal from bells.[5] Henry needed money, and he was able to drive through this extraordinary measure because two years earlier, in his momentous Act of Supremacy, he had assumed authority over the church in England. From that moment on, England was no longer answerable to Rome. In 1532, the English clergy, outwitted and intimidated by the tactics of the Crown, abdicated their independence to the king in an act known as the Submission of the Clergy—a capitulation described by one scholar as 'the suicide of ecclesiastical authority'.[6]

The first benefit for Henry from the Act of Supremacy was his long-delayed divorce from Catherine of Aragon; the second was a financial windfall from church property. Both turned out to be illusory gains. Just three years and four months after their marriage, Henry's new wife, Anne Boleyn, went to the scaffold without producing the longed-for male heir. As for the monastic wealth, it went initially to the Crown, and thence, much of it, to the Crown's cannier subjects. Henry was assured by the recipients that he was buying support for his assumption of supremacy over the country's religion—the wider the circle of beneficiaries, argued Henry's vicegerent, Thomas Cromwell, the more stakeholders there would be in the new order, and the more irrevocable the break with Rome. Thus the wealth originally destined for the reformation of the church infrastructure went largely to those quickest on their feet when it came to the division of spoils. A wide-ranging recent study of eighteen thousand dispositions by Cromwell's Court of Augmentations, a model of bureaucratic efficiency, found that only 27 per cent of the new acquisitions went to church institutions; 70 per cent went first to the nobility, then to the royal household and government officials, then to gentry and yeomen, and finally to London merchants and traders.[7] The money that went into the royal coffers did not create the stable landed endowment for the Crown that reformers hoped would ensure the stability of the new order—instead, it was frittered away on ruinous vanity projects by an increasingly irresponsible king.

The acquisitive momentum continued under Henry's son, Edward VI, a young and fervent Protestant. During his short reign all 'idolatrous' practices were banned—thus churches, chantries, chapels, cathedrals, shrines, indeed all religious establishments, were required to yield up their candlesticks, pyxes, crucifixes, altar cloths, vestments, chalices, and anything bearing an image or even an illuminated letter. The nature of this ugly rush is nicely caught by the staunchly Anglican historian

Thomas Fuller in 1655, who describes the free-for-all in terms of a frenzied feast at the royal table, ending with a race for the chantry revenues by greedy courtiers, 'knowing this was the last dish of the last course, and after chantries, as after cheese, nothing to be expected'.[8] Shakespeare's contemporary Michael Sherbrook, a vicar writing in Yorkshire in 1591, gives a vivid description of the sacking of Roche Abbey in his father's time: 'It would have pitied any heart to see what tearing up of the lead there was, and plucking up of boards, and throwing down of the spars; and when the lead was torn off and cast down into the church, the tombs in the church all broken . . . and all things of price, either spoiled, carried away or defaced to the uttermost.'[9] Private houses and estates rapidly took the place of old abbeys and their lands. What was not melted down or sold was publicly destroyed and burned. It looked as though reform had indeed become irrevocable.

In a brief period following Edward's early death, however, his half-sister Mary attempted to roll back the clock and return England to Rome, discrediting her cause by her barbaric treatment of 'heretical' reformers, hundreds of whom were burned at the stake. When she, too, died, after a six-year reign, her Protestant half-sister, Elizabeth, came to the throne. Sickened by the executions, rebellions, burnings, and doctrinal contradictions that had accompanied the early stages of England's 'Long Reformation', the country settled for Elizabeth's promise of moderation. Nonetheless, the Crown retained the supremacy, and the dismantling of the old religious order resumed, albeit at a slower pace. By 1610, according to the British art critic Andrew Graham-Dixon, well over 90 per cent of England's art had been destroyed. In his view, the only comparable historical period of state vandalism is the Cultural Revolution in Maoist China. There was a final burst of iconoclasm in the middle of the next

century, when the country erupted into civil war, Parliament
against Crown, and the final traces of superstition and popery
were razed to the ground by militant fundamentalists. Centuries
of religious and political debate were to follow over the exact
nature of what had happened to England in the course of this
social and cultural upheaval.

Viewed purely in economic terms, and setting aside questions about the loss of what we would now call the nation's cultural heritage, modern historians have taken a broadly positive
view of the dissolution. The argument goes that the monasteries, often lax, undermanned, and over-endowed, were in urgent
need of reform, and the secularization of church property, however crudely executed, empowered a new landowning class that
would contribute much to the subsequent wealth and security of
the nation. But opinion is divided. At the other extreme, some
historians, including John Bossy, argue that the accompanying
loss of common land and community life in England amounted
to the very 'revolution of the rich against the poor' that Cobbett
so passionately denounced, bringing in a ruthless market econ-
omy and breaking up age-old models of social life. This opinion appears to be gaining ground. According to a recent study,
'the destruction of the monasteries probably damaged England's
structures for social welfare more than any other single event has
ever done. . . . In upland regions, where parishes were large and
the monasteries' role had been that much more vital, the effect
was catastrophic. Archeological research on childhood mortality
suggests that it leapt in the years around 1540 and remained high
thereafter.'[10]

Of these two views, it is, perhaps unexpectedly, the second that becomes more insistent and vocal the further back in
time we go towards the fateful 1530s, when Henry took his
irrevocable step. It is curious that until the publication of a

groundbreaking article by the historian Margaret Aston in 1973, the common assumption was that a Protestant critique of the dissolution was rare, almost freakish.[11] But the truth appears to be that evangelicals, Protestants, and even Puritans were often aghast at what had been done to the physical and spiritual infrastructure of their own country.

The reformers themselves were among the first to throw up their hands in horror at Henry's 'reforming' course of action. Traditionally, historians have tended to belittle one of the major functions performed by religious houses—that of providing care and hospitality for travellers, the sick, the aged, and the unemployed. But disinterested voices at the time, many of them vigorously anti-Catholic, suggest that England's monks and nuns had not been nearly as idle as later sources made out; on the contrary, they insisted, monastic charity was part of the very fibre of the country. One of the first warning shots fired across Henry's bows as he meditated his takeover came in an anonymous play written for court performance in 1529, *Godly Queene Hester.* In a thinly veiled attack on the proposed dissolution, Queen Hester begs her husband, King Assewerus, to allow his Jewish subjects to continue to perform works of charity. If pious giving ceases, she argues, wealth will fall into the hands of a privileged few, and his subjects will be too impoverished and weakened to do him service. In the case of England, her warning was to prove prophetic.[12]

Leading evangelicals, such as Hugh Latimer, bishop of Worcester, had expected reform of the monasteries, not suppression. In 1536, Latimer urged the king to 'revert the abbeys and priories to places of study and good letters and to the continual relief of the poor'.[13] The reformer Henry Brinkelow made an impassioned defence to Parliament of monastic hospitality: 'Every man knoweth that many thousands were well received of them', but now 'I do not hear tell that one halfpenny worth of alms or any other profit cometh unto the people from these parishes'.[14] In a 1537 pamphlet another reformer, Thomas Gibson, brought a similar tone of firsthand outrage to his protest that the Reformation had been hijacked, and 'that a great hurt and decay is thereby come and hereafter shall come to this your realm, and great impoverishing of many your poor obedient subjects'.[15]

This body blow to the nation's well-being continued to be lamented down the ages: 'Tut tut, almshouses will make good stables', writes Shakespeare's contemporary the satirist Thomas Nashe in a typical late-Elizabethan swipe at the calculating mindset of the new owners, 'and, let out in tenements, yield a round sum by the year'. He continues: 'A good strong-barred hutch [gaol] is a building worth twenty of those hospitals and alms-houses; our rich chuffs will rather put their helping hands to the building of a prison than a house of prayer.'[16] The seventeenth-century antiquarian John Aubrey laments 'the vanished convivial inns', mournfully adding, 'I wish the monasteries had not been put down.'[17] Cobbett graphically evokes what the roads around him would once have looked like, leading off to religious houses every few miles where anyone could take shelter or receive assistance, bearing witness to what Aubrey called 'the Piety, Charity and magnanimity of our Forefathers'.[18] The nineteenth-century poet Robert Southey, like many of those in his intellectual circle, believed that the abbeys had been the spiritual centres of their communities, and sources of paternalistic charity. Samuel Coleridge called for the restoration of all abbey lands to what he called 'the Nationality'.[19]

Almost more agonising for the reformers—and for all the antiquarians, historians, and writers that followed them—was the destruction of the monastic libraries. For centuries religious houses had been the main repositories for precious books, as well as producers of exquisitely illuminated manuscripts. John Bale, chief propagandist for the Reformation, writing in 1549, speaks for many: 'I utter it with heaviness', he says, as he lists the uses to which these papers have been put. The burning of priceless books or their reuse as wrapping paper, rags, and bungs for beer barrels was considered not just among English scholars but 'among the grave seniors of other nations' as 'a horrible infamy'. He continues: 'Neither the Britons under the Romans and Saxons; nor yet the English people under the Danes, and Normans, had ever such damage of their learned monuments, as we have seen in our time. Our posterity may well curse this wicked fact of our Age, this unreasonable spoil of England's most noble antiquities.'[20] The Anglican clergyman and historian Thomas Fuller takes up the lament a century later in the same anguished tone: 'What soul can be so frozen, as not to melt into anger hereat? What heart, having the least spark of ingenuity, is not hot at this indignity offered to literature?' He grieved over the loss of Bibles as well as works of history and mathematics: 'All massacred together', he mourned.[21]

Sacrilege was the term for all this: 'the diversion of holy and ecclesiastic things to profane and secular use', in the words of Shakespeare's contemporary, the highly respected antiquarian Sir Henry Spelman.[22] The fact that Spelman's own family had profited from the dissolution filled him with anxiety and guilt; he believed that the many misfortunes that had befallen him were vengeance from heaven for his forebears' ill-gotten gains. He spent much of his life researching and compiling an influential book titled *The History of Sacrilege*, an account of the impact of the dissolution on the families who had benefitted from it, the prime example being the childless offspring of Henry VIII. The book circulated privately and remained unpublished until after his death. Spelman pulls no punches, writing with passionate intensity about 'the ocean of iniquity and sacrilege, where whole thousands of churches and chapels dedicated to the service of God were by King Henry VIII . . . sacked and razed as by an enemy'.[23] John Donne compared the emptying of the monastic buildings to the emptying of the body after death—deprived of the soul that created and sustained them, the buildings themselves became nothing but 'heaps of stone'.[24]

Michael Sherbrook's account stresses the communal involvement in the destruction of an abbey in 1591. Everything left behind by the commissioners was removed by local people, including his own father and the monks themselves. He details the trading in books, pewter vessels, locks, iron hooks, cell doors: 'and every person had everything good cheap; except the poor monks, friars and nuns that had no money to bestow on anything'. He marvels at the sudden change of heart of those who worshipped at the abbey church and 'thought well of the religious persons and of the religion they used', wondering 'that they could this day think it to be the house of God, and the next day the house of the Devil'.[25]

Records survive of the immense logistical challenge of the operation, which often entailed gunpowder, mines, skilled engineering, and considerable planning.[26] Those in the workforce paid themselves from the spoils, and were accompanied by swarms of looters who took away glass, timber, bricks, tiles, and bedding. The remaining structure was not always razed to the ground or rebuilt as a private dwelling; often it was left as a mutilated reminder of the materialism of the old church. On most observers, these ruins left a different impression. Thomas Fuller again, writing in 1644: 'These cruel cormorants with their barbarous beaks and greedy claws, rent, tore and tattered these inestimable pieces of antiquity.'[27] As Michael Sherbrook wrote, 'No doubt there hath been Millions of Millions who have repented the thing since; but all too late.'[28]

Most surprising of all, perhaps, is the indignant verdict of the great Elizabethan historian, antiquarian, and humanist teacher William Camden, a mentor of Shakespeare's fellow writers Edmund Spenser and Ben Jonson. His masterwork, a three-volume survey of the country's history and geography titled *Britannia*, would not be translated into English until 1610, but the Latin version, appearing in 1586, was reprinted six times before that, and was immensely influential. In line with other Elizabethan accounts, it shifts the blame to Cardinal Thomas Wolsey for authorising the initial dissolution of small houses, but the scale of the subsequent plunder is feelingly described. In Camden's view the religious houses were 'monuments of the piety of our ancestors, erected to the honour of God, the propagation of Christianity and learning, and support of the poor'. He begins this sentence with the guarded phrase 'If I may be allowed to say so'. But decorum is quickly forgotten as eloquence and emotion take over: 'About the 36th year of Henry VIII', he goes on, 'a storm burst upon the English church like a flood breaking down its banks, which, to the astonishment of the world and grief of the nation, bore down the greatest part of the religious with their fairest buildings.' The revenues, as well as that of all colleges, chantries, and hospitals, 'under the specious pretence of destroying the remains of superstition', were surrendered to the king. 'These were almost all shortly after destroyed', he adds, 'their revenues squandered away, and the wealth which the Christian piety of the English had from the first conversion of England dedicated to God, in a moment dispersed, and, if I may be allowed the expression, profaned.'[29] That the iconic Elizabethan scholar William Camden can talk of such events in terms of 'the grief of the nation' should give pause to glib assumptions that only Catholics lamented the passing of the monasteries and all that went with them.

Who was ultimately to blame for all this? Camden's attack indicates that the safest target, while Elizabeth I was still alive, was the worldliness of the old church. King Henry VIII's ostentatiously wealthy chancellor, Cardinal Wolsey, came to embody the vices of the Catholic hierarchy, and indeed could be seen as the inadvertent initiator of the whole process. By dissolving a number of small monasteries to finance his own grandiose building schemes, he alerted Thomas Cromwell and the king to the accessibility of the vast wealth of the English monasteries and abbeys. Thus the case could be made that the dissolution was the fault of a church increasingly fixated on wealth, power, and display.

A strong case could also be made that the whole thing was masterminded by cunning profiteers—'ambitious men' who sought a 'deluge of wealth'. This was the opinion of Sir William Dugdale in *The Antiquities of Warwickshire*, a book published in 1656 that brought him admiration and acclaim. Dugdale cautiously positions his trenchant analysis of each stage of the takeover towards the end of the volume, appending it to an account of a saintly nunnery at Polesworth, probably because the descendants of those 'principal ambitious men of that age'—and the 'active gentry' who had brought about this 'great and strange alteration'—were by then in positions of power.[30] Dugdale, a meticulously accurate scholar with access to resources now lost to us, gives vivid detail: Lord Audley, one of those profiteers, 'hunted eagerly after the Abbey', and threatened to charge those who didn't surrender voluntarily with adultery and sodomy. Centuries later, Cobbett pounces on Dugdale's account, arguing that these were the sort of 'voluntary surrenders' which men make of their purses when a robber's pistol is at their temples or his bloodstained knife at their throat'.[31]

But though the scenario of hungry courtiers and neighbouring landowners eagerly assisting the royal visitors goes some way to explain the speed of the capitulation, and though Thomas Cromwell himself, who acquired immense wealth, took much of the opprobrium, no one was in any doubt as to the root cause of the catastrophe, the man without whom none of this would have happened. Wenceslaus Hollar's frontispiece to Dugdale's *Monasticon* shows a double image of England. On the right is a king kneeling piously at an altar. On the left is Henry VIII, straddling the landscape in his most characteristic pose, legs planted wide apart, hands on hips, with the words 'Hic Volo' (This is my wish) issuing from his mouth. Apart from a group of wide-eyed onlookers, the landscape has just one feature—a ruined church.

For most writers, it was the role of the monarch that was the most shocking aspect of the whole business. How could a king inflict such wanton damage on his own country? 1n 1640, in his poem 'Cooper's Hill', John Denham wrote,

> Who sees these dismall heaps, but would demand,
>   What Barbarous invader sackt the land?
> But when he heares, no Goth, no Turk did bring,
>   This desolation, but a Christian King . . . ?[32]

A biographer of Henry VIII, Lord Herbert of Cherbury, had to begin his largely favourable account of the king with a disclaimer that he is aware of the public criticism of the subject of his book. Like many others, he describes the takeover of the church as 'rapine', and notes that the clergy who fled abroad told tales of the 'ruins of themselves and house in such terms that the Christian world was astonished'.[33] 'The tyrant, Henry VIII', wrote the great political thinker and orator Edmund Burke, in his 1791 *Reflections on the French Revolution*, dissolved monasteries on grounds 'no voice has ever yet commended'. 'I cannot conceive', he added, 'how any man can have brought himself to that pitch of presumption to consider his country as nothing but carte blanche upon which he may scribble whatever he please.'[34] In the same year, the fifteen-year-old Jane Austen was merrily committing her own thoughts on Henry VIII to paper, satirising in one breath both the king's actions and the English taste for ruined monasteries: 'Nothing can be said in his vindication, but that his abolishing religious houses and leaving them to the ruinous depredations of time has been of infinite use to the landscape of England in general, which probably was a principal motive for his doing it, since otherwise why would a man of no religion himself be at so much trouble to abolish one which had for ages been established in the kingdom?'[35] For William Cobbett, there were no half-measures when it came to Henry VIII—he is simply 'the tyrant'.[36] Cobbett echoes many earlier exclamations at the tyrannical actions of a monarch who sacked his own country more thoroughly than any enemy could: 'The whole country was thus disfigured: it had the appearance of a land recently invaded by the most brutal barbarians. . . . Nothing has ever yet come to supply the place of what was then destroyed.'[37] The two words 'Hic volo' issuing from Henry's mouth on the frontispiece of Dugdale's *Monasticon* daringly connect Henry's acts of self-willed tyranny with Martin Luther. When Luther was criticised for adding the word 'alone' to his translation of St Paul's statement that man is justified by faith (in order to stress his belief that 'faith alone' saved men), he struck back with a quotation from Juvenal's fourth satire: 'Sic volo, sic iubeo, sit pro ratione voluntas': 'This I wish, this I command, let my will stand as a reason.' Though Henry was no Lutheran, Dugdale represents him as a destroyer who quoted Luther's challenge to the church as a precedent when it suited him.[38]

We know Shakespeare was familiar with the work of at least one of these protestors, because he drew on it for his own play *Henry VIII*, first staged for the Jacobean court in 1614: George Cavendish. Cavendish's *Life of Thomas Wolsey* is an eyewitness account of the early stages of the takeover as they unfolded before his fascinated eyes. He was gentleman-usher to the cardinal, and, like many who work for celebrities, he was simultaneously awed and scandalised by the immense wealth accumulated by his master, itemising clothes, ceremonies, banquets, and, above all, key political encounters. The book has been of intense interest ever since—not least because of his fresh and engaging style. 'Startlingly modern', the novelist Hilary Mantel calls him. Though he was the inspiration for her own novels about Thomas Cromwell, she omits his verdict on the king. Cavendish portrays Henry VIII just as Dugdale, Cobbett, and Burke do—as an irresponsible tyrant. Like others, he equates the physical cupidity that attracted him to Anne Boleyn with the mercenary desire that drew him to the monasteries.[39]

Cavendish catalogues the harms perpetrated in a heated passage about Henry's lustful actions. Since the takeover, he writes,

> what surmised inventions have been invented, what laws have been enacted, what noble and ancient monasteries overthrown and defaced, what diversities of religious opinions have risen, what executions have been committed, how many famous and notable clerks have suffered death, what charitable foundations were perverted from the relief of the poor, unto profane uses, and what alterations of good and wholesome ancient laws and customs hath been forced by will and

willful desire of the prince, almost to the subversion and dissolution of this noble realm.[40]

For Cavendish the tragic consequences extend into the present: the 'plague' continues. Half a century later, Shakespeare's
contemporaries shared the view that the malign effects were
still spreading. Thomas Nashe writes, 'Would he that first gelt
[taxed] religion or church-livings had been first gelt himself or
never lived.' He predicts that those who did so have incurred
'punishment yet unpaid' which will be 'required of their posterity'.[41] The urbane John Harington, godson of Elizabeth I, took
the same apocalyptic view of the consequences of what he, like
others, had begun to call a 'deformation'. The injustice was ongoing: 'For law with lust and rule with rape is yoked / And zeal
with schism and simony is choked.'[42]

The final word on this subject goes to the outstanding classical scholar Edmund Campion, whose rhetorical skill was admired by Elizabeth while he was at Oxford, but who was in the
end executed for ministering in England as a Jesuit. Here Campion, one of the many who died for their conscience as an indi-
rect result of the king's policy, sums up everything that has been
said in this chapter about Henry VIII and his legacy. Noticing an
inscription on a wall at Christchurch attributing to Henry the
dazzling building actually erected by Wolsey, he suddenly ex-
plodes. The king, he says, was 'a man who has destroyed all honesty, completely confused the human and divine, and destroyed,
root and branch, both the religion and the commonwealth of
Britain'.[43]

This is the single recorded instance of intemperate language
from the normally equable Campion. The indictment is more
extreme, but the reaction is the same as that of all the others: a
rush of rage and indignation at the memory of what had been

lost forever under Henry VIII. Campion, a proscribed Catholic priest, was condemned to death as a traitor; but the rest of the men and women who have spoken in these pages are not dissidents, malcontents, or subversives: these are the voices of English patriots robbed of their patrimony.

CHAPTER FIVE

THE POETRY WAR

I F SO MANY people felt so strongly, for so long, that King
Henry VIII's appropriations ripped the heart and soul out of
England, why does their protest not figure more emphatically in
the literature of the sixteenth century?

One answer is censorship—and its accompaniment, self-
censorship. In the early days, as we have seen, it was relatively
safe for reformers to protest in Parliament as they saw vast funds
intended for the public good being diverted for private use. But
towards the end of Henry's lifetime, both reformers and tradi-
tionalists were executed for voicing dissent. From then until
the close of Elizabeth's reign, open criticism of the actions of
the Tudor monarchy was not an option. Henry Spelman's book
would not be published until late in the seventeenth century;
nor would George Cavendish's biography of Wolsey, though
both circulated widely in manuscript. Historians and antiquarians included their own views on recent events cautiously, anon-
ymously, or not at all: in Walter Ralegh's preface to his 1614

History of the World, he excuses himself from including a history of his own time on the grounds that 'whosoever in writing
a modern history, shall follow truth too near the heels, it may
haply strike out his teeth'.[1] But there was another way.

At all periods, and in all societies, oppression gives instant
rise to covert forms of communication. The longer the period
of repression lasts, the more complex and allusive the hidden
language becomes. Recent studies have revealed the speed with
which literature responded to Henry VIII's stringent requirement for loyalty.[2] Equivocation, allegory, and code proliferated
right through the sixteenth century. One scholar, Annabel Patterson, has gone so far as to state that 'literature, in the early
modern period, was conceived as a way around censorship', and
she and others demonstrate the widespread use, by the mid-
sixteenth century, of a 'cultural code . . . by which matters of
intense social and political concern continued to be discussed in
the face of extensive political censorship'.[3]

Among the first to make systematic use of it were the indignant reformers after the downfall of their champion, the 'lov-
ing' Edward Seymour, Lord Protector in Edward VI's minority.
When the Catholic Queen Mary acceded to the throne in 1553,
a group led by the Protestant propagandist William Baldwin
put together a collection of apparently harmless verse histories
from England's past, featuring famous figures who returned
from the dead to give moralising accounts of their lives. They
were based on the mini-biography format of *The Fall of Princes*
by John Lydgate, a medieval poet who was rudely dismissed by a
later critic as 'a voluminous, prosaick and driveling monk'.[4] The
poetic quality of their own *Mirror for Magistrates* was not much
better; the work has tried the patience of later literary scholars
who have been compelled to take it seriously because of its wide
popularity in the sixteenth century. This small but immensely

influential book was read by everyone from courtiers to shop-
keepers; in the early seventeenth century, the erudite Lady Anne
Clifford scribbled admiring comments in the margins. Academics today react to *Mirror* much as they do to *The Rape of Lucrece*.
'What did the Elizabethans find so fascinating about this poem
that the rest of us have been missing?'[5]

It now turns out that poetic quality was not the authors' primary concern. The dissenters who put together the first edition were using the tales as cover for the dangerous history
of the immediate past that Ralegh prudently avoided. So neat
was their work, and so dull much of the verse, that it is only
recently that scholars have woken up to their true content. Contemporary censors were smarter. Under Queen Mary, the first
publication attempt was quashed, the Catholic authorities rightly
suspecting that beneath the tales of the downfall of great men,
there lay messages of advice and encouragement for those who
sympathised with the evangelical cause.[6] When Elizabeth came
to the throne in 1558, the book finally went into print, and
thereafter it was frequently republished, with contributions by
new authors and additions by a series of new editors. The format, however, remained the same: one by one, penitent ghosts
of English historical figures return from the grave to edify the
reader with stories of their sensational and tragic lives; and each
is followed—in the early versions—by a short, animated editorial discussion.

Between 1559 and 1562, just after Elizabeth's accession to
the throne, three momentous Parliamentary Acts affirmed her
claim to supremacy over the English church. They included
stringent and wide-ranging penalties for those who refused to
conform to the newly established Protestant practices, many
of which were opposed by evangelical reformers like Baldwin.
Writing or preaching against the royal supremacy was forbidden

on pain of prosecution for treason. There is an immediate impact on the next edition of the *Mirror*, in 1563. Ghostly visitants now crowd in from the reign of Richard III, the classic English embodiment of tyranny, lamenting their complicity with the usurping king, or, in the case of the king himself, warning him that nemesis would follow. In spite of its loud anti-Spanish patriotism, the *Mirror*'s growing hostility to the new regime was clear. Elizabeth's enemies used the fact that she had been disinherited by her father, Henry, to portray her as a usurper, like Richard; for the *Mirror* writers, tyranny and usurpation become consistent themes. As time goes on, attacks on the Reformation 'rape' are slipped in, cleverly disguised. One short but startling poem from a 1578 edition tells the tale of a community of Anglo-Saxon nuns who follow the example of their abbess, Lady Ebbe, cutting off their noses to avert the 'lust and lawless love' of marauding Danes.[7] The ploy fails—the Danes rape and kill them anyway. On a quick reading, this looks like an anti-Catholic morality tale, a jibe at the gratuitous 'beauty' of the old church. But the story doesn't quite work that way. The virtuous nuns are described without irony—even disfigured, they are 'vessels garnished gay before god's sight'.[8] As for the Danes: 'There was no sin from which those men did shun. . . . They churches burned, they pluckt the Abbeys down.'[9] The undoing of the commonwealth, the plucking down of abbeys—these might bring more recent acts of tyranny to readers' minds and prompt thoughtful reflection on the fate of the English church. Here, too, was a figure painfully stripped of its beauties, but powerless all the same to resist the brutal 'lust and lawless love' of a brutal predator.

The 1563 edition of the *Mirror* carried a manifesto for all poets writing under tyranny. One of the plaintive ghosts, William Collingbourne, returns from the dead after being hanged, drawn, and quartered for penning a rhyme lampooning Richard

III and his followers Catesby, Ratcliffe, and Lovell. The verse was famous in the fifteenth century: 'The cat, the rat and Lovell the dog / Ruled all England under the hog.' The blood-soaked victim begins with a message for fellow poets: 'Beware, take heed, take heed, beware, beware', he cries, denouncing tyrants as enemies of freedom and ending with the very line which would be used, as we have seen, by Dugdale to remind readers of the way Luther's words sanctioned the actions of Hollar's swaggering Henry VIII: 'Sic volo, sic iubeo, sit pro ratione voluntas.' For Collingbourne, poets are champions of truth, duty-bound to inform the monarch of the real feelings of their subjects, to regulate those in authority, to correct errors, and to do all this with lightness, wit, and tact. Drawing on a long line of classical precedents, he compares the poet to Pegasus, the winged horse born from Medusa—brave, unswerving, strong-witted, capable of plumbing the earth, sounding heaven, travelling the world, researching trades and occupations, discerning things of import, and uttering the truth. Though his own attempt failed, he recommends code and allegory as the best way of speaking truth to power: 'I name no man outright / But riddle-wise, I mean them as I might.' But if he does get caught out by a tyrant, then the poet, like Pegasus, must have the wit 'to gallop thence, to keep his carcass safe'.[10]

Collingbourne is doing more here than airing the *Mirror*'s cleverly allusive technique. He is giving it status and dignity. There is nothing base or furtive, he claims, about the role of the oppositional poet, and certainly nothing treacherous; on the contrary, the supple, perceptive, courageous writer is essential to the good governance of the realm. If the poet has to resort to coded writing, that is the fault of the tyranny he is addressing.

Collingbourne is William Baldwin's final contribution before handing the project over to younger editors—and if he hoped that the *Mirror* would continue to attract a popular readership and inspire oppositional writers, his hopes were more than fulfilled. Educated Elizabethans of all classes devoured the many successive editions right through to the end of the century. Philip Sidney's *Defence of Poesie* gives it high praise, and Shakespeare's generation of writers continue to show signs of its influence.[11]

By the time the 1587 edition came out, when Shakespeare was in his early twenties, the increasingly intransigent hierarchy of the state church was battling a rising tide of dissent. Catholics attacked them for innovating a new religion, reformers for appropriating the old one, and some of those who maintained a neutral pose, such as John Harington, bitterly satirised the divisiveness, corruption, and rampant materialism of the new order. Central to the argument now raging between reformers, Catholics, and the Elizabethan clergy was the true nature of England's church.

In those days, the church was widely portrayed as a living being. Early Christian commentators on the Old Testament book the Song of Solomon, or Song of Songs, read the protagonists in this sensuous love poem as symbols, or 'figures', of Christ and his beloved bride, the church.[12] But as always in the commentaries, the allegory was shimmering, changeable, complex. For some scholars there was just one bride, the fair Ecclesia. But others detected a second, dark-skinned sister, who rejected the bridegroom at first, only to return to him at the end of time. She was often depicted in medieval art and sculpture standing next to the obedient Ecclesia, as the equally beautiful but wilful Bride who refused Christ, 'Synagogua' (the Jews), or, in some versions, 'Haeresis' (heresy).[13] There is a scarf, sometimes a snake, over her eyes. Later preachers and polemicists adapted these early symbols of the two church brides to their own causes.

The sixteenth-century reformers, making full use of the printing press, combined the figure of a blowsy Ecclesia flourishing a chalice with the image in Revelations of the Whore of Babylon, and cast her as the Roman church. Catholics, meanwhile, presented the opposing bride as blinded Protestant heresy.[14] In England, the clamour of competing female voices became louder still, because, as the two great poets of the period demonstrate at the turn of the seventeenth century, England was faced with the bewildering choice of three, not two, church brides.

John Donne's early poems, circulating in manuscript in the 1590s, agonise over the difficulty of choosing between the Roman, Genevan, and English churches. The predicament is lightly caricatured in his third satire and dramatised with real desperation in his eighteenth sonnet. In the satire, one seeker finds her in Rome, 'richly painted'; a second falls for an unprepossessing bride in Geneva—'plain, simple, sullen, young, / Contemptuous yet unhandsome'; the last submits to an arranged marriage at home in England for purely mercenary reasons.[15] The tone of the sonnet is quite different. Here the quandary is expressed as an impassioned prayer:

> Show me, dear Christ, thy spouse so bright and clear
> What! is it she which on the other shore
> Goes richly painted? or which, robed and tore,
> Laments and mourns in Germany and here?
> Sleeps she a thousand, then peeps up one year?

George Herbert lines up the same trio of rivals in his poem 'The British Church'. For him, writing over a decade after Donne, the established church is the clear solution: she is the acceptable compromise, 'neither too mean nor yet too gay'. The Roman bride, up on the hills, is painted and disreputable; down in the valleys, the Genevan bride goes half-clothed or even naked, her hair dangling carelessly 'about her ears'.[16]

Not surprisingly, in view of this acute dilemma over central questions of allegiance and belief, a mood of deep depression overtook the English lyrical impulse in the 1590s, saturating with tears and sobs the sonnet sequences and madrigals that flourished throughout the decade. The most distinctive expressions of this peculiarly English form of angst, which are known to literary critics as 'complaints', occur in the *Mirror for Magistrates*, and the genre was taken up by many other poets. The complaint was a tale of woe usually uttered by a weeping woman returned from the dead; she is often encountered lamenting by a river, and is always eager to regale the passerby with a full recital of her miseries. In many cases, the woman is a victim of royal lust. Whether she submits or resists, disgrace, suicide, or murder eventually follow. Her sorry story is never simple; it involves many digressions, and much soul-searching, breast-beating, and indictments of tyrannical abuse. There is not much sisterhood among these fallen women. Their tragedies are oddly competitive; they belittle the woes of their fellow victims and attempt to outdo them. They are rarely read now. But at the time, the business of penning complaints and laments was so fashionable that one contemporary admiringly listed the group that he considered 'the most passionate among us to bewail and bemoan the perplexities of love'. They included Thomas Churchyard, Edmund Spenser, Samuel Daniel, Michael Drayton, and William Shakespeare: all masters of the art of complaint.[17]

For some scholars, the fact that Shakespeare's Lucrece finds herself in such company is yet another nail in her literary coffin. Critics are usually dismissive of the whole genre. 'In the last decade of the century the story of the sinning woman became something of a fad', yawns one recent scholar.[18] But we now know that such tales are more than mere titillating anecdotes. The first of them, *Shore's Wife*, written by Thomas Churchyard, appears five years after Elizabeth's accession, in the same 1563 edition of the *Mirror* that featured Collingbourne's advice to poets on how to oppose tyranny and yet survive. It concerns Jane Shore, the popular mistress of Edward IV, who, according to Thomas More, was cast out of the court to beg on the streets by the tyrannical Richard III, who succeeded Edward. Churchyard's tearful fallen woman gets an enthusiastic thumbs-up from the editorial discussion that follows, and *Shore's Wife* was widely admired by later poets. Thomas Nashe warmly complimented Churchyard as his generation's guru, whose aged muse was 'grandmother to our grandiloquentest poets at this present'.[19]

The reason for their admiration becomes clear when we trace the subtext which that generation might have detected beneath Churchyard's iconic tale. Like the young John Donne, Nashe was caustic about the course taken by the English Reformation and undecided about the nature of the true spiritual 'Spouse of Christ' over whom the Crown had so arbitrarily assumed marital rights. This uncertainty was profoundly unsettling at a time when most people still believed their salvation hung on the right answer. Unlike twenty-first-century readers, for whom Churchyard's poem is simply puzzling, Nashe and his contemporaries would have looked for parallels with the most pressing debates of the day: parallels which explain the poem's digressions and which give it the artistic coherence it otherwise lacks.

Churchyard's humbly born Jane Shore begins by reminding us of her pristine beauty and innocence. She recalls a golden time when her light outshone the sun, illuminating a dark world. Things began to go wrong when she gave in to the pressure of friends and consented to an arranged marriage to a merchant. An attack on forced marriage follows: there is, of course,

a personal cost, but also, oddly, an international one: it is a practice that wrecks not just an individual, according to Churchyard, but entire countries. So far, to readers alert to allegory, this
slightly tarnished figure would chime with the reformers' view
of the Spouse of Christ. To them, the church had been intact and
perfect only for the first few centuries. Under the later Roman
emperors she was fatally espoused to temporal power, a move
never intended by her founder. The damage incurred by this
'forced marriage' dimmed the original light of the gospel and
compromised its spread across the world. But a second, 'adulterous', entanglement happened in sixteenth-century England:
and this second liaison occurs in the poem. The king himself
makes advances. Shore's wife shrinks and crouches like a hound
before its master, a fowl beneath an eagle; she makes excuses to
her readers: 'Who can withstand a puissant king's desire?'[20] In
the end, she consents to become his mistress: 'I agreed the fort
he should assault.'[21]

At first all goes well. She uses her exalted position for good,
helping the poor, taking nothing for herself, promoting justice,
and acting as the king's conscience.[22] But she is now at that dangerous point, the pinnacle of Fortune's wheel, perilously exposed to wealth, admiration, and earthly pleasure. Before long,
Edward dies, and she plummets downwards, exiled from court
by Richard III. Churchyard embellishes her disgrace and destitution with details that would have resonated with those who
had seen the human casualties of the secular appropriation of the
church in England. She is now mocked, discarded, and despised
by all those she once helped.

Beneath this human tragedy, many contemporary English readers would have discerned their own country's tragedy. Churchyard has been criticised for complicating Thomas

More's straightforward biography of Jane Shore, on which he based his poem. But his alterations position the story within the then familiar framework of the Reformation debate. The poem laments both the 'enforced marriage' of the early church with temporal power and, much later, her enforced adulterous union with the English Crown. A brief interlude of charitable, enlightened reformation under the English monarch proves stillborn, and Tudor tyranny destroys the sorry remnant of the original true Spouse of Christ.

Churchyard's poem triggered a debate of which Baldwin might have been proud. The publication of works in which one weeping woman after another steps forward with her own story climaxed in the 1590s and included works by, among others, Edmund Spenser. The details of the stories were dependent on their authors' views of the sequence of events that followed on from Henry VIII's Reformation: they form an early, largely forgotten contribution to one of the most contentious debates in English history, one which remains unresolved to this day.

In 1591, Spenser, author of the English epic poem *The Faerie Queene*, published the extravagant laments of no less than eleven weeping women in a volume he called simply *Complaints*, which got him into serious trouble for satirising leading government figures.[23] Nine of Spenser's women are the muses, 'exiled from their native heritage' (341), who line up by the springs of Mount Helicon to bewail a cultural wasteland in which beauty, art, and learning are wrecked by ignorance and error. Each muse ends her lament with torrents of salt tears and 'yelling shrieks throwne up into the skies' (24).[24] The other two are ruined Roman cities personified as weeping women—one is Rome herself, the other Verulamium, or St Albans. Tellingly, Verulamium invokes William Camden as the one truthful recorder of 'my long decay which no man els doth mone'.[25] Camden does, indeed, record the first-century destruction of the Roman Verulamium, the apparent subject of this poem; but he also denounces the more recent destruction of the great Abbey of St Albans, which, he says, was dissolved under Henry VIII 'by the persuasion of those who preferred private reasons and their own fortunes to their king and country, nay to their God, under the specious pretence of reforming religion'.[26] Reminded of this familiar historical viewpoint, we can begin to see the point of Spenser's otherwise bewilderingly passionate laments in this volume— laments for 'the light of simple veritie / Buried in ruins' (171– 172), for 'antique monuments defaced' (179), for steeples turned to 'an heap of lyme and sand' (128), for the loss of 'endowments rare' (87), 'faire pillours and fine imageries' (96). 'Of that brightness', he mourns, 'now appears no shade' (124).[27] The cultural and historical losses detailed by Verulamium, Rome, and the muses echo similar laments by John Bale, John Stow, and many others for the cultural damage incurred by the dissolution. Here, and at points throughout the *Faerie Queene*, Spenser gives hauntingly lyrical expression to the heartache so evident in the pages of contemporary historians.

A year later, another famously melodious and sophisticated poet, Samuel Daniel, takes up the running, with another royal mistress returned from the dead to tell her weeping tale, this time beside the river Styx.[28] Before her death, Henry II's Rosamond, once a byword for the glamorous fallen woman, was concealed by her royal lover in a labyrinth, but his jealous wife finally tracked her down and forced her to take poison. Rosamond begins by reminding us peevishly of the complaint of Churchyard's heroine, Jane Shore, who 'passes for a saint', while Rosamond's own situation has been ignored. Yet she, too, was once an unspoilt beauty who briefly had a king at her feet.

The story that follows of her seduction and fall is full of angles developed from Churchyard and picked up by the many later admirers of the poem. Influential passages include her anguished inner monologue as she deliberates on how to respond to the advances of Henry II. Here she uses the classic language of the victim of tyranny: 'But what? He is my King and may constrain me / Whether I yield or not I live defamed' (337–338). Daniel is harder on his subject than Churchyard. Although Rosamond was coerced, in the end 'glittering pompe my vanitie did winne' (354), and 'Lost me the goal, the glory, and the day' (361). Immured by a jealous king for his own private use, Rosamond becomes in her own eyes a 'Minotaur of shame' (378). She is concealed in a 'stately' maze of 'confused errors' (465)—an echo of the theological arguments that surrounded the introduction of the new doctrines.

Daniel's careful development of these ideas can be read as an elegant articulation of one widespread view of the English Spouse of Christ. Originally an embodiment of universal truth, she has evolved into an expedient political hybrid after her appropriation by the Crown. Beauty like Rosamond's, says Daniel, should not be privatised. It is intended to be universally accessible 'by ancient charter' (515). The phrase is a reminder of early medieval charters guaranteeing the independence of the English church from illegal interference by the Crown.

The most interesting aspect of Rosamond's story is what happens to her after death. The penitent, reproachful ghost that accosts Daniel is stranded between one world and the next. Charon, who ferries souls to Hades in Greek mythology, refuses her passage over the river Styx because she is totally forgotten. Her soul can never pass, he says, until it is assisted by sacrifice and lovers' sighs in the world of the living. At the end of the poem we find out why no one remembers her. Henry's beloved

Rosamond was 'richly tombed in honourable wise' (704) at the nunnery at Godstow, outside Oxford. But, like so many grave-stones, hers vanished in Camden's 'storm'. Now, she says,

> . . . scarce any note descries
> Unto these times, the memory of me
> Marble and brass so little lasting be
> (717)

Like Spenser, Daniel deftly merges the ravages of time with the ravages of the Reformation plunderers. The marble and brass of Rosamond's tomb were destroyed by human hand, not by the elements, and vanished with the marble and brass is the crucial reminder to passersby to pray for her soul.

Rosamond, it seems, is one of many displaced spirits for whom, thanks to the loss of their gravestones, the world has for-gotten to pray. Daniel is specifically reminding us of the Cath-olic doctrine that those who must expiate their sins after death in purgatory can be assisted into heaven by the living—the doc-trine that was a prime target for the reformers, and the prime excuse for profiteers making a grab for the wealth of the old church, much of it acquired through countless donations to the church offered on behalf of the dead, to shorten their time in purgatorial suffering. Rosamond even asks Daniel's muse to grant her an 'indulgence' (47)—the theological term for the diminution of the soul's term in purgatory. This is the whole point of the poem—poor Rosamond's fate depends on a resump-tion of the prayers lost to her when her tomb vanished. Driving home the same protest at mindless and ignorant destruction as Spenser's, Daniel protects himself from accusations of papistry by ironically adopting the crude language of iconoclasts as he laments the loss of buildings consecrated to prayer:

For those walls which the credulous devout
And apt-believing ignorant did found
With willing zeal that never called in doubt
That time their works should ever so confound,
Lie like confused heaps as underground.
    And what their ignorance esteemed so holy
    The wiser ages do account as folly.

(708–714)

The tone may be coolly balanced, but the gist of this poem is a criticism of the effect on England of the royal takeover of the church. Daniel's urbane, sophisticated versification, and his skill in ventriloquizing both the compromised church and the friendless, unprayed-for sinner in a single, dramatic monologue, had a deep impact, both in drama and in poetry. Other poets followed suit with increasingly eloquent and introspective weeping women, and with them, opposing views as to what exactly had happened to the Spouse of Christ in sixteenth-century England.

Michael Drayton's *Matilda the Fair* comes next, in 1594. Set in the thirteenth century, the poem is partly narrated by Matilda Fitzwalter, a beautiful noblewoman who unluckily caught the eye of King John. But Matilda is quite unlike Rosamond, Jane Shore, Spenser's defeatist women, and the many other women who appeared in such poems. Far from surrendering in despair, she escapes, is pursued, and resists to the death. When she dies, it is not as another guilty victim, but a martyr.

Drayton's story differs from the narratives of his poetic predecessors and from the accounts of antiquarians and historians described in the previous chapter. For all the commentators so far, the tragedy of the English church was that it yielded to political pressure and precipitated a tide of greed and plunder deplored by all civilised onlookers—in short, that it became complicit with the state. Women like Rosamond and Jane Shore perfectly embodied this poignant capitulation, and Spenser gives memorable voice to the anguish caused by the ensuing loss. On the theological level, the church's beauty, truth, and virtue vanish with her shameful surrender.

The unflinching Matilda, however, departs emphatically from her sisters from the start, dismissing previous targets of royal lust as 'looser wantons', including Jane Shore, Rosamond, and, in what may be an early reference to Shakespeare's poem, Lucrece herself.[29] Drayton dwells at length on the sacred nature of Matilda's beauty, which, unlike that of her predecessors, remains unchanged and pristine throughout the poem. In a lengthy introduction, Matilda is given the clear theological overtones of the universal church, attracting 'all men's hearts' like a 'stately' lighthouse (115). Her face is a heavenly book, a map of Elysium; her brow displays tables of heaven's divine law. Her eyes—synonymous, in allegory at this period, with leaders, or guiding lights—guard her treasure, which is the tree of life. Describing the beauty of her face in terms of a heavenly coat of arms, she is, she tells us, the creation of the divinity, 'that great king of heavenly heraldry' (133). King John, alerted to her beauty by the 'jealous monster' rumour, is at once seized by 'controlling love' (183). He addresses Matilda in terms that identify her still further with the church. He recognises that in her, sorrow's wounds are healed, 'abstinence keeps virtue in a diet', 'wisdom, grown wealthy', lives 'at quiet' (344–350). Healing, silence, abstinence, and the pursuit of wisdom were among the chief purposes of monastic life in particular. Contemporary readers would have been well aware that King John was seen both by reformers and Catholics as a prototype of Henry VIII: his break with Rome, his excommunication by the papacy, his seizure of church lands and income, and the resulting interdict of England were dramatised by writers from John Bale to William Shakespeare, and portrayed as either heroic or misguided, depending on the standpoint of the author.

To begin with, just as the church originally wielded supreme spiritual authority in England, Matilda's beauty inspires respect, indeed submissiveness, in John: she holds the reins 'which ruled his princely will' (182). But not for long. John resolves to overpower Matilda, seize her identity, and adopt it as his own: 'Thy name as my impreza [device] will I bear' (414). But Matilda's father, Robert Fitzwalter, warns her that if she loses her virtue she will also lose her beauty: the two are indissoluble. The king banishes him and confiscates all his possessions. As he leaves, he bids his country a poignant farewell, calling it a 'rich isle', now 'taken from me by yonder tyrant's theft' (572–573). His followers and friends are denounced as traitors, imprisoned, and exiled. Drayton is here describing exactly the fate of opponents of the royal supremacy, who argued that their own country had been unjustly taken from them, and hoped to return to reclaim it, as the historical Robert Fitzwalter did. Matilda flees. In a vivid passage, the air, wind, and grass spy on her as she is hounded through the country by the king's men.

Drayton now departs from the chronicles of King John to align the story in striking detail with the events of the 1530s. Eight years later, Drayton would demonstrate detailed knowledge of the Henrician period in his poem *The True Chronicle of the Whole Life and Death of Thomas Lord Cromwell*, in which a gleeful Cromwell returns from the grave to tell the story of his life, in particular his pivotal role in the dissolution of the monasteries, a process the poem presents as a disastrous own goal by the English church. The same knowledge is evident here. When Matilda takes refuge in a priory, where she becomes a nun, King John sends his messenger, 'a devil walking in a human shape', to persuade her to submit to him. The messenger uses exactly the methods deployed by Henry VIII's commissioners to enforce the surrender of religious houses to the Crown—persuasion, followed by bribery and threats (730).[30] The messenger brings a letter from the king described as a 'black Commission'; it requests assent to a 'Bloody Act' (743–745). At first, as he asks her to sign the papers 'to make the Prince assurance of thy love', his tone is civilised and reasonable (807). He explains that Matilda has been deluded into resisting by 'foolish superstition' derived 'from old folk by tradition'; her scruples are 'trivial toys of reputation . . . whose ceremonies have the world infected' (791–800). 'Reason roots out what error erst hath sown', he explains; chastity is one of those outdated ideas 'the wiser have neglected' (802). It could be an English reformer speaking, pointing out the errors, superstitions, follies, and empty ceremonies of the Catholic Church, and ridiculing the clerical vows of chastity.

But Matilda disagrees. What the monarch demands is immoral. She argues that kings are God's vice-regents, and should act accordingly. The messenger's mood darkens. 'Minion', he snaps,

> 'Tis now no time to prate,
> Despatch, or else I'll drench you presently.
> Of this, nor that, I stand not to debate.
> Expects't thou love where thou rewards't with hate?
> (834–838)

If she refuses to sign, she must drink poison. In a moving passage, Matilda accepts the poison rather than 'live an abject in the world's disgrace' (858). Though she calls the king 'the Tyrant', she thanks him for showing her the way to salvation and prays for his conversion. She is confident that the shedding of her blood in God's cause will earn her 'everlasting bliss', as hers is a 'precious, sweet, perfumed sacrifice, / Hallowed in my almighty maker's eyes' (893, 922). This is the classic speech of the Tudor martyr facing death.

News of Matilda's death spreads like wildfire, reaching her father in France. Heartbroken, Fitzwalter asks God the agonised question so often asked by Drayton's countrymen: 'If so for virtue these rewards be due / Who shall adore or who shall honour you?' (972–973). His instant reaction as he sees the blood of innocents 'staining the glory of fair Albion' is to wreak revenge; but he restrains himself. Revenge is God's, he reflects: 'We must await heaven' (1009). In the dilemma voiced by Matilda's father, a dispossessed exile, lamenting the cruel treatment of 'innocents' at home and considering armed invasion, Drayton dramatises the conflicted reaction of English Catholic exiles to the persecution in their own country. Fitzwalter did in fact return with an army and was one of the barons who forced the king to sign the Magna Carta, an early attempt to curb the powers of the monarch.

What Drayton has done is to identify the true Spouse of Christ not with the raped, compromised, and desecrated figures depicted by Churchyard and Daniel, but with the followers of the traditional church who refused to compromise, and with those who, throughout the rest of the century, were persecuted for maintaining that stance. He passes over the whole question of the capitulation of the clergy, focusing instead on the fate of those who resisted with increasing determination right through to the 1590s. His poem ends not with shame, but with apotheosis, the elevation of the saintly martyr to heaven. Martyrdom was considered one of the marks of the true church, and the truth and purity of the Catholic Spouse is vindicated by Matilda's martyrdom. This is exactly the way Catholic dissident writers described the trials and triumphs of the church in England.

Drayton later deepens the Catholic identity of his Matilda in a reworking of the same story of King John and Matilda. In his *Heroicall Epistles*, written around 1596, but published in 1619, the king writes Matilda a frivolously blasphemous love-letter identifying her physical attributes with those of the old church, and portraying their imagined love-making in terms of sacrilege. Matilda's breast will be his altar, her lips his 'sacring bell', her curls his beads, his bed her shrine. 'Wert thou the Cross, to thee who would not creep / And wish the cross, still in his arms to keep?' (70–80). His salacious, lingering sexual proposition evokes a desecration of sacred objects and practices which would have had irresistible political overtones at the time. Drayton here develops the most explicit possible identification of the royal takeover of church property with the physical lust to which it was so often compared.

The entry of Matilda into the literary ring of competing women widens the debate dramatically. The puppet-masters of these afflicted women now include the full range of late Elizabethan dissident opinion. There are those reformers who hark back to the early church, seeing all Christian compromise with temporal power as wrong. They dated the first 'Fall of the Church' to the time of Constantine, or even earlier. Thus Jane Shore, her youthful perfection marred by an arranged marriage, was doomed almost from the beginning, according to Churchyard, and she falls further when she becomes the king's mistress, in spite of her brief period of virtuous influence on the country. Then there are those for whom the English church remained intact until her surrender to the English Crown, when, like Daniel's Rosamond, she became the possession of the state, cordoned off, vulnerable, and imprisoned in a temporal labyrinth. Rosamond is severed from traditional English religious practices: her tomb is destroyed, her soul unprayed for. There are those, like Spenser, for whom the cultural and artistic damage that followed the takeover is the real tragedy, amounting to a new age of barbarism. And finally, there is Drayton, who maintains that in spite of the desecration, the true Spouse remains inviolate, in the form of those in England who refused to capitulate.

Common to all these poems is condemnation of the takeover and its results. John Harington is typical of these late sixteenth-century English intellectuals. He remains studiedly detached on the surface, but at heart, as his privately circulated book of epigrams reveals, he is scandalised by the country's 'schism'. Like others before him, he compares the rift to the rending of Christ's seamless garment at the foot of the cross, the preservation of which, he laments, had always been the special care of 'our reverend elders'.[31] But beyond this, there was no consensus. Who was to blame? Could the garment—the fabric of the one, true, apostolic church—be repaired? If not, where was the true church? What had become of the Spouse of Christ? By the end of the century, the apparently naïve verse allegories of William Baldwin's circle had morphed into sophisticated inner monologues giving voice to the depth of thought and intensity of feeling that the late Elizabethans brought to their spiritual and religious predicament.

To this passionate argument, in the year 1594, the sixtieth anniversary of Henry VIII's Act of Supremacy, William Shakespeare introduced the sorrows of his own weeping woman. The choice of the Roman heroine Lucrece raised the tone of the debate. Unlike the royal mistresses of his contemporaries, she has ancient, distinguished, classical credentials, and she brings in her train centuries of arguments over the very issues now exercising the Elizabethan public—issues of tyranny, resistance, compromise, submission, ambiguous motivation, and martyrdom. In his *Defense of Poesie*, written a few years earlier, Philip Sidney mentioned the figure of Lucrece as the quintessential example of allegory. Here was the perfect vehicle for an analysis of England's most momentous historical upheaval—ready to be exploited by her greatest writer.

CHAPTER SIX

LUCRECE: THE ACT

A T THE END of *The Rape of Lucrece*, Shakespeare invents an
odd family quarrel over the victim's corpse. The first to
react after the shock of Lucrece's stabbing is her father, Lucretius.
With her life, he cries, his own life has ended too. She was his
image, his 'glass', his very identity, and now that the glass has
shattered he 'no more can see what once [he] was' (1751–1757).
But he is elbowed aside by her husband, Collatine, who col-
lapses histrionically onto Lucrece's corpse and initially appears
to die as well. Back on his feet, the 'pale fear' in his face now
covered with her blood, he struggles to speak, to call for revenge. But he can't find the words (1775–1780). At last he pulls
himself together, only to round on his father-in-law, displaying
the possessive streak that caused all the trouble in the first place.
He alone has the right to mourn Lucrece, he bursts out. His
wife belonged exclusively to him: 'I owned her' (1793–1803).
For the next two verses he and old Lucretius compete for possession of the dead woman. The effect is absurd. 'She's mine'; 'O

mine she is'; 'She was only mine'; 'tis mine that she hath killed' (1795–1802). The family row continues until Brutus cuts short their display of 'childish humour'.

What is going on here? None of this competitive mourning occurs in Ovid, in Livy, or in any of Shakespeare's other sources. There husband and father lament briefly, with dignity, and in unison. But if we set Shakespeare's *Lucrece* in the context of the Reformation debating chamber we have just left, which echoed with rival figures claiming to represent the assaulted spirit of the country, this passage not only makes sense, but gives us insight into Shakespeare's own political standpoint. If Lucrece is his late entry to this doctrinal and poetic arena, then the purpose of a tug of love between her father and her husband becomes clear. For those living through the aftermath of the Reformation in England it would have been a parody of the all-too-familiar dispute dividing England, which increasingly, in the 1590s, had become a debate about authority. The need to resolve this futile and ultimately disastrous rift, one of the main factors behind the bloody civil war half a century later, may well have been the inspiration behind the whole poem.

If Lucretius and Collatine represent the polarized positions of Catholic and Protestant, both laying claim to England's dying spirituality, which of them represents Roman Catholicism, and which the English Protestant church? Read in isolation, this final passage merely conveys the futility of the dispute; but by the time Shakespeare's original readers reached it, they would have been in no doubt as to the two identities.

Throughout the narrative, Collatine's behavior matches the fluctuating profile of the English Catholic leadership as its position altered from that of unquestioned spiritual authority over the church in England in the 1530s to the uncertainties and controversies of exile on the Continent in the 1590s. His often curious actions differ from all previous versions of the story of Lucrece, but accurately mirror the actions of successive leaders of English Catholicism throughout the sixteenth century. At first, like the princely Cardinal Wolsey under Henry VIII, Collatine flaunts the unrivalled prestige 'lent' to him by the 'priceless wealth' that is Lucrece. At the end of the poem, he is paralysed by indecision. His apparent inertia reflects the view in England of the exiled Elizabethan Catholic leadership under Cardinal William Allen. Unable to decide on an effective course of action and divided over the practicalities of a military solution, Allen and others resorted to conducting a cross-Channel war of words with the new Protestant church in a barrage of controversial books and pamphlets.

After Lucrece's account of the rape, she appeals in vain to Collatine for guidance. He offers her no support. Torn between powerful, conflicting emotions, he is unable to utter a word. The same reaction occurs after her death. He is first silent, then inarticulate: 'No man could distinguish what he said' (1785). When at last he manages to speak coherently, his main concern is to proclaim the dead Lucrece as exclusively his own property. The disedifying quarrel over who has the greater authority over her remains echoes the pamphlet war between the Catholic and Protestant leaders over which church displayed the theological 'marks' of the true Spouse of Christ.[1] This was of little comfort to English Catholics hoping for an end to persecution.

Old Lucretius, denying Collatine's superior claim to his daughter, represents the native English Catholic Church, supposedly founded at Glastonbury by Joseph of Arimathea before the primacy of Rome. What reformers saw as her independent identity was lost when her buildings and hierarchy were seized by the Crown in 1534. For those who were on the side of reform, but opposed to the royal supremacy, this English bride was fatally compromised by her subjection to the state. Lucretius, then, mourns the loss of national identity that occurred when the English church lost both its autonomy and much of its infrastructure in the 1530s. For him, the desolate images of a splintered mirror and a dying colony of bees sum up the sense of social collapse which is one of the major themes of the poem.

Shakespeare's masterstroke was to combine these two brides in a single figure. The Roman heroine Lucrece was raped, and yet she resisted; she submitted, and yet she defied; she was a complicit, guilty victim, but also a martyr. She is at once guilty, like Rosamond and Jane Shore, yet redeemed, like Matilda. In this poem Shakespeare reconciles the opposing camps of Drayton and Churchyard in the raped and vindicated figure of Lucrece. He demonstrates that the English Spouse need not be either the appropriated 'English' church or the oppositional 'Roman' church. They were the same, a single identity: both of them were England.

But Shakespeare presents an England in two moods, separated by around sixty years—the 1530s, the age of compliance, and the 1590s, the age of growing resentment and resistance. And the tricky depiction of England's evolving reaction to the supremacy is made possible by a second feature unique to the tale of Lucrece. There is an interval between Lucrece's rape and her decision to kill herself. This is the agonising period of reflection Rembrandt depicts so well. Shakespeare makes a daring alteration to this interval, in the process running the risk of losing the attention of the uninitiated reader. He greatly extends it so that Lucrece's period of indecision and mourning appears to take far longer than the forty-eight hours or so of the traditional story. The actual length of time is not stated, but it occupies almost half the poem. We are given not just an overdose of moral sententiae, not just a traditional debate about suicide, but leisurely reflections on Time, Night, and Opportunity, on the nature of sorrow, on music, on painting. We get slow, mannered interchanges between Lucrece and her servants, and the long digression on the fall of Troy, the whole thing amounting to almost a thousand lines of densely packed, often difficult verse during which the modern reader is tempted to give up. The rape itself has passages of rapid, vivid action and gripping suspense—but not the far longer section of the poem preceding Lucrece's suicide.

Shakespeare does this because the story of Lucrece, perfect though it is as a parallel to the royal takeover of the English church, is useless as a parallel to what happened next. What Sir William Dugdale called 'the great and strange alteration' that followed the takeover was a vast social upheaval that in the end, and in many different ways, affected almost everyone in England.[2] The kaleidoscope of material at the centre of the poem, which ostensibly describes Lucrece's fluctuating mental state, allows Shakespeare to explore these many consequences and to create a chronological timeline covering the period between the Act of Supremacy and its sixtieth anniversary in 1594, when he writes his poem.

If we line up the characters and events of the poem alongside the characters and events Shakespeare's contemporaries considered to be the chief landmarks of England's history between 1534 and 1594, we will begin to get a sense of what he was doing in the poem, and why the result was so admired by his readers. The following sections align each phase of the poem with its topical subtext to give us Shakespeare's perspective on the real-life drama that drove so much of his own work and the work of his literary contemporaries: the slow, tragic disintegration of a once unified England.

THE CARDINAL AND COLLATINE:
LIGHTING THE FIRE

The first landmark was the larger-than-life character of Thomas
Wolsey, who was intimately associated in the Tudor mind with
Henry VIII's divorce and takeover of the church. He was widely
viewed as the inadvertent initiator of the English Reformation.
Sixteenth-century readers of the 'wiser sort', who were as engaged with the causes of the Reformation as we are with the
causes of the First World War, would have been immediately
alert to Wolsey's ghostly presence behind the first few verses of
the poem. But the once famous hallmarks of Thomas Wolsey's
period of supremacy over church and state are now all but forgotten. If he does figure at the beginning of the poem, to us he
remains invisible. To try reading the poem as Shakespeare's contemporaries would have done, we need to recover their memories of this man: a cardinal, the Lord Chancellor, a candidate for
the papacy itself, and an awesome embodiment of hubris, whose
career epitomised the sudden plunge of a great man from the top
of Fortune's wheel to dust. 'If I had served God as diligently as I
have done the king he would not have given me over in my grey
hairs': these were his last words as he died, destitute en route to
the Tower, stripped of all symbols of the great offices of church
and state.[3]

Wolsey's commanding profile hangs in the Oxford college
in whose foundation he took such pride, Christ Church, once
Cardinal's College. Working from some lost original, the painter
presents us with a powerful, fleshy face, thick neck, heavy jowls,
sensuous mouth. Here is the infectious master of ceremonies,
the statesman, the visionary, the bon viveur who captivated the
king but then fatally outdid him at his own game, celebrating

peace treaties, building houses, conducting processions with a lavishness that left the king behind. 'Ego et meus rex', he would sign documents—'I and my king'.[4] His revived Star Chamber, a neglected judiciary chamber named after its star-spangled ceiling, was the place where he literally held court for much of his energetic working day, dispensing a form of direct justice much resented by the nobility but welcomed by commoners across the country; the place became synonymous with his name. Everywhere he went, he was preceded by two great silver crosses and two silver pillars; his Mass was served by noblemen, sung by matchless choirs to music by the composers he patronised.

As with all great celebrities, everything about his life caused gasps. At his death he was worth millions, and even more sensational, this dazzling wealth, itemised in all its gorgeous detail by his faithful supporter George Cavendish, went straight into the royal coffers after his fall. The London base for the Archdiocese of York—a house indistinguishable, when Wolsey had finished with it, from a Renaissance palace—would shortly become the Palace of Whitehall. It was a huge windfall for Henry VIII.[5]

How had Wolsey accumulated such wealth? Largely by collecting rich benefices and bishoprics; but also by a new stratagem, in which he was ably assisted by the rising star Thomas Cromwell, whose many skills included that of land conveyancing. To build his new foundations at Ipswich and Oxford, between 1524 and 1529 Wolsey closed down nearly thirty small monasteries and liquidated the proceeds. In a phrase highly significant for later literature which attacked the dissolution in veiled terms, Wolsey hotly denied that he had acquired these monasteries 'ex rapinis'—as a result of rape, or illegal seizure.[6] His unobtrusive legal manoeuvre had momentous consequences. Cromwell learned his lesson well and passed it on to a grateful king:

within ten years, there were no more monasteries in England. In his 1602 poem *The Legend of Cromwell*, Michael Drayton has no doubt that all this was 'ex rapinis': he, like many others, uses the word 'rape' for the raid on the church: 'And what their fathers gave her being dead / Her sons raped from her with a violent hand' (749–750).[7] Thomas More uses the same image of rape, with the sequel of eventual extinction at the hands of the king, in response to leading bishops who attempted to persuade him to accept Henry VIII's Act of Supremacy by attending Anne Boleyn's coronation. More warned them that they would first be deflowered that they might later be devoured.[8] Drayton's Cromwell revels in the irony that the church's own clergy initiated her downfall:

> Thus thou, great Rome, here first wast overthrown, . . .
> And in this work they only were thine own
> Whose knowledge lent that deadly wound to thee.
> (377–380)

Wolsey's personal downfall, however, was caused by his failure to secure Henry a divorce from his first wife, Catherine of Aragon. Fatally, he was caught in the marital crossfire, blamed by Henry for failing to plead his cause in Rome, and by Catherine for trying to plead it in the first place. Catherine attacked Wolsey at the divorce hearing, and the historian Edward Hall recorded her words: 'But of this trouble I onely may thanke you my lorde Cardinal of Yorke, for because I have wondered at your high pride & vainglory, and abhorre your voluptuous life, and abhominable Lechery, and little regard your presumptuous power and tyranny, therefore of malice you have kindeled this fire.'[9] Shakespeare seems to have been struck by this concept of

Wolsey kindling a fire. In his later play *Henry VIII*, he highlights it. 'For it is you', says Queen Katherine, 'Have blown this coal betwixt my lord and me / Which God's dew quench!' (2.4.79–80). Wolsey answers: 'You charge me, / That I have blown this coal: I do deny it' (2.4.93–94).

This play stages a second reason for Wolsey's downfall. In a single dramatic moment of furious discovery, Henry suddenly wakes up to Wolsey's vast riches and regal pretensions:

> What piles of wealth hath he accumulated
> To his own portion! And what expense by th'hour
> Seems to flow from him! . . .
> Forsooth, an inventory, thus importing
> The several parcels of his plate, his treasure,
> Rich stuffs, and ornaments of household; which
> I find at such proud rate that it outspeaks
> Possession of a subject!
>
> (3.2.108–128)

Shortly after this, Wolsey realises he is finished, as 'all that world of wealth' is shown to have been gathered 'for mine own ends' (3.2.211–212).[10]

For the dramatists, poets, and historians who were far closer to the events than we are, these were the main charges against Wolsey. He flaunted ecclesiastical wealth to an outrageous and unprecedented extent; he began the practice of dissolving monasteries to generate cash; he used his status as cardinal and papal legate to outrank his peers, and, on occasion, his king; the disrepute into which all this brought the church assisted what Drayton's poem on Cromwell called Rome's 'sad ruin' (720); and he kindled the fire of divorce, division, and dissolution.

Shakespeare's play on the subject picked up on the 'high-proud' aspect of the cardinal, Henry's affront at the discovery of his shocking wealth, and Catherine's image of the fire, which Shakespeare turned to a 'blown coal'.

The Collatine of the original story of Lucrece is a straight-forward, blameless soldier. In no way does he resemble Wolsey. He is not an instance of hubris, he is married, he becomes a re-publican rebel. But in Shakespeare's hands, his first appearance can, and does, powerfully evoke the notorious cardinal. We now see why the story is altered so that it is Collatine who initiates the whole process by which his wife will be raped. His boasting inadvertently kindles the 'lightless fire . . . in pale embers hid' that drove Tarquin to 'leave the Roman host' (243). By drawing attention to the riches he has in possessing his wife, he inflames Tarquin's lust for her, just as Wolsey drew attention to the riches of the church, inflaming the king's lust for its holdings. The hid-den flame in *Lucrece* has momentous consequences. It becomes a glowing 'coal' in the seventh verse and will continue to burn unforeseeably: 'O rash false heat, wrapped in repentant cold, / Thy hasty spring still blasts and ne'er grows old!' (48–49).

As soon as Collatine's name is mentioned, Shakespeare's nar-rator embarks on a stream of exclamatory speculations about his motives: 'haply', 'perchance', 'What needeth . . . ?' 'Why . . . ?' As Collatine himself blurs into a fog of possibilities, the pro-file of Wolsey sharpens. The narrator's restless queries build up a portrait of a rashly boastful, mercenary character who sees his 'beauteous mate' not as a woman, or even as 'Honour and Beauty', but as a commodity, a 'rich jewel', something of 'price-less wealth', a 'treasure' which outclasses the possessions, and in-deed the 'sovereignty', of the king (15–42). Shakespeare tells us Collatine's mate is not, strictly speaking, his own—she is 'lent' him by the heavens—but fatally, he appropriates her, reckoning her at a 'high-proud rate' and bragging provocatively about his 'possession'. There is a subtle allusion here to the borrowed nature of ecclesiastical wealth, which belongs, of course, to the church, not to churchmen, however princely. Like Wolsey throughout, this character 'unwisely' publicises what he sees as his own, unaware that it is 'weakly fortressed' and vulnerable to 'thievish ears' (10–35). Not surprisingly, this arrogance piques the interest of Tarquin, the 'proud issue of a king' (37). Tarquin is stung by the fact that his inferior appears richer than him, that 'meaner men should vaunt / That golden hap which their superiors want' (41–42).

So Shakespeare opens his poem with an unmistakable and dramatic Reformation chord, announcing the momentous theme of England's break with Rome. The lit coal that prompts the king to 'leave the Roman host';[11] the picture of the extravagant, overweening subject; the resulting threat to a vulnerable, unprotected object of great beauty; the possessive, mercenary language; the foolish lighting of a fire which would never die— all this would have been instantly recognisable to his readers.[12] The urgent questioning would have drawn them into the great debate, promising that this poem would not be a lecture or a polemic like those of so many of his predecessors, but a wide-ranging exploration of the whole complex subject. If Collatine represents Wolsey at this point, and Lucrece the inviolate church, then the exclamations and queries become the intelligent observer's reaction to the opening stages of Henry's reformation. Why did Wolsey run the risks he did? How did he view the wealth of the church? What kind of rival did Henry think he was? Did Wolsey inadvertently initiate the dissolution of the monasteries? How responsible was the king? Did Wolsey really light the fuse that meant he would be the last Catholic cardinal to live in England for the next three hundred years?

HENRY AND TARQUIN: THE GREAT GAMBLE

The historical Tarquin was a prince: yet time and again, Shakespeare's poem refers to him as a king, and a king who is assumed by Lucrece to be as engaged as Henry VIII was in the nature and obligations of kingship.[13] One of the aspects of the poem singled out for criticism by the scholar Colin Burrow is a long passage in which Lucrece tries to argue Tarquin out of raping her using high-flown humanist arguments that she somehow thinks will appeal to a responsible ruler. Burrow calls this 'a textbook example of political oratory' drawing on commonplaces from the work of the Renaissance humanist Desiderius Erasmus which would anyway have sounded 'decidedly old-fashioned' by the 1590s.[14]

But if we switch to the poem's secondary, political level, learned disquisitions on the virtues required of an enlightened ruler were just the kind of thing the younger Henry VIII enjoyed in the works of Erasmus and More, discussed with his courtiers, and indeed, commissioned from writers such as Thomas Starkey and Thomas Elyot. Well aware of the power of the new royal printing press, Henry went to great lengths to ensure that his reign would be portrayed as a golden age of humanist debate, in which he himself, the model Renaissance prince, attended to fearless advice from those around him about ideal governance. A number of his councillors advised against the takeover of the church—but when it came to actions rather than words, the king proved deaf, like Tarquin. 'By heaven, I will not hear thee', is Tarquin's impatient response, as he silences Lucrece and treads on the candle by her bed to extinguish it: 'This said, he sets his foot upon the light' (667–673).

Equally accurate, this time as a portrayal of Henry's private motives rather than his public image, is Tarquin's sleepless debate with himself before the rape. He considers the problem in terms of a risky financial gamble. The potential reward is 'great treasure' (132), he reflects, but it involves a threat to what he already possesses. He may 'scatter and unloose' what he has in the quest for more, he worries. He has enough—why risk everything for 'the profit of excess'? He may 'prove bankrupt in this poor-rich gain' (136–140). In other words, he will risk 'Honour for wealth, and oft that wealth doth cost / The death of all, and all together lost' (146). Continuing to ponder his own motives, he reflects that he has 'much', but that great wealth 'torments us' with the idea of what we don't yet have. We reach out for more, and 'all for want of wit / Make something nothing by augmenting it' (151–154).

Here, in painstaking detail, Shakespeare mirrors the thinking behind the failed gamble of the dissolution of the monasteries, drawing on analysis by the historians of his own time. The primary motive was financial—it looked like a winner—but in fact, Henry lost on many fronts, and indeed he wasted the capital he already had. Once the church's assets had been sold, the royal profits were soon spent, and the income and support the Crown had previously gained from the huge endowment of the church vanished. Neatly telling is the reference to 'augmenting', in his concern that he might 'make something nothing by augmenting it'. Thomas Cromwell set up the Court of Augmentations specifically to transfer the monastic gains into private hands and pass the proceeds on to the Crown, among many other pressing clients. In the eyes of many, it did literally make something nothing: the monastic network was liquidated, much of the estate destroyed, and the cash quickly squandered. The line can be read as a darkly ironic pun.

Shakespeare's insistent image of risking current assets in a bid for future profit does little to throw light on the mentality of a rapist, but it conveys with great sophistication the perception at the time, and among many historians to this day, of what Henry did to the Crown's finances. After the rape, Tarquin's worst fears are realised. He slinks off, a 'bankrupt beggar' (711), 'far poorer than before' (693), 'a captive victor that has lost in gain' (730).

Trading, deals, and unwise investment are the insistent themes of the first part of the poem, themes that end, as time moves on in the extended aftermath of the rape, with a portrait of an unhappy, avaricious old man, one of the many passages less relevant to Tarquin than to Henry VIII:

> The aged man that coffers up his gold
> Is plagued with cramps and gouts and painful fits;
> And scarce hath eyes his treasure to behold,
> But like still-pining Tantalus he sits.
>
> (855–858)

The lines evoke the overweight, gouty, pain-wracked Henry in old age. The children of such a man gain little: 'Their father was too weak, and they too strong / To hold their cursed-blessed fortune long' (865–866). The term 'cursed-blessed' echoes succinctly Spelman's view of the blighted legacy of those who profited from sacrilege. Furthermore, if we interpret those 'too strong' children as Mary, Elizabeth, and Edward, Henry's children from different wives, each destined to wrench the country in a different religious direction, this whole verse brims with political significance.

THE VIOLATED PRINCESS:
ENGLAND'S CONFLICTED RESPONSE

Images of spiritual catastrophe accompany images of material catastrophe as Tarquin resolves on rape. Meditating his 'loathsome enterprise' (184), he begins to worry about the fate of his soul. Out of habit, he finds himself praying that the rape will succeed, but then starts guiltily—praying is out of the question.

> . . . I must deflower
> The powers to whom I pray abhor this fact
> How can they then assist me in the act?
> (348–350)

He reminds himself, an anomalous pre-Christian Catholic, that 'the blackest sin is cured with absolution', a line that is followed by a rhyme suggesting what that sin might be—'fear's frost hath *dissolution* / The eye of heaven is out' (emphasis mine). This whole passage, rhyming on act, or Act, absolution, and dissolution, emphasises the topical subtext (351–356).[15]

As Tarquin approaches Lucrece, religious awe alternates with greed, just as would have been the case for the king and many of the iconoclasts and profiteers as they meditated their course of action. Tarquin tries to dismiss his qualms as superstitious—like a simple believer, he tells himself, he is being kept in awe by a 'painted cloth' (245). Like Henry, who sought opinion from universities across Europe on the question of a dispensation of his marriage to Catherine of Aragon, he holds a 'disputation' between will and conscience, which ends in 'dispensation' by his 'good thoughts', who manage to make 'what is vile' look virtuous (246–252). But Tarquin still hesitates. Henry remained a believing Catholic: and Tarquin to the end uses Catholic language in relation to Lucrece, whom he views as spiritual and inviolable:

> Die, unhallowed thoughts, before you blot
> With your uncleanness that which is divine;
> Offer pure incense to so pure a shrine
> (192–194)

Lucrece is a 'heavenly image' (288), a 'blessed thing' (340). He has debated the assault, he tells Lucrece, 'even in my soul' (498).

In the context of Tarquin's soul, critics point out a remarkable feature of the poem. The effects of the rape on his own soul, and, later, on Lucrece's, are described in almost identical terms. The language is so similar that some critics wonder if this curious repeat is carelessness on Shakespeare's part. There are subtle differences, but Shakespeare's phrasing suggests that they are two aspects of a single identity; almost, two ways of reacting to the same event. Tarquin's soul, a violated, 'spotted' princess, protests at once that her rebel subjects have 'battered down her consecrated wall' and 'defaced' her 'fair temple' (719–723). Lucrece's soul is also a princess, but one that remains inviolate in spite of Tarquin's assault. Her mansion has also been 'battered', and her sacred temple 'spotted', but by enemies, not her own subjects (1170–1175). And whereas Lucrece's violated princess seeks a hole by which she can escape from her 'spoiled' and 'blemished' fort through death, Tarquin's soul suffers a different fate. His princess complains that she has been captured and imprisoned by her own rebellious subjects, that she cannot escape, and that she is fated to 'living death and pain perpetual' (726).[16]

Shakespeare here distils into a few densely packed lines decades of reflection on the damage England was thought by many to have inflicted on herself in the course of the Reformation. In his two near-identical images of a violated princess within a fortress, he portrays the tragedy of a sacred infrastructure despoiled and violated, its spiritual occupants either escaping or guiltily submitting to the rule of the invader. By repeating the image first from Tarquin's point of view, and then from the point of view of Lucrece, Shakespeare distinguishes between the two different responses within the assaulted English church: those who remained loyal to the king, and made peace with their conscience, and those who resisted and died.

Many who profited from the windfall or co-operated with it paid for their actions with their integrity. Spelman himself fell into the category of those who had second thoughts, and returned their families' appropriations to the church. And indeed, like Spelman—and, above all, like Henry VIII—Tarquin regrets his actions. Just as Henry reasserted traditional Catholic practice ever more stringently towards the end of his life, alarmed at the headlong and unintended course of the Reformation, so Tarquin is portrayed as 'a heavy convertite' (743), a 'faultful lord of Rome' who as a 'guilty rebel for remission prays' (714–715).

PLUNDER

The full fury of writers like Cobbett, Dugdale, and others was reserved not for the king, but for the opportunists and profiteers who hijacked royal policy and the reforming impetus of the time for their own ends. Shakespeare joins them. Tarquin the rapist is a composite figure, and his very first actions encompass those of Henry VIII's self-serving ministers as well as those of Henry himself. Alongside Tarquin's strengthening resolve and final commitment in the buildup to the rape, one can detect the shadowy actions not merely of Henry, but of the highly placed cabal who capitalised on Cromwell's executive skill. They were vehemently denounced at the time.

When Tarquin first sets eyes on Lucrece, Shakespeare evokes elements of interrogation, of someone making an observant inventory. This was the task of the small group of government agents, known as royal visitors, commissioned by the Crown in 1535 and 1536 to investigate the communities of all the religious houses in the country and, more covertly, to assess their wealth.[17] Shakespeare's Tarquin deviates from the original Lucrece story by keeping her up late into the night when he arrives—'For, after supper, long he questioned / With modest Lucrece, and wore out the night' (122–123). Unsuspecting, she gives him 'reverent welcome', oblivious of the hungry eyes of one who 'having all, all could not satisfy' (90–96). The heads of religious houses, welcoming the king's servants, were often similarly unsuspecting, welcoming, and compliant.

Burrow highlights the element of aesthetic discrimination and excitement at this point, comparing Tarquin to 'a rich patron drooling over a costly work of art', as he visualizes Lucrece in terms of ivory, alabaster, and precious stones.[18] Like the commissioners and others surveying ecclesiastical possessions, he assesses the worth of each tantalising detail: 'What could he see, but mightily he noted? / What did he note, but strongly he desired?' (414). The repetition of the idea of 'noting' is a reminder of a strikingly similar scene in the much later work, *Cymbeline*, in which the voyeuristic villain, Iachimo, actually notes down the contents of a bedchamber: he goes through an 'inventory' in which he itemises the details of the sleeping Imogen's room, which he compares to a 'chapel', including pictures, fabrics, and even, as he removes a bracelet from Imogen's wrist, a five-spotted mole on her breast (2.2.10–51).

These highly worked scenes could not fail to bring familiar sights and stories of plunder and sacrilege to mind. Both Iachimo's and Tarquin's stealthy intrusions are fraught with religious language, evoking 'monuments', precious jewels, incense, candles, and untouched beauty, and both works stress the word 'canopy' as the intruders approach the holy of holies at the centre of the room. The term had religious overtones. A manuscript in circulation in the 1590s entitled *The Rites of Durham*, written by the antiquary William Claxton, recalls the central place and significance of the canopy in pre-Reformation churches, when the host hung in a shrouded container above the altar, believed by Catholics to embody the very presence of Christ: 'Within the second quire over the high Altar did hang a rich and most sumptuous canopy for the Blessed Sacrament to hang within it.' Inside was 'a marvelous fair pyx that the holy blessed sacrament did hang in, which was of most pure fine gold, most curiously wrought of goldsmith's work, and the white cloth that hung over the pyx was of very fine lawn all embroidered and wrought above with gold and red silk'.[19] The pyx, containing the host, often ornamented with golden rays, was one of the most elaborately ornamented objects in the church, and the canopy was often richly embroidered and tasseled with gold thread. When Tarquin opens the curtain around Lucrece's bed, we have the image of what a round, white host in a pyx still looks like, for the canopy hides a 'silver moon', and yet the immediate impact is of a brilliant 'fiery pointed sun' (371–372).

At the very centre of this sacred space, both Iachimo and Tarquin find something that delicately symbolises the passion of Christ. Iachimo compares the five spots to 'crimson drops' at the bottom of a cowslip—an irresistible reference for the contemporary reader to the ubiquitous English medieval image of the five wounds, which was used as the banner of Catholic resistance

in the 'Pilgrimage of Grace', the 1536 protest against Henry
VIII's supremacy.[20] Similarly, the sleeping Lucrece shows 'life's
triumph in the map of death, / And death's dim look in life's
mortality' (402–403). Rapidly read, this is a conventional image
of sleep; pondered on, it evokes the central Christian mystery of
redemption mysteriously contained, it was believed, within the
suspended pyx.

When Tarquin finally makes his move, the language is the
standard language of rape, which was often described in literature of the time as a military assault—but Shakespeare adds
elements of acquisitiveness and possession. Tarquin's swelling
veins are described as 'straggling slaves for *pillage* fighting' (428,
emphasis mine), and Tarquin, recalling the original fault of the
church, repeatedly blames Lucrece's beauty for provoking his
lust—'the fault is thine', he tells her. 'Thy beauty hath ensnared
thee to this night' (482–485). He is not just a rapist, but a new
owner: 'like a foul usurper', Tarquin intends 'from this fair
throne to heave the owner out' (412–413).

OPPORTUNITY: THE NEW OWNERS

In order to put a face on the raiders as they take possession of
their gains, Shakespeare calls up the three personifications of
Night, Opportunity, and Time. Images of predators and prey
give way to images of intrusive and destructive occupation—
wasps stealing honey from bees, worms entering buds, cuckoos
occupying nests—all of them new occupants who replace virtue
with vice: 'The adder hisses where the sweet birds sing; / What
virtue breeds iniquity devours' (871–872). Lucrece's 'weak hive'
has been invaded. She has lost the 'perfection' of her summer
and is 'robbed and ransacked by injurious theft' (837–840).

Opportunity acts out all the accusations Cobbett would later level at what he called 'the plunderers'. Opportunity facilitates the whole thing to start with: he makes the 'vestal violate her oath', plants 'scandal', and displaces 'laud' (883–887). Here Shakespeare details the process required to dissolve a reluctant abbey. The ground was first laid with persuasive visitations and discreet pressure; next, the occupants were induced, either by promises or by threats, to renounce their vows. Resistance was met with the spread of scandalous reports about the life of the community. And finally, 'laud', the ancient cycle of ordered prayer and daily ritual, was brought to a close, and displaced by new, private owners. Shakespeare joins Nashe, Camden, and others in the virulence of his attack on these intruders. Hypocritically feigning virtue, Opportunity ignores supplicants, the sick, the wretched, widows and orphans. Instead, he feasts, sports, grants 'no time for charitable deeds', and indulges in every kind of vice, 'spending the dowry of a lawful bed'— appropriating what was endowed for the poor and needy for his own purposes (897–908). These passages are full of tremendous rhetorical power. Cumulative questions pile up and explode into repeated denunciations. Shakespeare moves up a gear with the same ascending tone of incredulity and anger which seems to overtake so many of those, from his own time to Cobbett's, who contemplated the takeover:

> Guilty thou art of murder and of theft
> Guilty of perjury, and subornation
> Guilty of treason, forgery, and shift
> (918–924)

An intriguing question arises here. The man to whom this poem is dedicated, the young Earl of Southampton, was

descended on both sides of his family from just such opportunists. What could he have made of this thunderous denunciation
of the very men who had brought him his wealth and his title?
His maternal great-grandfather was Sir Anthony Browne, one of
a long line of courtiers who became trusted intimates of Henry
VIII and remained, like the king, conservatives in religion. His
Catholicism, however, was no bar to joining the rush to dissolve
the monasteries and benefit from the takings. The king granted
Browne one of the jewels in the crown, Battle Abbey, built on
the site of the Battle of Hastings, in Sussex; he also acquired
Cowdray Castle in Hampshire. His son capitalised on his inheritance under Queen Mary, acquiring further property along with
the title of Viscount Montague, and emerging on Elizabeth's
accession as one of the foremost Catholic noblemen in England.

More famous, however—indeed notorious—was Southampton's grandfather on his father's side. The red-haired, handsome
Thomas Wriothesley was an unscrupulous man of outstanding political gifts. He rose from undistinguished origins to become Lord Chancellor and almost single-handedly governed
the country in the years of Henry VIII's decline. He began his
public career as a vigorous suppressor of monasteries alongside
Thomas Cromwell, amassing abbeys and manors in eight different counties, as well as three houses in London. Titchfield
Abbey in Hampshire and its eleven manors lay at the centre of
his domain in the south of England, a critical area in terms of
defence against invasion from the Continent. As Cromwell's
man, he was a reformer, energetically destroying tombs and rel-
ics, including the tomb of Alfred the Great and the shrine of
St Swithin in Winchester Cathedral, to the indignation of his
old friend and tutor, Stephen Gardiner, who was bishop there.
But after Cromwell's fall, an adroit U-turn saw him becoming

Bishop Gardiner's traditionalist ally, and turning his energies to the burning of heretics.

A contemporary described him as 'an earnest follower of whatsoever he took in hand', one who 'very seldome did miss where either wit or travail were able to bring his purpose to pass'.[21] Holbein painted a miniature of this quintessential Tudor courtier, who embodied the relentless self-interest that scandalised men like Fuller and Dugdale. He has the lean, fit face of an athlete, a tight mouth and determined chin just visible under the red beard. The most striking features are the pale green eyes, wide open as if fixed on some distant object which has just caught his attention. A delicately rendered collar, made from the spotted fur of a lynx, completes the impression of a predator arrested mid-prowl. He was also a ruthless investigator and interrogator, once turning the rack with his own hands and dislocating the limbs of a woman accused of heresy. In a move that disgusted many of his contemporaries, he devised treasonous charges against the admired poet and soldier Henry Howard, Earl of Surrey, which sent him to the scaffold.

Wriothesley's most valuable skill lay in reading the mind of the increasingly unpredictable king, and it was partly this, and his ability to understand the king's religious inclinations, that made him, in the words of the historian Geoffrey Elton, 'manifestly the most successful civil servant of his day'.[22] In spite of the occasional prudent compromise, he remained a traditional Catholic throughout his life, effortlessly rising from one office of state to the next to become the king's secretary, knight, privy councillor, foreign envoy, Lord Chancellor, and Baron of Titchfield. Towards the end of the king's life the imperial ambassador was under the impression that Wriothesley 'almost governs everything here'.[23]

We do not know how Southampton regarded his eminent grandfather. Like many others of his generation, including Henry Spelman, he may have felt the need to distance himself from what had been done by his forebears, even to atone for it. Southampton's cousin, the Catholic poet and martyr Robert Southwell, viewed his own life as an expiation for that of his grandfather Richard Southwell, another unscrupulous fixer who had made a fortune out of the dissolution, and had assisted Wriothesley in the destruction of the Earl of Surrey.[24] Shakespeare's attack on Reformation opportunists in *Lucrece* must have echoed Southampton's own attitude to his family's past. Men and women like him, growing up at the end of the sixteenth century, were in an unenviable position. Their awareness of the negative impact of Opportunity on the social fabric of the country was complicated by the fact that their own grandparents were very often among the chief culprits.

NIGHT: THE PRICE OF CONFORMITY

Less well-known is the psychological impact right across society, across the country, and throughout the century on those who reluctantly yielded to government pressure and 'polluted' their own souls, as Shakespeare's Tarquin and Lucrece did: whether by submitting to the royal supremacy, unsaying their vows, yielding up their abbey or religious office without protest, reluctantly renouncing proscribed beliefs, capitalising on a windfall that many believed in their hearts was sacrilegious, or simply conforming for the sake of advancement. In the passage immediately following the rape, Shakespeare, who we know lived and worked among many who were struggling with just these dilemmas, gives us a persuasive picture of their state of mind.

The first ally on whom the fallen Lucrece calls is Night, 'image of hell'. Lucrece wants Night to hide her; indeed, she 'prays she never may behold the day' (746). Light sickens her: bring on concealment, she implores, rotten damps, musty vapours, anything but the 'life of purity, the supreme fair', which she begs Night to infect with his 'exhaled unwholesome breaths' (779–780). In a shocking reversal of her previous chaste and holy innocence, she speaks dully of the sun reaching the 'weary noontide prick' of the dial (781). Her shame is such that she cannot bear even the light of the moon and stars, and wishes Tarquin had raped them, too, 'so should I have co-partners in my pain' (789). Shakespeare dwells on this deeply human emotion, something his generation must have known well—the need for fellowship among the guilty, cowed, and oppressed.

Isolation and loneliness set in with her silence and guilt, along with a constant nagging anticipation of posterity's unforgiving view of her actions. These fears are genuinely prophetic if she speaks on behalf of the compromised church. She will be 'martyred', she predicts, not with fire or on the scaffold, but 'with disgrace' (812). 'Charactered', or written, in her face, people will see 'the story of sweet chastity's decay'—an epigrammatic summary of the prevailing later narrative of church corruption (807–808). Even those unable to read will 'quote my loathsome trespass in my looks' (812). The mutilation of images and the destruction of religious buildings were intended to convey this very message—the old church was disgraced, decayed, rightly taken in hand by the Crown.

Lucrece dwells at length on the way her meek compliance with rape and her betrayal of her marriage will become accepted truth by everyone, from orators to street singers. And she uses the sad words later antiquarians used to describe the destruction: her husband 'in peace is wounded, not in war' (831).

TIME: ALTERING THE RECORD

Time is as darkly ambiguous as wicked, protective Night. In a great passage invoking all the classic actions of Time the destroyer, Shakespeare repeatedly brings in the human destroyers who assist Time in its work as the decades go by, those who perpetuate the 'endless date of never-ending woes' (935). These woes include, of course, the ruin of 'proud buildings', of 'stately monuments', of 'antiquities of hammered steel'; but they also include the doctored historical record complained of by later scholars—Time's task, says Lucrece, is 'to feed oblivion with decay of things, / To blot old books, and alter their contents' (939–951). Shakespeare here touches on a theme to which he returns repeatedly—the fragility of historical truth, a major issue under a government which went to extraordinary pains to bolster its legitimacy by the deployment of censorship and propaganda, making full use of pamphlets, reports, chronicles, pictures, and plays.[25] This is where Lucrece, reaching the climax of her impassioned attack on her rapist, describes the event of the rape as a 'storm', and a 'wrack' (966)—the very image deployed by Camden and others for Henry's Reformation. The image of the storm triggers the most brilliant of all the variants in the poem on the theme of 'undoing'.

After begging Time to undo his own work, and rewind just one hour so that, somehow, the wreck never happened, a newly vindictive Lucrece prays for a different type of undoing in a prayer that is in fact a curse: 'Teach me to curse him that thou

taught'st this ill', she demands of Time (996). She asks that the
effects of Tarquin's crime—sleeplessness, sorrow, destitution, os-
tracism, madness—will recoil onto his own head. She prays, in
fact, for the very nemesis Spelman believed haunted those who
had profited from the dissolution, a nemesis which undid the
'plunderers' in all the many ways they themselves undid the abbeys and their evicted occupants.[26] In a linguistic tour de force,
her very words go back on themselves, enacting the idea of poetic justice:

> Disturb his hours of *rest* with *restless* trances;
> Afflict him in his *bed* with *bedrid* groans.
> Let there *bechance* him pitiful *mischances*
> To make him *moan*, but pity not his *moans*.
> *Stone* him with *hardened* hearts *harder* than *stones*
> (974–980, emphasis mine)

Finally, in a great litany, each line beginning 'Let him have
time . . . ', she completes the picture of inversion, of an assailant
suffering the grief he inflicted on others. The injuries are those
endured by the evicted, unemployed monks and nuns rather the
raped Lucrece. The whole section would have brought to mind
the widespread superstitions about the curse the monastic gains
brought with them:

> Let him have time to live a loathed slave
> Let him have time a beggar's orts to crave,
> And time to see one that by alms doth live
> Disdain to him disdained scraps to give.
> Let him have time to see his friends his foes,
> And merry fools to mock at him resort;

> Let him have time to mark how slow time goes
> In time of sorrow . . .
>
> (983–991)

Shakespeare repeatedly slips in a plural instead of a singular noun in these passages, so that Lucrece appears to be addressing multiple tragedies, not simply her own—Time would buy itself 'a thousand thousand friends', she urges, if it would only, just this once, rewrite the past (963).

In one of his last plays, *The Winter's Tale*, a work which has many parallels with *The Rape of Lucrece*, Shakespeare again introduces the persona of Time (4.1). The allegorical figure appears on stage halfway through the action. He reminds us of his power to create, preserve, and destroy; but his chief function is to fast-forward the narrative. He refuses to apologise for gliding over the 'wide gap' between one generation and the next, claiming authority to 'turn my glass, and give my scene such growing / As you had slept between' (4.1.16–17). Time also appears almost exactly halfway through *The Rape of Lucrece*, and Lucrece's repeated stress on the effects of the passing of time has a similar function. Image after image of growth and decay succeed each other, creating a hypnotic effect similar to time-lapse photography recording the passing of seasons on a screen. She awakes almost with a jerk from the reverie (1016), and, as in *The Winter's Tale*, we find we have moved on from the story of the remote past, the time of Southampton's grandparents, to his own present. In *The Winter's Tale*, written some fifteen years later, the present is conjured up in a vivid, infectious depiction of earthy English country life, and, after a first half which evokes the sudden and brutal division of England as a result of one man's passions, the conclusion of the play is redemptive. But in *The Rape of Lucrece*, written in the dark 1590s, there is no escape from the past, which has left many in England in an impossible situation. 'As the poor frighted deer that stands at gaze / Wildly determining which way to fly' (1149–1150), Lucrece tries desperately to block out her miseries with every kind of distraction—but nothing works. Increasingly, it seems that debate, music, 'the helpless smoke of words' (1027), even, Shakespeare will suggest, drama, are not enough. The only resort is that chilling path offered by the dagger, and championed by Lucius Junius Brutus: direct action.

CHAPTER SEVEN

LUCRECE: THE AFTERMATH

W E KNOW THAT Shakespeare, Southampton, Sidney, and thousands like them were intimately acquainted with the despairing state of mind described in the passages on Night and Time. In the finest passage in *The Mirror for Magistrates*, the courtier and writer Thomas Sackville, Lord Buckhurst, head of a wide family network which included many Catholics, situates an unusual allegorical figure, 'Remorse of Conscience', at the gates of hell. He describes her mind 'continually in fear / Tossed and tormented'. With 'her eyes unsteadfast, rolling here and there', she is 'wishing for death, and yet she could not die'.[1] Sackville, a relative of Southampton's, was a wealthy and successful outward conformist whose loyal stance protected his more exposed dependents. The 'remorse of conscience' that he portrays with such feeling was a peculiarly English condition which altered and deepened over the sixty years that passed between Henry VIII's Act of Supremacy in 1534 and the year 1594.[2] Reformers, but more particularly, Catholics who came of age in the 1590s, such as the Earl of Southampton, inherited a bitter legacy. This Elizabethan inheritance is explored in detail in the second half of *Lucrece*; to understand it, we must briefly revisit the fluctuating fortunes of the English church after the death of Henry VIII, and in particular their impact on Southampton himself, whose family and situation become an increasingly integral part of the poem.

DAY: THE ELIZABETHAN AGE

Though the church's infrastructure suffered a mortal blow under Henry VIII, it was only under his son Edward that the state religion changed from Catholicism to Protestantism. Thousands rose up in rebellion, but many more kept their heads down, silently condoning the surge of iconoclasm as reformers set about eradicating every trace of what was now condemned as idolatry and superstition from the liturgy, the churches, and the social life of the country.[3] When, after Edward's brief reign, his sister Mary ascended the throne, Catholicism once more became the country's religion. The reversal was widely welcomed, but her five years in power exacerbated sectarian hatred. Almost three hundred Protestants were burned as heretics: the memory of this horror was kept alive for centuries by John Foxe's *Acts and Monuments*, a graphically illustrated indictment of Marian cruelty distributed from 1571 to all the cathedral churches in England. After Mary's death, the supporters of Elizabeth I steered a third change of religion through Parliament: Protestantism again, but this time with the promise of moderation. The promise turned out to be hollow. Elizabeth's advisors calculated that only the complete eradication of dissent would permit the survival of the

new state compromise, a religion that was doctrinally Calvinist, but which retained controversial 'popish' elements. Warily
introducing statutes that at first were barely enforced, the new
men set about the extinction of England's old religion while
others worked to silence the extreme reformers who had pioneered the new.

Following the momentous introduction of the Acts of Supremacy and Uniformity in 1559, Catholic gentry and commoners were excluded from public office of all kinds, which
now required an oath of allegiance specifically denying the spiritual authority of the pope. Failure to attend the state church
was punished by monthly fines amounting to a schoolteacher's
annual salary. 'Recusants'—those who refused to take the oath
or attend church services—faced confiscation of their goods or
imprisonment if they were unable to pay. In 1570, the papacy
responded by excommunicating Elizabeth and absolving her
subjects of loyalty to their queen, even if they had sworn oaths
to her. The effect on English Catholics was disastrous: they were
now perceived as potential traitors. As time went by, new laws
were passed: educating children as Catholics became a crime;
Catholics were confined to within five miles of their homes; a
crippling 'loan' was imposed on recusants to defend the country
against Spanish invasion; further fines and loans were exacted to
provide for military expeditions to Ireland. Sheltering a priest,
converting others to Catholicism, returning to the country as a
priest—all these were punishable by death. In 1581, Lord Burghley even proposed a scheme to remove children of Catholic gentry from their homes in order to bring them up as Protestants.[4]

Inevitably, most took the oath and conformed, becoming
'church papists', and attending the occasional Catholic Mass in
secret. All the same, the numbers of recusants ran into thousands,
requiring the building of new prisons right across the country,

while the flood of Catholic exiles stoked fears of foreign invasion led by Sir William Stanley, one of England's most formidable military leaders, who had defected to Spain while fighting in the Low Countries in 1587.[5] Meanwhile, reformers were also on the run from government authorities. At the end of the 1580s, a series of caustic satires on the new church by an anonymous Puritan, 'Martin Marprelate', began to issue from a secret printing press. The press was eventually found and destroyed, the printer racked, and by the 1590s, the church authorities had hounded dissident clergymen out of their church livings and, in many cases, out of the country.

The crisis of conscience that reluctant religious conformity entailed in an age of faith is difficult to recapture now. In a letter in 1580, Philip Sidney, who was well-acquainted with the milieu of families like Southampton's, warned Queen Elizabeth about the ferment within them and the threat they posed. They were, he said, 'men whose spirits are full of anguish; some being forced to oaths they account damnable; some having their ambition stopped . . . ; some in prison and disgrace; some whose best friends are banished practisers; many thinking you a usurper; all burdened with the weight of their consciences; men of great number, of great riches'.[6]

Though to be a Catholic was politically unwise, the nobility were at least exempt from the oath. For ordinary people, life was harder. Desperate members of Shakespeare's own family broke cover briefly in 1583, when his young relative John Somerville, whose sanity cracked under the restrictions imposed on Catholic recusants, rode down from Warwickshire to London wildly threatening to kill the queen. He died in prison, his distinguished father, Edward Arden, was executed, and many others suffered in the aftermath. The fall of the Ardens was only one of hundreds of similar small-scale local tragedies among

commoners and gentry throughout the country. More conspicuous were the struggles of those noblemen who attempted to retain both their faith and the great gains they had acquired under
Henry.

Southampton's parents and grandparents were high-profile
examples of these casualties of conscience. During Mary's reign,
Southampton's father made the most of the wealth and status he
had inherited from the great 'plunderer', Thomas Wriothesley,
but he gradually fell from grace under Elizabeth as he obstinately refused to change his religion. Implicated, like the Duke
of Norfolk, in Catholic plots, he was periodically put under
house arrest and spent almost two years in the Tower in 1571–
1573. His marriage fell apart, and he died at the early age of
thirty-six, possibly of an illness contracted during a second spell
in the Tower in 1581.

Southampton's maternal grandfather, the 1st Viscount Montague, was more cautious. A forceful character, he began Elizabeth's reign by speaking out vehemently against the Act of
Supremacy in Parliament in 1559—the only temporal peer with
the nerve to do so. His hard-hitting speech was, in the words of
one scholar, 'as thorough an indictment of the regime's policy
as it is possible to imagine'.[7] Once the bill was passed, however,
Montague prudently took the line of outward conformity to the
new order. He attended the new Communion service and for a
while prospered at Elizabeth's court.

But, like Buckhurst's, Montague's conformity was decep-
tive. It concealed an extensive network of Catholic activity right
across the south of England and beyond, ranging from chap-
lains almost as conformist as he was to missionary Jesuits, activists, and hot-headed separatists.[8] Government nervousness
with regard to his various households is understandable, most
particularly with regard to his wife, Magdalen. An even more

dominant character than her husband, she remained a figure-head for English Catholics right through to the next century, firmly repelling all attempts to put a stop to flagrant Catholic practices in Montague House in London and in the great family houses in the south-east of England—Cowdray, Battle Abbey, and Titchfield, all situated in a swathe of south-eastern England dominated by a broad, if often covert, Catholic kinship network.

These were the surroundings in which Southampton spent his early childhood. As he grew up he would have been aware not only of quarrels between his warring parents, but of constant, heated debate among his relatives over exactly how the family of which he would shortly be the head should respond to increasingly invasive government pressure to conform. 'Politically radical' is the way Michael Questier describes many of his Catholic relations. They included the notoriously determined Thomas Pounde, a onetime favourite of the queen, who spent his entire life in and out of prison for his beliefs.[9] There were activists on the Montague side of the family as well, some of them supporters of the 1580 Jesuit mission by the celebrated scholar Edmund Campion, who called for a public debate with Elizabeth's divines. Instead, he was captured after a year on the run, and hanged, drawn and quartered at Tyburn in the winter of 1581. The mission was regarded by some Catholics as a spiritual lifeline; for others it was needlessly divisive. Southampton's great-uncle, Francis Browne, concealed the Jesuits' printing press at his house in Southwark, and his own generation included three boldly oppositional cousins, John, William, and Anthony Browne, who inherited the title of Viscount Montague. The brothers were pictured arm-in-arm by Isaac Oliver in 1598 in a strikingly defiant group portrait, in which they are dressed identically in the 'mourning' black favoured by English

Catholics. Significantly, there is a cross incorporated into the design through the use of window bars, just as in Southampton's slightly later Tower portrait.

Most notorious of all was the poet Robert Southwell, another of Southampton's resolutely Catholic cousins, who also rejected the option of compromise. He became a Jesuit, returning from the Continent in his late twenties to spend six perilous years working underground in England. He had dedicated his life to reviving the spirits of waverers who had, by falling away from the faith, 'long sowed in a field of flint' that brought them 'nothing . . . but a crop of cares and affliction of spirit, rewarding labours with remorse, and affording for gain eternal damages'.[10] Southwell's prose and poetry can be read as a searching analysis of the torn psyches of the many people he met and knew in England—men and women who were often paralysed by confusion and doubt. In spite of his remarkable empathy, Southwell himself was not one of them. Before setting foot in England, he knew exactly what awaited him. He was captured in 1592, tortured periodically over the next three years by a psychopathic priest-hunter, Richard Topcliffe, and kept in solitary confinement until his execution in 1595 for high treason at Tyburn.

The fate of men like Pounde and Southwell was a terrible option that most of Southampton's family, however committed to their faith, did their best to avoid. Michael Questier's study uncovers the many ways in which the Montagues, in particular, attempted to reconcile their consciences with a conformism that the Catholic Church condemned as perjured and damned.[11] Southwell analysed their cruel dilemma with sensitivity but warned against compromise. The same inescapable predicament of all those who could not, in conscience, accept the Elizabethan Settlement clearly absorbed Shakespeare as well. As he approaches the final phases of his poem, he moves on from the days of capitulation and submission under Henry, Edward, and Mary to the growing quandary under Elizabeth as a new wave of highly educated missionary priests like Southwell preached dogged resistance, and the number of recusants, prisoners, exiles, and bloody executions grew. Shakespeare's portrayal of the problem is broader and more nuanced, however, and the solution he proposes is more radical, than Robert Southwell's.

LUCRECE'S DILEMMA:
1594, THE DIVIDED RESISTANCE

Tarquin has slipped away and dawn is now breaking. Lucrece, frantic and undecided, 'like a poor frighted deer', knows that only suicide, from which she recoils, will demonstrate her loyalty to Collatine. As she steels herself to the terrible decision, Shakespeare introduces another of his unique details to the story. Her death will show that her virtue was enforced, says Lucrece, but it will also ensure that any child she may have conceived will not survive. She will never have to swear an 'infringed oath' to her husband that the child—the 'bastard graff'—is his. It is in odd interpolations like these, which, if anything, reduce the drama of the original story, that the topical level intrudes. At this period, inevitably, English Catholics were acrimoniously divided over the Oath of Supremacy. Conformists urged formal acceptance of the oath in return for toleration. But the mainstream held out: the result would be a 'bastard' Catholicism, nominally Roman Catholic, in fact subject to the English state. The long-running dispute would shortly split the English Catholic cause. To the conflicted Catholic circles examined by Questier, there was an immediate and painful relevance in Lucrece's reflections on the dangers of a perjured oath and its long-term consequences.

Also familiar to such people was a sense of unease and alienation, of being under surveillance in their own country, of being a stranger in familiar surroundings. The rising sun seems to spy on Lucrece and mock her with its 'peeping'; its light brands her forehead.[12] Angry and irritable, she shuts out the birdsong: 'sad souls are slain in merry company' (1110). Instead she turns to the nightingale, the classical image of Philomel, the raped woman. They will sing together in the forest at night to soften the hearts of the 'creatures stern' they find there, she says, and harmonise the sad tune with several voices (1147). The purpose of these songs, and their setting, also sounds topical. The school of English madrigals flourished briefly in the 1590s, patronised particularly by the Earl of Essex and written for the most part by Catholic composers: their laments and pleas are often the veiled utterances of afflicted English Catholicism.[13]

Lucrece still cannot decide, like Hamlet, 'to live or die, which of the twain were better' (1154). Finally, she calls her maid. A long, stylised account of their weeping encounter evokes the late Elizabethan vogue for female complaint, and the fondness of Catholic poets and lyric writers for elaborate images of tears and weeping, exemplified by Robert Southwell's widely imitated poem 'Mary Magdalen's Funeral Teares'. At last she lays her 'plot of death'; she writes a letter to summon Collatine, so that he can hear her story and witness her death. But what can she do in the long hours before his return? Worn out by sorrow, Lucrece is desperate for distraction, or at least for a means 'to mourn some newer way' (1365). At this point, under the guise of praising a painting, Shakespeare reminds his readers where most Londoners went to find distraction: not in poetry or the visual arts, but on the stage.[14]

ROMAN ART, ELIZABETHAN DRAMA

If Shakespeare had not lived, the proliferation of stage dramas at the end of the sixteenth century in England would still have been considered remarkable. The appetite for plays across the country, but particularly in London, was insatiable. Playwrights could not keep pace with demand. Theatres sprang up all over the capital, many of them on former church properties that lay outside the jurisdiction of the City of London. Great ingenuity went into finding sites and dramatic methods that would allow politically engaged writers and their patrons to escape the censorship of the city and the Ecclesiastical Court of High Commission. To counteract the pernicious influence of dissident drama, members of the Privy Council funded a state theatre company, the Queen's Men, to travel the country proclaiming the orthodox political and religious line.[15] The more all these plays are examined in the light of the complex politics of the day, the clearer it becomes that drama was just as much a forum for religious and social debate as poetry was, and clearly, in Shakespeare's view, it was a more effective one. If Baldwin, in his poem about Collingbourne, championed the poet as the single figure able to speak truth to power with impunity, Shakespeare, an actor-dramatist briefly experimenting with a poetic career, disagrees. When Lucrece writes her note to Collatine she despairs of setting down her tragedy on paper. Such a tale needs 'sighs and groans and tears', 'the life and feeling of her passion', and she withholds words 'till action might become them better' (1316–1323). And live performance has another advantage. It can tell the truth. Much earlier, as she vainly tried to argue with Tarquin, Lucrece reminded him of the one group of people who will expose his crime: not poets, but actors:

O, be remembered, no outrageous thing

From vassal actors can be wiped away;

Then kings' misdeeds cannot be hid in clay.

(607–609)

Hamlet, who employs actors to expose his uncle's crime, calls them 'the abstract and brief chronicles of the time', dangerous men, in other words, capable of holding a mirror up to the present (2.2.517–519).

In *The Rape of Lucrece*, Shakespeare is about to show us that even painting, however accomplished, is inadequate to portray the conflicting passions aroused by certain tragic events. Only the playwright, with living actors at his disposal, has the capacity to air, explore, and to some extent heal the agonies of an intolerable situation like that of Lucrece, and of his own generation. In 1599, Southampton was described by an onlooker as passing his time in London 'merely in going to plays every day'.[16] But going to plays was no longer an idle or harmless pastime. It was an escape, but it was also a vital stimulation: obliquely, deniably, daringly, the latest developments in an increasingly repressive decade were being dramatised and discussed on stage by 'the abstract and brief chronicles of the time'.[17]

Lucrece gives us an example of the kind of exhilarating catharsis experienced by late Elizabethans as they saw their own situation portrayed on stage, and often, not merely portrayed, but closely analysed and resolved. Waiting for Collatine's return, aware that her suicide will follow, Lucrece recalls a painting of the fall of Troy which hangs in her house. She goes off to look at it.

Shakespeare portrays the picture as a masterpiece. From start to finish as he takes us through this vivid aesthetic experience, we are kept aware of the genius of the painter and his impact on his audience. Nine times, we are reminded of the 'well-skilled workman'. His brilliance is almost cinematic. The peasants appear to 'quake and tremble' (1393); Nestor's beard 'wagged up and down' (1405). This magical artist can show us what is barely visible—the sadness of the distant eyes of defenders 'through loop-holes thrust' (1383). He can even depict what is not there at all, through 'conceit deceitful', by using a part to represent the whole, an essential part of the repertoire of the allusive artist or dramatist: 'A hand, a foot, a face, a leg, a head / Stood for the whole to be imagined' (1422–1428). Somehow the painter can convey not just the conflict between the Greeks and the Trojans, but the complex emotions behind it. The Trojan mothers, watching their sons march to war, display conflicting emotions beyond the reach of a painter, but not an actor—indeed, the striking lines almost sound like the advice to members of the cast by a theatrical director:

> To their hope they such odd action yield
> That through their light joy seemed to appear
> (Like bright things stained) a kind of heavy fear.
> (1433–1435)

Lucrece at last finds what she is looking for—Hecuba, the widow of the Trojan king, the very image of grief, gazing on her dead husband. Hecuba, like Lucrece, is more than a mourning woman. In her face, the painter has 'anatomised'—that is, analysed in detail—three giant forces, which amount to the destruction of a society: 'time's ruin, beauty's rack and grim care's reign' (1450). Lucrece is mesmerised—the image perfectly mirrors her own situation. But there is one thing missing. Hecuba is silent. Brilliant though he is, the painter cannot animate his pictures: 'And therefore Lucrece swears he did her wrong, / To give her so much grief, and not a tongue.' It would take a living being to give Lucrece the 'cries' that she needs to hear from Hecuba, she says, if the old woman is to be a true mirror to her own sorrows (1459–1464). The whole painting strains towards drama, and the impact on the unhappy Lucrece of its 'shows of discontent' is what a great dramatist aims for: she experiences the relief of catharsis, 'Being from the feeling of her own grief brought / By deep surmise of other's detriment' (1578–1589).

So this highly self-conscious description of a work of art, addressed to a patron who was known to be a great lover of plays, could have been understood at the time as a vindication not of painting, or even of poetry, but of drama as the greatest healer in times of personal and communal grief. Lucrece's response to the still images is to convert them into action—lamenting aloud with Hecuba, dropping balm into Priam's wounds, quenching Troy's flames with her tears, tearing out the eyes of the Greeks with knives, ripping Sinon with her nails. The therapeutic aspect of this passionate involvement in the tragedy is nicely caught at the end when Lucrece realises she is lashing out at a painted image: 'At last she smilingly with this gives o'er. / "Fool, fool!" quoth she, "His wounds will not be sore"' (1567–1568). 'Smilingly'—the word has extraordinary impact after so many pages of relentless melancholy. It heralds a newly decisive Lucrece. The agitation and indecision are gone; she is now able to face her returning husband, tell the tale of the rape with dignity, and ready herself for the last, fatal step.

Though it celebrates the potential of drama to air and heal the complex, largely suppressed grievances of the English in the late sixteenth century, this passage has an equally important role in the structure of the poem. It summarises the political subtext, using the tale of Troy to mirror the social wounds and cultural destruction of England.

CLASSICAL TROY, TUDOR ENGLAND

At a period when England was regularly hailed by poets and pro-pagandists as 'Troynovant', a second Troy, readers would have expected political allegory from this key passage. In this case, the parallel was a grim one. Just as the collapse of the civilisation and the beauties of Troy stemmed from the lustful actions of a single man, so, Shakespeare suggests, the collapse of much of England's culture and heritage stemmed from the lustful actions of a single ruler. The true parallel to Lucrece's destruction is not Hecuba, but Troy itself, victim of the actions of the Trojan prince Paris, who eloped with Helen, the wife of the Greek king, Menelaus, and thereby triggered the Trojan war. Shakespeare dwells on this particular aspect of the conflict. Paris is repeatedly viewed as the embodiment of a heedless, selfish passion which wrecked the lives of thousands. 'One man's lust these many lives con-founds', Lucrece laments, reflecting on the disaster that results from what she sees as Paris's unchecked 'desire' (1489–1490):

> Thy heat of lust, fond Paris, did incur
> This load of wrath that burning Troy doth bear,
> Thy eye kindled the fire that burneth here,
>   And here in Troy, for trespass of thine eye,
>   The sire, the son, the dame, and daughter die.
>   (1473–1477)

The stress on the disproportionate impact of one man's lust con-tinues: 'Why should the private pleasure of some one / Become the public plague of many more?' (1478–1479). Lucrece seems unable to drop the theme of the public repercussions of a private act of lust, revisiting it five times within two verses (1473–1491), and twice connecting it with the word 'plague'—regularly viewed on all sides in England as divine judgement on the religious changes.[18] All of this is less reminiscent of her own situation than England's.

Remarkably, the war is not mentioned. All the suffering in this passage could relate to the mutual persecution that disfigured England. Shakespeare details the anguish of bystanders and mothers as well as soldiers, and encourages the impression of an internecine conflict: 'Here friend by friend in bloody channel lies, / And friend to friend gives unadvised wounds' (1486–1487). He was not the first to compare the destruction of English society with the ruin of Troy. The link had already been made in a notorious pamphlet written by a Catholic exile twenty-two years earlier. In his *Treatise of Treasons*, John Leslie develops a long, explicit parallel between the two cataclysmic events, telling his fellow countrymen that he could find 'no story that doth more aptly resemble the false sleights that are now in the forge among you' than that of the infiltration of wooden horse into Troy.[19]

For Leslie, the evil genius behind the disaster is not Paris, but Sinon, the sweet-talking Greek whose deception persuaded the Trojans to accept the gift of the wooden horse in which were concealed soldiers who threw open the city gates to the besiegers. In a sustained and vitriolic attack on a man he sees as the deviser of a similar subterfuge, one which wrecked his own country, Leslie identifies Lord Burghley as the 'English Sinon', 'principal worker of all the Treason, one that had a deep wit, a smooth tongue, an aspiring mind. . . . A sly and subtle shifter to compass whatsoeuer he would.' Having identified her own woes with Hecuba and vented her fury on Paris, Lucrece, too, reserves her last and bitterest attack for Sinon, the deceiver whose act, like Tarquin's, completely hoodwinked his unsuspecting victims. The embodiment of Opportunity, Sinon is the plausible intruder through whom Troy perished, the final figure in the panorama.

Shakespeare's *Lucrece*, then, contains its own microcosm—a work of art that begins with the precipitating act of a lustful prince, proceeds to explore the many-faceted misery his actions created, and ends by tracing and lamenting the work of the opportunists who capitalised on the original crime.

Shakespeare's extended Trojan panorama is far more than a bravura rhetorical showpiece. It uses one of the oldest and grandest of all classical tales to restate a detailed analysis of the English Reformation in terms which, as we have seen, many of his contemporaries already recognised; and at the same time, it shows how art, in particular his own favoured art form, drama, could act as a channel and escape valve for the anguish this unhappy national story entailed.

RAPE REVISITED:
RECALLING THE ACT OF SUPREMACY

At last, Collatine arrives home with a group of others, including Lucrece's father, Lucretius, and Lucius Junius Brutus, who, though dismissed as a fool, is in fact a secret enemy of the Tarquins. The witnesses are assembled. A calm, resolved Lucrece has a dagger in a steadied hand. Much would be anticipated by a sixteenth-century reader from the crucial final scene, that of Lucrece's long-delayed suicide. If this reading is correct, then alongside a greatly expanded version of Lucrece's rape, Shakespeare's contemporaries would have been following a narrative of the opening phases of England's 'Long Reformation', accompanied by a searching analysis of spiritual England's enforced submission to the Crown. How will the discussion end?

An account of the rape by Lucrece, repeated by Brutus as he rallies support against the Tarquins, is essential to the most conventional conclusions of the story. And that is what Shakespeare gave us in his short prose 'Argument', or summary, at the beginning of the poem. There Lucrece revealed the name of the rapist and urged her supporters to avenge her death. Next, Brutus recounted the details of the 'doer and manner of the vile deed, with a bitter invective against the tyranny of the King' (37–40). Finally, 'with one consent', the Romans exiled the Tarquins and changed the state government 'from kings to consuls' (41–50).

As many critics have noticed, the ending of the poem itself is quite different. The expected punchline has gone. The result of Lucrece's death should be Rome's transition from monarchy to republic; here we are told merely that the Tarquins were banished. As Lucrece begins her sad final recital, other key Roman details vanish. Shakespeare erases much of the tale's original context in order to highlight the elements in the story that coincide with the history, the memories, and the current situation of his readers. His version builds up to a simple statement of Lucrece's famous case of conscience, deliberately couched in terms with which his readers were all too familiar: 'What is the quality of my offence / Being constrained with dreadful circumstance?', Lucrece asks her husband and the assembled company. 'May my pure mind with the foul act dispense?' (1701–1703). Were all those who submitted unwillingly to the Act of Supremacy spiritually undone? If so, what was the way to undo that undoing?

Selecting only what is relevant to his own time, Shakespeare keeps the contemporary parallels constantly in view. He omits the name Tarquin, for instance. Lucrece does not identify him in her simple résumé of the event. Her attacker was a 'stranger' (1620), a 'creeping creature with a flaming light' (1627). She asks for a vow of vengeance without naming her assailant—the only version of the tale in which this happens. When at last she tries to reveal the name at her death, she is oddly described as 'throwing forth' the word 'Tarquin' before making no fewer than five different attempts to utter it. '"He, he," she says / But more than "he" her poor tongue could not speak.' She goes on: '"He, he, fair lords, 'tis he / That guides this hand to give this wound to me"' (1717–1722). Collatine has the same difficulty: 'Sometime "Tarquin" was pronounced plain / But through his teeth, as if the name he tore' (1786–1787). Brutus, in his concluding call to arms, does not mention Tarquin. So here, more insistently than ever, and for the last time, Shakespeare encourages us to substitute something or someone else for the perpetrator of the rape.[20]

The word 'rape' itself is also omitted. Throughout the poem, and even in the original title (*Lucrece*), Shakespeare avoids connecting Tarquin's deed with rape or ravishment, though both words occur elsewhere in the poem. 'Foul enforcement' (1627) is just one of a series of euphemisms the characters use for the assault. The most significant substitution is the word 'act', which replaces the word 'rape' four times; twice, the original compositor gives the word an eye-catching capital 'A' in the first quarto.[21] It appears with a capital in the important final speech, when Brutus calls on Collatine to avenge 'his foul Act, by whom thy fair wife bleeds' (1824). And when Lucrece recounts the event to Collatine, she tells him that her 'enemy' threatened her with slander, and boasted that 'this Act will be / My Fame, and thy perpetual infamy' (1637–1638). By Shakespeare's day, fame and infamy were indeed the consequences of the events of 1534. The Act of Supremacy had become a cornerstone of English political identity, while often slanderous stories of the corruption and degeneracy of the Roman Catholic clergy and the long-gone monasteries had become part of the country's official history.

DEATH AND DIVISION

Shakespeare aligns the dead Lucrece with a very different identity from the sacred image of the first few pages. The poem begins with a highly worked association between her red and white colouring and the heraldic attributes of both her country and the English church. It ends with the tragic undoing of this intricate device. Instead of displaying the harmonious interplay of red and white, her colouring now divides and changes. Though the red stays the same, the white has undergone a tragic alteration. As she bleeds, 'Some of her blood still pure and red remained, / And some looked black, and that false Tarquin stained' (1741–1742). As at the beginning, the colours are minutely differentiated—Shakespeare describes in detail the way the red blood, 'still pure', blushes with shame at the putrefied, 'tainted' black. And he ensures that we see the 'mourning' black not as evil in itself, but as the victim of evil. A watery serum, then and ever after, he stresses, surrounds the corrupted black blood and 'seems to weep upon that tainted place' (1744–1750). These two connected emblems—Lucrece's red and white cheeks at the beginning, and her red and black blood at the end—are delicately symbolic. They show us England's identity before and after the events of Henry VIII's reign. In the first emblem, those who cling to the 'beauty' of tradition and those who press for the 'virtue' of reform are in equilibrium. In the second, an emblem of death, the red remains inviolate, but the reformers are the casualty. They are no longer white, pure, and unsullied: their cause has been taken over and betrayed by the state. The black, associated with the persecuted and derided Puritans in Shakespeare's day, is in this image the black of mourning.

Most explicitly of all, Lucrece's death is described in terms of the disappearance of life and beauty from an island. Shakespeare frequently refers to England as an island, most famously in *Richard II*, where John of Gaunt calls it 'a sceptered isle . . . this little world . . . a precious stone, set in the silver sea' (2.1.40–50). In *Richard II*, as here, the island is tragically damaged by a king's misdeeds. As Lucrece begins 'the sad dirge of her certain ending', she is portrayed as a pale, dying swan in a nest surrounded by water. After her death, her body, surrounded by streams of blood, 'like a late-sacked island vastly stood / Bare and unpeopled in this fearful flood' (1740–1741). The picture of a devastated island kingdom could hardly be clearer. The sense of social disintegration deepens in the scene where Lucrece's father and husband fight over her body.

ROMAN REVOLT, TUDOR REBELLION

Shakespeare ends his portrait of England not with a lament, but with a dramatic action plan. Brutus's response to Lucrece's suicide is startling: 'Thy wretched wife mistook the matter so / To slay herself that *should have slain her foe*' (1826–1827, emphasis mine). Shakespeare's is the only version of the story in which Brutus believes Lucrece should have fought back and even killed her assailant instead of herself. Her suicide was wrong, he asserts, and so are the pointless recriminations of Collatine and Lucretius, whom he rouses to anger, revenge, and rebellion. The 'abominations' that disfigure and disgrace Rome, he says, must be 'by our strong arms from forth her fair streets chased' (1834).

By the time the members of the determined company have knelt, prayed, sworn a solemn oath, and, in a muted final verse, banished the hated Tarquins, we can at last begin to apprehend something of the scale of Shakespeare's undertaking in this tremendous poem. It is no longer surprising that he, and others, referred to it so often in the years that followed. The complaints of assaulted England reiterated in earlier poems, the repeated jabs at tyrants driven by lust and lawless will, the fractious debate over the identity of the church bride—all these by now tired and clichéd elements are boldly swept up, set in a full and detailed historical perspective, and revolutionised in a tour de force of political analysis which in its ambition and scope dwarfs its predecessors. Add to this the inner music of the poem, the rhetorical suppleness and wit, the balance and sophistication of the arguments, and the powerful emotion of the many moments of indignation and anger, and we are looking at a political poem that rivals those of John Dryden, Andrew Marvell, and John Milton in its breadth, clarity, and intellectual command.

The Rape of Lucrece is a powerful indication that in the year 1594 Shakespeare either shared the increasingly oppositional standpoint of Southampton and Essex, or that he was, at the very least, deploying his formidable intelligence and ingenuity—the 'wit' that was so often associated with him—in order to popularize their views. There is of course an accepted wisdom among some distinguished literary critics that Shakespeare did not write allegory. This poem suggests not only that he did write allegory, but that he was an apologist for a particular party: the broad, amorphous group of dissidents, including Southampton's extended family, who were beginning to look to the Earl of Essex as the last hope of regime change. The poem gives eloquent voice and a considered context to the grievances Essex promised to redress: the horror at the destruction of the old social order, the lament at the spiritual division of the country, the disgust at its descent into an era of greed and corruption. And it was addressed to Southampton not because of his youth and beauty, but because he was one of the last remaining figureheads of the old order prepared to make a stand against what was increasingly seen as a tyranny. The poem may even have had a political impact. Six years after the publication of *Lucrece*, Southampton and the Earl of Essex did exactly what Brutus recommended: they took up arms to remove an unpopular regime from their country. This prompts the question: Did the Earl of Southampton take *Lucrece* to heart and cast himself as the noble, avenging Brutus? Could Shakespeare have said of this poem, as William Butler Yeats said of his own political drama, leading up to Ireland's 1916 Easter Rising, 'Did that play of mine send out / Certain men the English shot?'[22]

All the elements in the preceding discussion of *The Rape of Lucrece* have been explored over decades by exceptional literary scholars, to whom this book owes a great deal. But the long-standing disinclination to pursue topical commentaries in Shakespeare's works, particularly if they hint at dissident, or, worst of all, Catholic sympathies, means that scholars have avoided the necessary discussion about exactly what that topical commentary might be, and hung back from proposing full-scale political interpretations. Yet, as the next chapter will show, a very large number of educated, humane, and civilised people in 1590s England may well have shared the suggested standpoint of the poem.

This standpoint can only be retrieved if we are prepared to take the concerns of the Elizabethan opposition seriously, and to set aside the traditional reverence for the figure who dominated Elizabeth's age and, to a large extent, its historical record: William Cecil, Lord Burghley. Once we have looked at the queen's chief councillor as he appeared to his contemporaries, we will begin to understand why his ward, the Earl of Southampton, was the man to whom Shakespeare dedicated his two narrative poems.

Chapter Eight

The Guardian

B OTH ESSEX AND Southampton began their lives as wards of the Crown, the unenviable fate of those heirs to landed estates in Tudor England who were under the age of twenty-one when their fathers died. Like a number of other leading peers of the realm, their wardship fell to the Master of the Court of Wards himself, the treasurer and close advisor to the queen, William Cecil, Lord Burghley. Essex, the older by eight years, was Protestant, and spent little of his period as a royal ward with his guardian. But Southampton, a Catholic, was more of a liability. Shortly after the death of his father in 1581, he arrived at Cecil House in central London. He was just eight years old.

As Master of the Court of Wards, the sixty-four-year-old William Cecil took a keenly protective interest in young and fatherless earls possessed of considerable estates and surrounded by powerful Catholic relatives. Though Southampton was now the head of his large south country Catholic clan, it is often assumed that his own youthful Catholicism did not last long. He himself, his religion, and all the lands, houses, hopes, and expectations he inherited, lay vulnerable and exposed to the biggest and most rapacious beasts of Elizabeth's court. Prising open and extracting the possessions of the old English nobility was a skill Elizabeth's government had already raised to an art form.

The young earl must have looked an easy target. His earliest portrait, painted in his late teens, was only recently identified as the painting of a young man. For many years it had been labeled 'Lady Norton, daughter of the Bishop of Winton'. His skin is unnaturally white, the lips cherry red, the eyebrows form two fine arches, there is an elaborate red and black earring, and—the giveaway—Southampton's trademark lock of hair hangs down below the left shoulder. But if Burghley thought this effeminate, self-regarding youth would be easily led, he would have done well to look more closely. The artist Nicholas Hilliard painted a miniature of Southampton a little later, in 1594, the year of *The Rape of Lucrece*. The chin is still rounded, the hair is fairer and even more elaborately curled and dressed, and he retains the long lock over his shoulder, but the pale green eyes, looking directly at the viewer, are those of his grandfather Thomas Wriothesley, the fixer who 'very seldom did miss where either wit or travail were able to bring his purpose to pass'.[1] In an echo of portraits by Hans Eworth of the Catholic Queen, Mary I, a scarlet cloth hangs behind him, the folds of which form a cross—a conspicuous motif picked up, as we have seen, in the painting of his three cousins, and employed in his own Tower portrait.

Little evidence survives of Southampton's early years as Burghley's ward. We know that he somehow resisted the strong religious pressure to conform, as he is recorded by one of his contemporaries as publicly converting to the new religion only twenty years later, on his release from prison in 1603.[2] Financially, however, he was outmanoevred from the start. The administrative machinery that had swung so smoothly into action under Cromwell in order to supply Henry VIII with monastic spoils had a secondary role—that of stripping the gentry and nobility of rights, privileges, and money which, it was argued, belonged to the monarch under neglected feudal law. The system of royal wardship allowed guardians to retain all the revenues of a young man's estates, which they administered until he reached the age of twenty-one, when he had to pay the Crown a large sum to regain the property. Just as with the abbey lands, these new gains rapidly devolved into the hands, not of the Crown, but of the men who rose to power in the wake of the Reformation. These were a new and more formidable generation of opportunists, expert at relieving the early beneficiaries of the dissolution of their newly won lands and titles. Foremost among them was Lord Burghley himself: assiduous, pleasant, methodical, indispensable to the queen, and utterly focused on consolidating a position and amassing a fortune that encompassed and dwarfed even those of men like Thomas Wriothesley. Subjected to the governance of Burghley and his circle, Southampton would have witnessed the continuing workings of Shakespeare's predators at first hand: the concealment of Night, the avarice of Opportunity, Time's alterations.

Under Burghley's authority, about a hundred wardships a year were sold to petitioners on the Crown's behalf. The purchase of a wardship allowed a guardian full rights over his charge. These could be highly lucrative, as they ranged from administering estates and receiving their income to selecting a suitable marriage partner; unsurprisingly, would-be guardians were prepared to pay well. The Crown was in desperate need of money, and in the absence of consistent taxation, needed to maximise every available source of income. Though the system operated with increasing thoroughness throughout Elizabeth's reign, over the same period her income from the activities of the Court of Wards mysteriously fell. Only a fraction of the proceeds from the sale of wards reached the royal coffers. As recent studies of the court's workings has revealed, the rest passed into the private pockets of Lord Burghley, his children, and his dependents.[3] And the sums were considerable. A note to himself by Lord Burghley, marked 'to be burned', shows that he charged eager purchasers on average three times more for a wardship than the amount officially recorded; his son Robert would charge considerably more.[4]

Burghley's persistent, methodical tactics did much to increase national resentment at the excessive incursions of government. By the 1590s, each county had its own agent, or *foedery*, employing a host of informers tasked with tracking down and alerting the Court to impending wardships, a network that incidentally supplied Lord Burghley with invaluable local intelligence. Meanwhile, sweeteners were passed up the line by would-be guardians, usually local gentry, with the widow left at the back of the queue in the scramble for lucrative wardships. One typical landlord concealed the deaths of his tenants for many years to protect them from what his steward called the 'Argos eyes' of the foederies 'peering into all conveyances'.[5] The uneasy sense of surveillance by a many-eyed governmental organisation is something we associate more with the twenty-first century than the sixteenth, but it was clearly widespread. People from all walks of life resorted to ever more complex legal strategies to counter the incursions, so that before long the whole country had become entangled in a struggle over property and marriage rights requiring the services of the new and ingenious generation of Tudor lawyers currently passing through London's Inns of Court.

This vast scam, and others like it, lay behind many of the

veiled references to the parasites, or 'caterpillars of the commonwealth', as they were often called, who surrounded the aged queen, nibbling away at the ancient rights and privileges of landowners, and ensuring that the great and influential families, most of whom had strong ties with the old religion, were quietly neutralised by one means or another. One of the poems which circulated in the 1590s attacking the acquisitiveness of the new men was John Donne's second satire, bristling with shafts directed at Burghley's ally, the leading lawyer Sir Edward Coke. Coke was also closely involved in the trafficking of wards and in detecting and preventing the exploitation of protective loopholes by their families. By the turn of the century, he owned over a hundred properties and, like Burghley, was amassing a fortune. Donne accuses him of avarice and asset-stripping; more generally, he attacks the style of the new landlords, who ignored old agreements, sold ancient deer parks and woodlands once accessible to commoners, enclosed land, and raised rents. 'Spying out heirs', he writes, the greedy barrister Coscus 'piecemeal' deprives them of lands, 'wringing each Acre' with infinite pains, until 'Where are those spread woods which cloth'd heretofore / Those bought lands? Where's th'old landlords troops, and alms?'[6] Donne, like many others, equated the new landlords with a loss of the old social responsibilities to the community, the poor, the land itself. In Shakespeare's *Richard II*, a play where 'caterpillars' are twice mentioned, John of Gaunt voices a tragic note as he considers the state of England:

> This land of such dear souls, this dear dear land,
> Dear for her reputation through the world,
> Is now leased out, I die pronouncing it,
> Like to a tenement or pelting farm:
> England, bound in with the triumphant sea

Whose rocky shore beats back the envious siege

Of watery Neptune, is now bound in with shame,

With inky blots and rotten parchment bonds:

That England, that was wont to conquer others,

Hath made a shameful conquest of itself.

Ah, would the scandal vanish with my life,

How happy then were my ensuing death!

(2.1.56–68)

As well as accruing vast riches, Burghley used his position as Master of the Court of Wards to retain for himself the guardianship of the most distinguished royal wards, including that of ten noblemen—Lord Wharton, the Earl of Oxford, two successive Earls of Rutland, the Earl of Bedford, the Earl of Essex, Lord Sheffield, Lord Zouche, the Earl of Southampton, and Philip, Earl of Arundel, whose father, the Duke of Norfolk, was executed in 1572 for plotting against the Crown. The ancient families that continued to flourish at court owed their survival to marriages into the new order, very often into the widening Cecil sphere of influence. Lord Burghley, a meticulous forward planner, made the most of the right of a guardian to arrange the marriages of his wards. His daughter Anne was married to the Earl of Oxford—though the marriage was predictably unhappy, it connected her with the second-oldest earldom in the country. One measure of Burghley's success in providing for his family is that four of his five granddaughters became countesses, while his grandson William married another of his wards, Elizabeth Manners, the wealthy heiress to the barony of Ros. Another was the complete ascendency achieved under James I by his second son and political protégé, Robert. Also educated in the little academy at Cecil House, Robert easily outshone his older brother, Thomas, and later, as the Earl of Salisbury, greatly increased his father's gains by methods which set a new standard of corruption, even in the notoriously venal Stuart court.

As the estates of great noblemen like the Earls of Oxford, Essex, and Southampton shrank and their homes decayed or were sold on, spectacular new houses took their place in an increasingly competitive process known as 'The Great Rebuilding', in which Lord Burghley led the field. Cecil House in London was typically ambitious. Occupying two large blocks on the Strand backing onto what was then the open countryside of Covent Garden, Burghley's city base had a restrained, sober street façade. Like all his houses, however, this one was in fact built and furnished on a magnificent scale in the latest Renaissance style. Four stories high, with towers at each corner, it included two central courtyards, gardens, bowling alleys, and a tennis court. At the back of the house, airy, unglazed arches of an Italianate loggia looked out onto the elaborate gardens, from which gates opened conveniently onto the route to two of his other grand architectural projects, the immense and imposing Burghley House, a day's ride away in Cambridgeshire, and the spectacular palace of Theobalds, near Cheshunt in Hertfordshire, only twenty or so miles north of London.[7] Other ambitious Cecil developments included Wimbledon Palace, another magnificent mansion, set in gardens based on the Villa Farnese at Capranola, which was erected to the south of London by Burghley's oldest son, Thomas, and another spectacular town house on the Strand built by Robert, known as the Strand Palace.

In its time, Theobalds, built ostensibly as an occasional royal residence for the queen, was the most famous.[8] The elaborately landscaped gardens, filled with exotic plants, rare fruit trees, and antiquities, were modeled on Fontainebleu, and there are descriptions by stunned visitors of their fountains, temples, loggias, and graceful courtyards, the mile-long double avenue of trees, the banqueting house, the covered marble swimming pool, the grotto, the canals and moats 'large enough for one to have the pleasure of going into a Boat, and rowing between the shrubs'.[9] Within, the magnificently decorated rooms and galleries, easily capable of accommodating the entire royal court along with visiting diplomatic delegations, were hung with tapestries and paintings which often portrayed the leading role played by the Cecil family in English history, and featured spectacular effects, such as a ceiling composed of a working model of the solar system. Theobalds outshone anything owned by the Crown, and the queen and court stayed there many times, all at Lord Burghley's expense. Robert Cecil inherited the house, which was such a favourite venue for James I that Cecil eventually surrendered it to the Stuarts in exchange for a smaller site at Hatfield. After the English Civil War, this princely symbol of the long ascendancy of the Cecil family was dismantled and destroyed by the anti-royalist government.

Burghley's wards were schooled mainly at Cecil House with occasional visits to Theobalds. His various households, and possibly the schoolrooms, were overseen by his formidable wife, Mildred. She was Puritan, famously learned, as fluent in ancient Greek, it was said, as in English, and politically active, occasionally advising senior ministers on matters of state. But if Burghley and his wife hoped to inculcate their charges with the Protestant virtues of prudence, temperance, piety, and industry, they failed. At least three of the wards—Rutland, Oxford, and Southampton—became wildly irresponsible delinquents.[10] All three gambled, womanised, adopted foppish and ridiculous mannerisms, acted erratically, and, apparently unchecked by their guardian, spent lavishly from an early age, something only the immensely rich Earl of Rutland could afford to do. They were also dangerously unpredictable. In one fit of temper, the seventeen-year-old Oxford killed an unarmed serving man while fencing in the gardens of Cecil House—a crime his guardian managed to cover up.[11]

Nor did Lord Burghley improve their fortunes. In almost every case, his guardianship benefitted his own family at the expense of his wards. Oxford, inheritor of an ancient title and great wealth, began by incurring considerable debts to the Crown to pay for his wardship, fell out of favour with the queen, was denied office, and after a life of increasingly resentful dependence on Burghley died a ruined man, having lost all his estates and deeply in debt to the Crown. 'He never got rid of the Cecils . . . to the end of his days', writes his biographer, having traced his harrowing decline in meticulous documentary detail.[12] The Earl of Essex also struggled with inherited debts: by the time of his death he owed thousands.

Shortly after Burghley's death in 1598, an anonymous admirer wrote a glowing biography entitled *The Compleat Statesman*, which may have circulated in manuscript but had considerable impact on later historians after its publication in 1732.[13] Curiously, it has been received largely uncritically, even though it is more hagiography than biography. Much of the content is reminiscent of Burghley's own careful, pedantic style, and the fact that it ends with a seraphic death-bed scene, and wise words of advice to his son Robert, makes it look suspiciously like a father-and-son initiative to counter the various attacks on his reputation. These are indignantly rebutted by the writer: Lord Burghley was never miserly or covetous, we are told, he was a friend to the nobility, he was an honest Master of Wards, he cared for the welfare of soldiers, he did not monopolise access to the queen. He was a model of virtue, and his 'mildness' a constant theme—the word is repeated many times. Nothing ruffled him: 'When his mighty enemies were most violent, then was he ever most calm.' There is great emphasis on his 'painful service' to his country, so that although he reached the ripe old age of seventy-eight and died still in office, his life is cut short by his 'intolerable pains', 'his mind broken with care, and his body with sickness'.[14] Underpaid and overworked, it seems, he remained equable, sober, and selflessly industrious to the end. Altogether, he was a model of virtue as well as 'one of the sweetest, and most well-favoured, well-mannered old men that hath been seen'.[15]

The account ends with his habitual sayings, which include the statement that 'he who was false to God could never be true to Man'. A list of precepts addressed to his son are worldly-wise, however, rather than Christian. He is against lending, even to close friends; otherwise both the friendship and the loan are at risk: 'He that payeth another man's debts seeketh his own decay.' Borrow only on agreed terms, he recommends, and from moneylenders, not friends. Once drawn into a lawsuit, 'spare not for either money or pains'. 'Let thy hospitality be moderate', is his advice, and, towards fellow men, 'be thou familiar, yet respective'. And so on.[16]

This list of truisms, and the calculating mindset behind them, the reverse of the openhanded values idealised by the old nobility, are unmistakably parodied in *Hamlet*, which was staged shortly after *The Compleat Statesman* was written. The genial, devious, busy old statesman Polonius, chief advisor to the usurping king, Claudius, sends his son Laertes off on his travels with a stream of advice which, in its emphasis on 'husbandry' as opposed to charity, perfectly catches the tone, and often echoes the very words, of Burghley's aphorisms. 'Be thou familiar, but by no means vulgar', says Polonius. 'Neither a borrower nor a lender be / For loan oft loses both itself and friend.' If drawn into a quarrel, be ruthless. Be discriminating about your household guests. The final lines echo Burghley's saying that those who are true to God will never be false to man:

> This above all, to thine own self be true
> And it must follow, as the night the day
> Thou can'st not yet be false to any man
>
> (1.3.78–80)

Shakespeare alters the sentiment to reveal what many believed was the true, self-centred motivation behind Burghley's sanctimonious exterior. Those who are true *to themselves*, says Polonius, will never be false to man. So perfectly does all this mimic Burghley's sententious, authoritative manner that much of it has been taken at face value ever since.[17]

It is this very manner, and the outrageous hypocrisy they saw behind it, that must have been most aggravating of all for his debt-ridden wards. Educated amid the bustle of the vast Cecil building projects, each architectural development eagerly micromanaged by their guardian, they were yet subjected to constant reminders to be thrifty, godly, and prudent. Their guardian would 'often say', according to his reverent biographer, that 'riches were Godes Blessinge, to such as use them well; and his Curse to such as did not', or, even more irritating, for those who knew how these new buildings were funded, 'Private Gaine is the perverting of Justice, and the Pestilence of a Commonwealth.'[18]

Shakespeare's Polonius was by no means the first or last veiled lampoon of Lord Burghley. Edmund Spenser, in an extraordinarily bold move, satirised Burghley's corruption, his ambition, his extravagant building programme, and his monopolisation of all access to the monarch in a poem which circulated in manuscript in the 1580s. Entitled *Mother Hubberd's Tale*,

it recounts the attempt of a fox and an ape to take over the kingdom of the beasts while the lion sleeps. Once in power, the fox
pampers his cubs with ill-gotten gains, sells justice, and under
the 'cloak of thrift and husbandry' increases his own wealth at
the 'common treasure's' expense. While impoverished peers and
princes are forced to let great buildings fall to ruin which were
founded by their forefathers for the 'kingdom's ornament' and
their own memorial, the fox's lofty towers rise. He despises the
nobility, soldiers, scholars, and the common people. Just in time,
the lion wakes, and the fox and the ape are routed.

This apparently harmless beast-fable was clearly too close to
the bone. The book was instantly called in and repressed by the
Privy Council when it appeared in print in 1591. Biographers
believe that it was because of *Mother Hubberd's Tale* that Spenser
left England for permanent exile in Ireland. 'Fox' became a byword for Burghley at this period; Essex would refer to him as
'the old fox', and scholars point out that the central character of
Ben Jonson's most successful play, *Volpone* (The Fox), is a post-
humous satirical portrait.[19]

But the real reason why Burghley was so detested by so
many went far beyond the many accusations of corruption. His
greatest achievement—in the eyes of his opponents, his greatest crime—occurred at the very beginning of Elizabeth's reign,
when he was still only in his thirties. To him can be attributed
the extraordinary success of what has been called 'the revolution
of 1559': the skilful process whereby the English Parliament and
people were nudged, cajoled, and, according to opponents, deceived, into accepting a third change of religion when Elizabeth,
outwardly Catholic at that point, came to the throne.[20] The process was driven not by leading clergy or by popular demand,
but by an inner cabinet of experienced administrators on whom
the young queen was totally dependent. The group was led by

William Cecil and his brother-in-law Nicholas Bacon. It was they who devised the Acts of Supremacy and Uniformity, the Oath of Supremacy and the swingeing penalties that enforced it, they who drafted and pushed through the new religious changes and who, by chicanery, removed many of the dissenting bishops from the House of Lords so that the religious changes were passed in Parliament by the narrowest of margins.[21] Close analysis of exactly how this was done is an object lesson in dirty politics, and amply justifies the description of Burghley as a fox.[22] The historian Philip Hughes, author of one of the fullest and most scholarly studies of this period to date, is generous to Burghley as statesman and administrator, and accepts the *Compleat Statesman*'s account of his exemplary private life. But he goes on to summarise his political skills in unusually forthright and negative terms: 'But if lies matter, and treachery, plots to encompass innocent men whom it was desirable to remove, and ruthlessness towards such in the hour of mastery, then, despite his temperamental *sophrosyne* [the Greek quality of balance and self-control], Cecil is a very bad man indeed.'[23]

Similar assessments poured from Catholic presses abroad: 'Machiavellian' was the repeated charge, and the two Machiavels, Cecil and Bacon, were regularly blamed for secretly manipulating the queen and persuading her to take the fatal course of imprisoning the bishops, reconstituting the Privy Council, and instituting a new religion with herself at its head.[24] In 1592, Richard Verstegan, a Catholic writing in the Low Countries, published *A Declaration of the True Causes of the Great Troubles*, and it pulled no punches. Calling Lord Burghley 'King Cecil the First', Verstegan denounces him as 'the beginner, prosecutor and continuer of the ruin of England, and the disturbance almost of every Christian region'.[25] He goes on: 'It is he that, neither of conscience nor for any other cause but merely for his own ambition, hath wrought the mutation and change of religion, whereof such wonderful inconveniences have followed.'[26]

The story of the fox's rise to power in Spenser's *Mother Hubberd's Tale*, published a year later, repeats the charge, and even more scandalously, associates the queen with the fox's companion in crime, the ape. At the turn of the twentieth century it was common for historians to conflate William Cecil with the queen. The great Victorian scholar J. A. Froude saw the queen and her first minister as a single entity—'She was a woman and a man; she was herself and Cecil'. Others took the same line. 'From 1558 for forty years the biography of Cecil is almost indistinguishable from that of Elizabeth and from the history of England', wrote the British historian Albert Pollard in 1911.[27] Spenser also presents his monarch and first minister as equals: 'Ye shall have both crowne and government', says the fox, as they strike the deal, 'Upon condition that you ruled be / In all affaires, and counseled by mee.'[28] To his own surprise, the fox manages to persuade the beasts to accept the usurping ape as monarch. He then monopolises access to the sovereign, controlling 'all offices, all leases'; and 'all whatso he likte, he kept'.[29]

Michael Questier summarises the view that Cecil and his cabal coolly hijacked the English throne for their own ends: 'In particular, these polemics alleged, the Protestant Reformation was like a Trojan horse, introduced by stealth into the English church to advance the careers of these Machiavels and to destroy their enemies.'[30] Leslie, as we have seen, was one of these polemicists, conflating Burghley with Sinon in his *Treatise of Treasons*. If we look closely, Lucrece appears to do the same. As she concludes her tour of the picture of Troy, a particular character catches her eye. He is Sinon the Greek, who is depicted being escorted by shepherds into Troy to tell the 'enchanting story' that persuades 'credulous old Priam' to accept the gift of the wooden horse that famously brings about the ruin of the city (1521–1522). She loses all self-control and attacks the canvas. For her, his devastating act of deception parallels Tarquin's, just as the destruction of Troy parallels her own downfall, and the cause of it all is the diabolical Sinon (1564). Repeatedly she associates him with hell, with devils, with incomprehensible wickedness. But what really takes her breath away, what drives her to utter fury, is his hypocrisy. Lucrece pores over the picture of Sinon for some time before she can accept that he is indeed the classic embodiment of the deceiver. He looks so harmless, humble, saintly, plain, honest. She refuses at first to accept that he is vicious: 'It cannot be', she stammers three times, that 'such a face should bear a wicked mind' (1534–1540).[31]

At this point it might be useful to turn to Marcus Gheeraerts's portrait of Burghley, a statesmanlike contrast to the craftier painted versions of his younger self (see photo insert).[32] Here is the image Lord Burghley projected in old age, the embodiment of mildness and restraint, summed up in Philip Hughes's assessment of him as exhibiting the Greek quality of *sophrosyne*. We are looking at 'one of the sweetest, and most well-favoured, well-mannered old men that hath been seen'.[33] The image has remained so irresistible down the ages that we, like Lucrece, have difficulty seeing beyond it. What is intriguing is that Shakespeare ascribes the very persona constructed for himself by the elderly Lord Burghley to the fraudulent Sinon in the picture, who deploys precisely the same world-weary, mild, and pious appearance to deceive his hearers. Lucrece gasps at Sinon's act. He appears to be so convincingly harmless, so 'sobersad . . . weary . . . mild . . . seeming just' (1542). He has 'a brow unbent that seemed to welcome woe' (1509). 'His face though full of cares, yet showed content' (1503). This image of the mature, temperate man is in fact not the persona Virgil's Sinon adopted. The original Sinon was a youth who feigned panic and fear to deceive his hearers. But, following Leslie, Shakespeare retouches the character in order to conclude his sweeping review of the history of his times with a veiled depiction of Lord Burghley as seen by the 1590s opposition—a man outwardly statesman-like, 'mild', 'seeming just', but in reality a Machiavellian deceiver, responsible for the disastrous turn taken by the country on the accession of Elizabeth.

If the young Southampton wished to take on his guardian, then, he would be facing a truly formidable opponent. And at first, it appears, he did what he was told. At the age of twelve he went to Cambridge, leaving at fifteen in 1589, the year after the Armada. He wanted to travel to Italy, but was told by his tutor, the scholar John Florio, that his Italian was already quite good enough, and was sent instead to study law at the Inns of Court. In fact, his guardian, the queen, and the Privy Council were extremely reluctant to allow young Englishmen to travel that far from home. 'Suffer not thy sons to pass the Alps', was one of Lord Burghley's precepts to his son, 'for they shall learn nothing there, but pride, blasphemy and atheism.'[34] Southampton would later prove himself to be an accomplished swordsman and soldier: this, too, was discouraged by his minders, who had no time for the aristocratic values of chivalry, honour, and military renown. 'Neither, by my consent, shalt thou train them up in wars,' Burghley said, 'for he that sets up his rest to live by that profession can hardly be an honest man or a good Christian.'[35] In that same year Southampton's armour was confiscated from his family home at Titchfield as part of a nationwide crackdown on suspect Catholic nobility after the Armada. For a young English nobleman, this must have been the ultimate humiliation.[36]

As he turned twenty, Southampton began to appear at court; he went to plays at Gray's Inn; flatteringly, he was mentioned for the Order of the Garter, a much-sought-after honour; and at some point he met the Earl of Essex and his cousin, the petite, beautiful Elizabeth Vernon, with whom he fell in love, and with whom he was to enjoy a long and unusually devoted marriage. Their liaison, whenever it began, was kept secret for two reasons. Elizabeth was one of the queen's ladies-in-waiting, forbidden to wed without the queen's assent; and Southampton himself, against his will, was already officially engaged. When he was sixteen, his guardian had arranged his marriage: the future Countess of Southampton would be Lord Burghley's own granddaughter, the nineteen-year-old Elizabeth Vere. It looked as if the stealthy assimilation of the great dissident Hampshire clan into the new establishment was at last in the bag. But here Burghley came up against an unexpected obstacle. Southampton refused the proposed match; and he continued to refuse, even though the penalty once he reached the age of twenty-one would be £5,000. This sum was almost double his annual income from his estates: the modern equivalent would be close to £1 million.[37]

If this marriage had gone ahead, it would have greatly benefitted Lord Burghley's family. But more importantly, it would have been a major coup for the regime. Gaining the public loyalty of families like Southampton's was of crucial importance. Burghley understood the vital necessity of image, and of the significance of the message that might be sent out if Southampton continued to resist. The abject messages and romantic emblems at the Queen's Accession Day tournaments are often cited as stirring examples of the loyalty of the young nobility under Elizabeth. But as one sardonic foreign observer noted, attendance was enforced: those who did not take part were fined. Men whose ancestral role had always been the military defence of the realm chafed at these pasteboard chivalric displays. Returning from the battlefield in France in 1591 to plead for more arms, money, and men, the young Earl of Essex wasted days in mandatory dancing and flirtation; in the end, he had to pay his desperate men £14,000 (around £3 million) out of his own pocket while attempting to win the queen round with abject love-letters.

Equally humiliating must have been Burghley's skill in doctoring the historical record of events, ascribing fictional motives and deeds to noblemen whose political stance was being closely scrutinised at home and abroad. As the Armada threat receded, Lord Burghley, after several careful drafts which still survive, rushed out a pamphlet written ostensibly by a despondent Catholic, describing the gallant actions of leading English subjects.[38] It was published in several editions, in English, French, and Italian, and is an example of Burghley's ingenuity as a propagandist. The material rapidly found its way into popular post-Armada ballads. According to this 'eye-witness' report, Lord Oxford took ship and risked his life at sea for the queen. The Earl of Arundel, a Catholic prisoner of conscience in the Tower, offered his own life 'in defence of the Queen, against all the world'. And Lord Montague joined the queen at Tilbury at the head of his sons and two hundred mounted troops. Recently, it has emerged that this narrative of Catholic loyalty was entirely invented. Lord Oxford actually resigned his post and took no part in the country's defence. Lord Montague was kept well away from the action and was put under house arrest shortly afterwards. And the Earl of Arundel was found guilty of high treason for praying for the Armada's success.[39]

The man who took such pains to ensure that the public face of English Catholicism remained resolutely loyal during a period of sustained Spanish threat was not likely to give way on the high-profile issue of Southampton's marriage. In 1589, Burghley asked Southampton's mother and grandfather to put pressure on him. Viscount Montague reported that he had no success, and that the young earl had asked for 'further respitt of one yere to answere . . . in respect of his yonge yeres'.[40] But the year passed, and he continued to hold out. Southampton was now facing not only the usual crippling sum required to buy back his lands and possessions from the Crown, but the exorbitant fine for refusing his guardian's choice of marriage partner.[41]

By 1591, further shadows began to close in on Southampton's family. While staying at Cowdray Castle in the summer, where they were entertained by Viscount Montague and his wife, who laid on days of pageantry for the royal court, the Privy Council and queen worked on the toughest penalties yet against Catholics. New proclamations in the autumn announced close searches of all those households, like the Wriothesleys and Montagues, suspected of sheltering priests, and the execution of those who protected them. One of the first victims was Swithin Wells, who had been tutor to Southampton's father, and possibly, when he was a small boy, to Southampton himself.[42] In December 1591, after the discovery of a priest saying Mass in his house at Gray's Inn Lane while he was absent, Wells was hanged, drawn and quartered outside his own front door, very close to Southampton's home. The site of such executions was always carefully calculated: this would have been a warning both to the students of Gray's Inn and to the Catholic enclave in and around Southampton House.

On a practical level, Southampton now made a disagreeable discovery. Lord Burghley was neglecting his duty to his ward and permitting his estates to fall into disrepair, very likely a deliberate ploy to get Southampton to agree to the match with his granddaughter. He wrote quickly to Burghley's agent about remedying the 'great decay and daunger' of his inheritance.[43] Ahead of him lay the prospect of a life similar to that of the Earl of Oxford, who was now in his early forties: continual debt and the erosion of his possessions accompanied by ongoing dependence on the family of Lord Burghley, into which he would be forced to marry.

It was at this point that Burghley, ever conscious of the power of print, commissioned a short allegorical work dedicated to his ward that publicised the problems he was facing with the wayward and obstinate Southampton.

Lucretia. This painting, by Rembrandt in 1664, shows Lucretia on the point of committing suicide after her rape, her arms outstretched in an echo of the crucifixion. Shakespeare's contemporary Philip Sidney described her 'constant though lamenting look' as she 'punished in herself
another's fault'. Her rape by the usurping king's son Sextus Tarquinius ended a corrupt regime and
precipitated the first Roman Republic.

Frontispiece to William Dugdale's *Monasticon Anglicanum*. 'Hic Volo' comes from a line that the Roman satirist Juvenal puts into the mouth of a tyrannical wife: 'I want it—I will have it—let my will stand for a reason.' Wenceslaus Hollar depicts Henry VIII uttering these words as part of his frontispiece to William Dugdale's monumental work *Monasticon* in 1682. The detail is an indication of the widespread English condemnation of the dissolution of the monasteries.

Pegasus and Apollo. Like Apollo, the winged horse Pegasus was a classical image of the poet. They were often portrayed together in Renaissance paintings and sculpture. Certain writers, including Shakespeare, used the swift and fearless Pegasus as a symbol of the oppositional poet.

In the image, a plaque reads:

IN VINCVLIS
INVICTVS.

FEBRVA: 8: 1600: 60
602: 603: APRI:

Henry Wriothesley, 3rd Earl of Southampton (1573–1603). The picture at the top right indicates that Southampton is imprisoned in the Tower of London for his part in the Essex Rebellion. His eighteenth-century descendants had the picture copied without the incriminating Tower detail. The original was painted circa 1603 by the court artist John de Critz.

View of Troy Burning by **Johann Georg Trautmann, 1762.** Brutus, who according to myth was the first king of England, was a descendent of the Trojan hero Aeneas. Writers in sixteenth-century England made much of this glamorous classical identity, hailing England as 'Troynovant', a new Troy. Shakespeare associates Troy with tragedy and destruction.

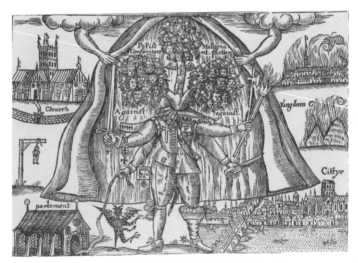

England Divided. This 1643 Puritan woodcut depicts the hidden enemies of the state—Catholics, Royalists, and the 'Bloodie Irish'. The composite three-headed figure, split down the middle and surrounded by the broken, isolated symbols of church and state, conveys the sense of social breakdown and mistrust in mid-seventeenth-century England.

William Cecil, 1st Lord Burghley (1520–1598). Attributed to Marcus Gheeraerts the Younger and painted in 1598, the year of Burghley's death, this is the public image of the great man who dominated Elizabeth's England. His hagiographer described him as 'one of the sweetest, and most well-favoured, well-mannered old men that hath been seen', but to his enemies he was 'the beginner, prosecuter and continuer of the ruin of England'.

Robert Cecil, 1st Lord Salisbury (1563–1612). Robert Cecil was physically undersized and hunchbacked; his political brilliance was underestimated for years by the more dynamic and popular Earl of Essex. But in 1602 the French ambassador noted that 'the English nobility were more afraid of this little man than they were of their consciences or their Queen'.

Robert Devereux, 2nd Earl of Essex (1565–1601). A visitor from Venice noted in late 1596, when this portrait was painted by Isaac Oliver, that Essex was 'fair-skinned, tall, but wiry . . . right modest, courteous and humane'.

Map of London, Georg Braun and Franz Hogenberg, 1572. Essex House, previously Leicester House, is situated between the Strand and the Thames just to the east of the bend in the river, midway between Whitehall and the city. Undecided which way to lead his followers out of the gates of his house on the fateful day of the rebellion, Essex made the wrong decision, marching east to raise the city.

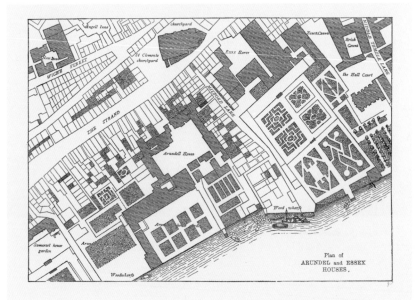

Plan of Essex House. Essex inherited this impressive house, full of fine pictures and furnishings, from his stepfather, the Earl of Leicester, Queen Elizabeth's first favourite. His mother, sisters, and many friends had lodgings there. Under siege on September 7, 1601, Essex and Southampton stood on the rooftops to negotiate with government forces. Cannon were drawn up in the street, and snipers were positioned on the roof of St Clement Danes, the church opposite.

CHAPTER NINE

RALLYING THE
OPPOSITION:
VENUS AND ADONIS

I N 1591, LORD Burghley's secretary, John Clapham, dedicated a condescending and slightly humiliating Latin poem
to Southampton entitled *Narcissus*, a reworking of the myth of
the beautiful young man who falls in love with his own reflection. The poem is set in a 'fortunate island' enriched by a 'vir-
gin queen' under whom it enjoys everlasting peace—England,
clearly.[1]

Clapham's Narcissus had an unlucky start in life. He was one
'whom Prosperity void of light engendered, vain Pride brought
forth, and Opinion nurtured with the warm milk of Error'—a
series of swipes at the wealth, pretensions, and deluded beliefs of
Southampton's family, from which he had been providentially
removed by his guardian.[2] But the Cecil rescue attempt clearly
failed. The youthful Narcissus enters Cupid's domain, the palace

of the blind—an alluring labyrinth of inextricable error, filled with dark shadows, where idle young men, 'unwilling to endure toil', cluster like crows around a corpse to learn about love.[3] Narcissus kneels, is sprinkled with water, and attends to the teaching of Cupid on his flaming throne ('cathedra'). He is initiated into evil ways—prodigality, wantonness, falsehood, self-love. Before long he is mistaking shadows for reality. 'You will be mine', Cupid exults as Narcissus bows like a slender reed before him.[4] Finally, Lust, in the form of an unbridled horse, gallops off with the spoiled, pampered Narcissus to the river of self-love, where, deceived by the shadow of his own reflection, he drowns.

Clapham's poem is a public portrait of Lord Burghley's view of Southampton at the age of eighteen—weak, immature, easily led, reared by his vainglorious family in an erroneous religion, and lured back again by wicked influences. Now, wilful, licentious, and obstinately papist, he faces ruin. The standard jibes at Catholicism—hedonism, homosexuality, the substitution of the shadows of idolatry and superstition for substance—are so transparent that, as one critic has commented, 'the surprise is it has never been decoded'.[5] Readers would recognise the sort of man it was who had returned to the old religion in spite of his upbringing in the Cecil household, and had rejected a marriage to Lord Burghley's granddaughter.

Two years later, in June 1593, a second work dedicated to Southampton appeared on the London bookstalls: *Venus and Adonis*, by William Shakespeare. Again, it was a poem, and again, it concerned the tragic fate of a beautiful young man accused of self-love. But there the resemblance with *Narcissus* ended. This time the youth was the victim not of a depraved teacher on a flaming throne, but of an overpoweringly possessive queen.

Riding off to a boar-hunt at dawn, a young man is accosted by a woman older and stronger than he is, who subjects him to a prolonged and grotesque sexual assault. She lifts him from his horse, forces him to the ground, and attempts to seduce him. When he refuses she accuses him of self-love, and, in terms suggestive of the unwelcome proposal of marriage constantly urged on Southampton at this point, begs him to yield. 'Say, shall we? Shall we? Wilt thou make the match?' (586). She tries everything to win him round. It is dusk before he manages to break free.

He races off to join the hunt. But his horse has gone, it is dark, he is fatally vulnerable, and when he finds the boar, it kills him. Bizarrely, the woman's lament equates her lust with the boar: her kisses would have gored him to death, she cries, had she been 'toothed like him' (117). Left alone, she curses love in a passage all the more chilling because of the powerful mythic identities of these two characters: she is Venus, the goddess of love, and he is Adonis, associated in ancient myth with the perennial beauty and fertility of the natural world. But Shakespeare has radically altered their roles. In the myth, familiar to Elizabethan readers through Ovid's *Metamorphoses*, Adonis responds to Venus's love. An Adonis who is desperate to escape an aggressive assailant, who argues that he is too young for love: there was a clear corollary here with the highly topical case of the Earl of Southampton.[6]

The new poem was more than a riposte to John Clapham. It was a work of genius that flew off the shelves from the moment of publication. Beneath the frustrated seduction, the poem has a deeper political resonance which would have brought Shakespeare instantly to the attention of people right across the country, but more particularly at court, who found themselves, metaphorically, in the position of the humiliatingly incapacitated Adonis, overwhelmed by the inescapable demands of a powerful queen, 'forced to content, but never to obey' (61). In an almost uncanny act of imaginative sympathy, Shakespeare has grasped every element of a complex national predicament and recast it in an irresistibly light, supple, learned, many-layered poetic form, which was to be constantly read, imitated, and reprinted over the next few decades, setting a new benchmark for sophistication and wit in the rapidly developing field of English Renaissance writing. Unlike the more cerebral *Rape of Lucrece*, which spans the whole gamut of Tudor despotism, this is above all a sensuous poem, which focuses on the here and now, on the immediate, felt impact of the 'great and strange alteration' on those born and brought up at the very end of the Tudor period. Here is the visceral reaction to oppression missing from the more intellectual and mannered *Lucrece*. Elegantly printed in almost identical quarto volumes, and published just over a year apart, these two works complement each other, the earlier *Venus and Adonis* exposing the symptoms of England's disease, in all its pain and humiliation, and *Lucrece* providing its considered diagnosis and cure.

Two hundred and sixty lines into *Venus and Adonis*, Shakespeare, in a long and celebrated digression, inserts his own manifesto, proclaiming with magnificent verve and elan his own political intent as he launches out as a public poet, and at the same time demonstrating his literary mastery. In literary terms, this passage was a triumph: it is the only extract from his narrative poetry which has been regularly anthologised ever since. Less often noticed is the political charge that it carries. It looks very much as if Shakespeare is deliberately picking up the baton handed on to his heirs by the founding editor of the *Mirror for Magistrates*, William Baldwin: that of the bold but circumspect oppositional writer.

Improbably, the passage concerns a horse. But this is not just any horse. As Baldwin explains to his readers, the figure of the perfect poet for classical writers was Pegasus, and he goes through the reasons why. Like Pegasus, the truly great poet cannot be constrained; he has wings of skill and wit that take him to heaven, or 'where him liketh best', he explores countries and the trades of men, he contemns worldly possessions.[7] When his hooves strike the earth on Mount Helicon and release the waters of Hippocrene, the river of the Muses, Pegasus, like the poet, frees grace and truth from the darkness of earthly error. Above all, his speed and skill allow him to escape the wrath of tyrants. As a warning, Baldwin puts this speech into the mouth of a poet who failed to escape—the horribly mutilated ghost of the poet Collingbourne, who was hanged, drawn and quartered by Richard III for an unwise libel.

Shakespeare pays homage to Baldwin in his own equestrian passage. Just as the escaping Adonis is about to seize his courser's reins, the animal bolts after a mare. The interplay between the two horses, as the courser goes through his paces to woo the reluctant mare, and at last gallops away with her to the woods, is an exhilarating piece of natural description. But at every turn, Shakespeare includes details from Baldwin that turn his real, living horse into the classical image of the poet, Pegasus. Like an imaginary animal, Adonis's vividly realised courser transcends nature, we are told; his beauty almost appears to be the work of an artist. He strikes the hollow womb of the 'bearing' earth as he rears up, so that it resounds 'like heaven's thunder', a powerful image of creativity recalling the birth of Hippocrene (265–270). His headlong gallop is like flight as he challenges the wind to a race, his hair and tail waving 'like feathered wings' (306). He crushes his bit and breaks the reins, like Baldwin's horse, who scorns bit and bridle. He is completely directed: 'He sees his love and nothing else he sees / For nothing else with his proud sight agrees' (287). Though Shakespeare effortlessly eclipses Baldwin, he echoes ideas, phrases, intonations, and key words in a passage which is a model of the surreptitious skills that Baldwin recommended to those writing under tyranny.

So, of course, is the rest of *Venus and Adonis*. Much has been written about the poem's wit, its many layers of lyricism and irony, its characterisation, all the elements that make it more accessible, to modern readers, than *The Rape of Lucrece*, and which filled John Keats with envy and awe.[8] But the highly effective use of one simple device distracts attention from its topical level. Throughout the poem, the tender, ironic narrator ignores Adonis and sympathises with Venus; the drama is seen through her eyes. Passionate and frustrated, she is, in her own view, the poem's victim. Baldwin would have approved of this artful piece of dissimulation. Once we set aside the amused voiceover and focus on the action, we find we are watching an imperious, cruel, self-centred woman overpowering a youth who weakly contrasts her devouring lust with real love at one of the few points where he is allowed to speak. But by detaining him until he has lost his horse and night has fallen, she brings about his death. So confident is Shakespeare of his skill in deflecting attention from the gist of his poem that he can afford to come dangerously close to identifying Elizabeth I herself as Venus in a passage where Venus denies, at great length, that she is an unattractive old woman (133–138).[9] With similar daring, he uses the politically loaded language of imprisonment, robbery, extortion, and enforcement to describe the situation of Adonis, who pleads, like so many of Elizabeth's subjects, 'You crush me, let me go' (611).

The sensation of often painful physical helplessness is the keynote of the poem. It permeates the whole narrative, from the squirming, protesting Adonis to the hunted hare, the shrinking snail, even the 'poor flies' bitten by the impatient horse (316). If this dark undercurrent is detectable even now, it would have been doubly evident to the eighteen-year-old Southampton struggling to break free of the many and varied constraints that, in the year 1593, threatened to wreck his life—and not only to Southampton and encircled noblemen like him, but also to the whole spectrum of the opposition of the day. It would have spoken to the Earl of Essex himself, who in 1593 was the frustrated and impatient favourite of the ageing, temperamental queen, and it encompasses the grievances of all those for whom he was beginning to be the one hope of redress: reformers, writers and thinkers, soldiers, and English Catholics. As the critic Richard Wilson has pointed out, the poem is full of sophisticated reference to the complex relationship between Elizabeth and her Catholic subjects, who at this point in her reign were approaching despair.[10] Philip Hughes comments on their 'utter lack of leaders' at the start of Elizabeth's reign, even though they were 'the great majority of the nation'.[11] The Privy Council, with great ingenuity, ensured that it stayed that way. By now the practice of the old religion was completely outlawed, and its remaining adherents were being hunted down ever more relentlessly.

Just over halfway through the poem, a poignant cameo of a hunted hare evokes the predicament of these desperate Elizabethan subjects. The setting is 'the downs'—a reminder, perhaps, for Southampton of the South Downs in his own suspect counties of Sussex and Hampshire. Venus begs Adonis to hunt the harmless hare rather than the boar. Yet she is oddly sympathetic to the 'poor wretch' as she imagines him doubling and redoubling his tracks to confuse the hunter, taking on the scent of a flock of sheep, merging with a herd of deer, hiding in rabbits' burrows: 'Danger deviseth shifts, wit waits on fear' (690). But the hounds are on his track. As he hears their cries,

Each shadow makes him stop, each murmur stay

For misery is trodden on by many

And being low, never relieved by any

(706–708)

There is a familiar ring to Venus's advice to Adonis to hunt down a fugitive with whom she has a sentimental sympathy. Throughout her reign Elizabeth maintained the fiction that she was not, at heart, opposed to Catholicism, and toyed more than once with the idea of a Catholic marriage. In fact, she took an intense personal interest in the hunting down of priests, and along with her Privy Council encouraged others to do the same. One of the ways local grandees in Elizabethan England were expected to prove their loyalty, particularly those with Catholic or Puritan leanings, was by zealously stamping out dissidence and identifying and prosecuting recusants in their area. Most did so, but beneath a parade of patriotic officiousness they often turned a blind eye to the legal loopholes and physical escape routes devised by people trying to evade them, especially when they were old friends and neighbours. As everyone knew, the terrors and tensions of everyday life for the underground priests and their protectors were almost worse than execution. They exploited every kind of subterfuge to elude capture, from adopting disguise to hiding in priest-holes or secluded attics, cellars, and caves: and it is this tension and fear that Shakespeare captures so well in his portrait of the weaving, dodging hare.

The same beleaguered Catholics would also have recognised their enemy in the very different creature who dominates the second half of the poem. Shakespeare's boar is not the wild creature who starts from a bush and almost accidentally kills the original Adonis, who runs fearfully away. This monster comes from a different part of Ovid's *Metamorphoses*, and its pedigree greatly deepens the political significance of the poem.[12] The Calydonian boar, which Shakespeare's boar resembles in every detail, is the terrifying servant of the goddess Diana. Furious when the king of Calydon forgets to offer libations on her altar, the vengeful Diana lets loose the boar to ravage the country-side. The boar slaughters everyone in his path until at last he is killed by Meleager, one of those who take part in a great boar-hunt which attracts heroes and champions from all over Greece. Shakespeare's poem stresses the strange intimacy between Venus and the boar and explores this paradox at some length. Gazing on Adonis's mangled body, which, distorted by her tears, looks as if it is actually dismembered, the grief-stricken Venus sees his wounds as the consummation of her own deathly love-making.

There is a connection between Elizabeth and the goddess incensed by those who forget to worship at her altars, and there are further links between the boar, 'a mortal butcher bent to kill', and the terror squads of Elizabeth's regime (618). The arch-persecutor of papists was the extremist Puritan Richard Topcliffe, whom Catholics often described as a 'butcher' and who personally supervised the grisly process of hanging, drawing and quartering his victims. Topcliffe was directly answerable to the monarch, not the Privy Council, and boasted in lewd detail of his close personal relationship with the queen. The boar's indiscriminate vandalism, as he destroys meadows and digs 'sepulchres' (622), recalls the continuing iconoclasm by the same sectarian persecutors deplored by such pillars of the new Protestant church as Richard Hooker and William Camden. The boar looks very like the dark side of the late Elizabethan state, an embodiment of the destructive forces it harnessed with a seductive queen as its gracious public image. The poem adroitly conflates the two.

If Essex was seen by Catholics as their last hope, humane and scholarly reformers were equally confident that he was their man. They were as profoundly engaged as Catholics with the issues of oppression raised in *Venus and Adonis*: they, too, felt that tyranny and acquisitiveness, or 'lust', had replaced religion in England and, in the words of Adonis,

> . . . hath fed
> Upon fresh beauty, blotting it with blame
> Which the hot tyrant stains and soon bereaves
> As caterpillars do the tender leaves.
> (796–798)

In February 1593, four months before the publication of Shakespeare's first narrative poem, their resentment exploded into a public row with the government when a representative group decided to speak out in Parliament against what they perceived as the tyranny of the Crown—and 'the tyranny of the clergy of England', who had, in their view, changed the church structure but not its abuses, hijacking true reform for their own ends.[13]

For the past ten years, Protestants who did not adhere at every point to the doctrine of the state religion had been silenced or removed by the queen and her archbishop, John Whitgift, who used the controversial powers of the Ecclesiastical Court of High Commission to enforce orthodoxy. Yet even in Parliament, reformers found they were unable to voice their protests. In 1593 they spoke out. For too long, they argued, the queen had restricted the 'ancient liberties' of the Commons by confining freedom of speech to 'matters propounded', and intimidating members by threats, bullying, and rumours. Like the old nobility, the House of Commons was being robbed of its traditional role of giving advice to the monarch.[14]

The tumultuous 1593 Parliament was conducted amid a spate of house arrests and imprisonments, including the incarceration of one determined champion of freedom of speech, Peter Wentworth, who died still in captivity five years later. Parliament had been summoned by the queen to provide subsidies for her runaway military expenditure, and to supplement her income by extending the fines for recusancy to Protestant as well as Catholic dissidents. The result was uproar. James Morice, an experienced lawyer briefed by Wentworth and supported by Essex, proposed two bills restricting the runaway powers of the ecclesiastical courts, which Morice correctly maintained were contrary to Magna Carta.[15] He was arrested and silenced, but his written letter of protest survives: 'I will not be ashamed in good and lawful sort to strive for the freedom of conscience, public justice and the liberties of my country.'[16] Southampton's later career suggests that the momentous clashes of this Parliament made a deep impression. As a member of the House of Lords, he was to become for the rest of his life a dedicated parliamentary opponent of the incursions of the Crown, along with others who, like him, followed in the footsteps of Morice and Wentworth.

The earliest written reaction to the publication of *Venus and Adonis* comes from a member of another group who saw the Earl of Essex as their champion. William Reynolds clearly read his own situation into the poem and took it for granted that Venus represented the queen, relishing, in particular, the passage in which Venus denies that she is old, lean, and wrinkled.[17] He was one of the many soldiers who had lost everything in Elizabeth's wars. Penniless and half-mad, he hung about court pressing long, rambling letters on anyone who would listen, itemising the crimes of the government and begging for relief. One of these letters, written to the queen the same year that *Venus and Adonis* was published, mentions the poem, and gives us an insight into how such men felt. He is destitute, and, in a reminder of how families suffered when their men were conscripted, cannot afford to leave his widowed mother for the wars 'in these uncharitable times', the old charitable institutions having been privatised long ago. All around him he sees abuses— poor petitioners, callous courtiers, prosperous lawyers—while in the London shops the talk is all of the covetousness of Lord Burghley, who, 'robbing you, . . . robs your subjects'. Reynolds angrily attacks the queen for her 'negligence' and reproves her and the wheedling Privy Council for trying to win him over: 'By your devices and printing of books you pretend great good to me, as though if I would come to the Queen, then you would do wonders for me'.[18] A fantasist he may have been, but his comments had a grain of truth. His response to the poem shows how attentively he read it, and how natural it was for men like him to read topical meanings into such writings.

The Earl of Essex spent huge sums out of his own purse on the well-being of soldiers like Reynolds, whose circumstances bring us on to a disturbing aspect of the late Elizabethan state which has only recently come to light: the full extent to which it recruited and devoured its young men. These Tudor victims were not the comparatively small number of dissident nobility and intelligentsia, or even the missionary priests who died on the scaffold, but the many thousands of ordinary people—countrymen, tradesmen, yeomen, vagrants, and the dispossessed—who died in the course of Elizabeth's increasingly discredited religious wars or returned penniless.[19]

England had been continually at war for most of Elizabeth's reign, and by the 1590s it had become a militarised state. The public was subject to continual musters and curfews and had suffered a vast casualty rate in multiple indecisive campaigns abroad—some to support the Protestant movements in France and the Low Countries, others to fend off potential Catholic invasion from Ireland and Spain. In 1586, two of England's most distinguished generals defected to Spain with their men, driven to desperation by the lack of pay and support from home.[20] Worse was to come. Between 1587 and 1591, Elizabeth and her council invested a colossal £345,000 (roughly £85 million today) in the French Protestant cause alone, emptying the national coffers and sacrificing many hundreds of lives in a bid to establish a neighbouring Protestant buffer against the Catholic European bloc.[21] Soldiers, often wounded, ill, and unpaid, now thronged the London streets, becoming a dangerous and disaffected presence. Thousands of others were lost, more to disease, poor food, and forced marches than to actual combat. Of the two thousand troops levied from Sussex and Hampshire for a single campaign in 1589, for instance, the Privy Council reported that 'few of the men returned againe'. By this time, 'men had come to dread service in France . . . soldiers went to all lengths of excuse and desertion rather than serve'.[22] By 1591, the queen was selling off Crown lands and treasures from her Jewel House to stay solvent. But in 1594, England's one major Protestant ally, Henri IV, converted to Catholicism in order to gain the French throne. It had all been for nothing.

Those at court like Essex, with first-hand experience of fighting in the field, blamed the loss of money and life on womanish indecisiveness, meddling, and lack of commitment on the part of the queen and Lord Burghley. Others saw the ruinous wars as yet another result of Henry VIII's fatal decision to isolate England from the Continent in the first place. In 1592, the exiled Richard Verstegan blamed Lord Burghley for the country's destruction of manpower. He jokes grimly that before long the country would be populated entirely by women, 'if ye shall now consider what infinite numbers of the inhabitants of the land

he hath by one means or other consumed, and daily intendeth
to consume'.[23] Verstegan's image of leaders callously devouring
their country's own subjects coincides with repeated images of a
murderous love in *Venus and Adonis*, as the voracious queen falls
on Adonis again and again, like a hungry animal or bird of prey.
She is a 'vulture' (551), an 'empty eagle' tearing at 'feathers, flesh
and bone' (55–56); 'Glutton-like, she feeds, yet never filleth'
(547). It was among these particular casualties of the Elizabethan state, ordinary people sent out to the wars, and their often
destitute families back at home, that the open-handed Essex was
most popular—in fact, he was often pilloried by his enemies for
his sympathy for the poor and underprivileged. His readiness to
further their suits at court was lampooned as a populist policy to
win over the common people for his own ambitious ends.

One aspect of the poem has led critics to doubt that Southampton and Essex, the potential figureheads of these dissident
groups and factions, would themselves have identified with
Adonis. Ignominiously, Adonis is killed by the boar. They
may have seen their own situation mirrored in the scenario of
a young man pinioned by a dominant queen who repeatedly
warns him to 'be ruled by me' (673). But when his horse dis-
appears, Adonis loses everything it symbolises—his vitality, his
ergon, his power-base. Once that has gone, the boar kills him.
If there is a moral, it is scarcely encouraging: death awaits those
who allow themselves to be diverted, delayed, and finally overcome by those in power.

A timely warning to the potential leadership of the opposition might indeed have been Shakespeare's purpose. Both of his
narrative poems present inaction as fatal, however excusable it
may seem at the time. Brutus's judgement of Lucrece is harsh—
she should have killed Tarquin, not herself. And Adonis is also
indirectly to blame for his own death. Shakespeare shows him

missing his one chance of escape. When he fails to recapture his horse, he gives up. Exhausted, angry, and discouraged, he allows Venus to talk him round, until, at last, 'Hot, faint and weary, with her hard embracing / . . . he now obeys, and now no more resisteth' (561, 564).

If the adoption of unhesitating, full-blooded, and determined methods of resistance was Shakespeare's political advice, it coincides with the line he takes in his plays, and the judgement of later historians, like Philip Hughes. 'In these centuries', writes Hughes, '—and for some time yet to come—there is only one way, even in England, for an opposition to triumph: by force of arms. And the classic way is for the opposition to become possessed of the nucleus of a powerful army outside the realm, and to conduct a successful invasion under the leadership of some kinsman of the sovereign.'[24] Shakespeare's popular and spine-chilling drama *Titus Adronicus*, published a year after *Venus and Adonis*, ends with precisely the kind of coup Hughes recommends: a successful invasion led by a relative of the unjustly displaced and persecuted leaders of Rome. Invariably, invasions in Shakespeare's plays are positive events. His rebellions, by contrast, are divisive and ultimately unsuccessful, unless they are supported from abroad.

But *Venus and Adonis* does contain a glimmer of hope that in some cases, home-grown resistance can succeed—only, however, with unified and determined support. The flower that springs from the blood of Adonis is not the anemone which Ovid describes. It is *Fritillaria meleagris*, the snake's head fritillary, then enjoying a vogue among Elizabethan gardeners, who enjoyed its striking chequerboard pattern. It is named after the hero Meleager, the member of the great boar-hunt who managed, finally, to kill the Calydonian boar. Shakespeare strongly suggests that, unlike Ovid's effeminate hero, his own Adonis actually kills the boar by running on it with his spear before he dies himself. When we last see it, the boar appears to be in its death throes, with its red mouth full of froth. The line 'Like milk and blood being mingled both together' (902) echoes the hissing foam and fresh blood of Ovid's Calydonian boar when it dies at the hands of Meleager.

So the poem has a heroic undercurrent that may have heartened chivalric young readers like Southampton and Essex, who would have picked up the thread of references to one of the greatest of classical hunts, and the conflation of Adonis's role in the hunt with that of the boar's killer, Meleager. More openly encouraging, however, is the finale of *The Rape of Lucrece* the following year, which ends with the republican champion, Brutus, taking on the Tarquins and surviving—though here, again, Shakespeare emphasises the need for unanimous support if such a rising is to succeed. In the opening 'Argument' he repeats the same crucial phrase twice: first the nobility and then the common people respond to Brutus's lead 'with one consent'. The word is echoed at the end of the poem itself, when the Romans, applauding, give 'consent' to the removal of the Tarquins. As we shall see, this cautious qualification was to prove prophetic.

The growing stress in the second narrative poem on the potential for successful rebellion prompts the question: Did Essex himself, attracted by the suavely oppositional stance of *Venus and Adonis*, have a hand in suggesting or devising the 'graver matter' of *The Rape of Lucrece*? As we have seen, successful rebellions are rare in Shakespeare's work, and it is just possible that there was input here from an Essex who, in 1593, was beginning to realise how entrenched the Cecil influence was at court and in government. The change in tone between the two poems, from light-hearted wit to almost statesmanlike gravity, may reflect the character of his new commission; so might the scholarly reach, intellectual ambition, and even some of the subject matter. Troy was, in the words of one scholar, 'the most famous backdrop for celebrating Essex'.[25]

Historians have painted Essex in such simplistic terms that it is difficult to believe that a man of Shakespeare's intellectual calibre could have taken him seriously. His image has always been that of a flashy, temperamental favourite: a proponent of an outdated code of honour and chivalry; a militant Protestant whose reckless campaigns failed in Spain, in France, and, most disastrously of all, in Ireland. Above all, according to this picture, he was an ambitious man who, Icarus-like, came to grief in a foolish bid for power. Around his story hovers the romance fostered by novels, films, and biographies of Essex as Elizabeth's last love, her 'wild horse', the beautiful, wilful boy who became first her protégé, playing cards with her 'till the birds sing in the morning', then her lover, and finally her nemesis, from whose rebellion and death on the scaffold she never recovered.[26] Scholars acknowledge positive references to figures resembling Essex in Shakespeare's plays, including the single explicit allusion to a contemporary figure when he compares Henry V returning in triumph from France to the Earl of Essex, returning in triumph from Ireland—a hope that was never fulfilled.[27] But even the eminent Shakespeare scholar Jonathan Bate, in a close study of the links between the Earl of Essex and what he believes came to be his 'signature play', Shakespeare's *Richard II*, concludes that Shakespeare himself was at best 'a little over halfway to being an Essex man'. For Bate, and for many others, Essex was essentially 'backward-looking', the champion of an outdated code of honour whose aim was to return the country to the days when the traditional nobility, not a centralised Tudor bureaucracy, set the tone at court and acted as advisors to the monarch.[28]

Until recently, however, the accepted view of Essex's

character and cause has depended on accounts by the faction that destroyed him, a group led by Walter Ralegh, Henry Brooke, Lord Cobham (known as 'Falstaff' among the Essex faction), the chief justice, Sir Edward Coke, and the two Cecils.[29] Thanks to painstaking work by recent scholars, another Earl of Essex is beginning to emerge, a man whose remarkable qualities explain the fact that he commanded the admiration and allegiance of a wide spectrum of the most enlightened of Elizabeth's subjects, a group which extended well beyond a small section of disgruntled nobility. 'No other nobleman living under a sixteenth-century monarch was so rapturously acclaimed in his lifetime for his great qualities', writes one biographer.[30]

It comes as a shock, for instance, to discover that the issue closest to the heart of this so-called Protestant warmonger was that of religious toleration. 'Christendom', the ecumenical concept of trans-sectarian Christianity, was a favourite term among his supporters, who included Puritans, Catholics, conformists, and men like John Harington, who described himself as a bit of all three—'a protesting catholic puritan'.[31] Common to all was a longing for the introduction of liberty of conscience in England, as 'amongst the people of Poland, Switzerland, and other Nations which give friendly entertainment unto a plurality of religions', according to the author of *The State of Christendom*, a Protestant appeal for toleration written in the mid-1590s and dedicated to Essex.[32] 'Men's consciences ought to be free and at liberty', the anonymous writer says. To be persecuted on religious grounds was intolerable: 'It should undoubtedly be a great tyranny to deprive them either of their lives or their country.'[33] Tolerant countries, the author argued, were secure and stable countries. At the opposite end of the confessional divide, the Catholic poet and diplomat Henry Constable, who worked tirelessly for the reconciliation of the churches, and who believed

Essex was 'the worthiest prince that this day liveth', wrote a treatise on very similar lines, arguing for toleration for both Protestants in France and Catholics in England.[34] Essex's supporters included distinguished Catholics, such as Southampton; the young Viscount Montague; the art collector, bibliophile, and antiquarian Lord Lumley; the Earl of Worcester, a leading courtier; the poet William Alabaster; and the dramatist Ben Jonson. He also attracted a wide range of prominent reformers and Protestants, including hard-liners like Archbishop Whitgift and Puritan dissidents like Thomas Cartwright, Peter Wentworth, and Henry Cuffe, a fervent Puritan and outstanding Greek scholar.[35] Toleration appealed to many on humane and religious grounds, but there was also an aesthetic dimension that affected all civilised Elizabethans, and that still affects us today. This was the continued, sustained assault by church and government on sacred and beautiful things. The period between 1534 and 1610 saw the almost total eradication of English art.[36] Daniel repeatedly refers to the 'barbarism' of the age, lamenting a period when 'all that holy was, unhallowed lies, / The scattered carcasses of ruined vows',[37] when beautiful, pleasure-giving things lie 'scattered, dashed, all broke'.[38] This was not mindless vandalism; it was the systematic state-sponsored extinction of 'idolotrous' images.

The brilliant and slippery Francis Bacon, a nephew of Lord Burghley and one of Essex's many dependents when he was court favourite, wrote the official account of Essex's so-called rebellion after his death; by that time, like many of the survivors among Essex's onetime followers, he had strategically changed sides. He portrayed Essex's ecumenism as a cynical ploy. It was, he said, 'a profane policy to serve his turn (for his own greatness) of both sorts of factions, both of Catholics and Puritans'.[39] But Bacon's account was a deliberate misrepresentation, written under duress, he later claimed, and then almost wholly rewritten by the Privy Council to blacken Essex's name still further.

Though, as Essex himself admitted, he was no saint—he had a number of affairs after his devoted wife, Frances Walsingham, retired from court life—he was at once an erudite humanist and a devout and active Christian. Many viewed him as 'the only nobleman that cared for religion'.[40] He mediated conscientiously between confessional groups, promoting talent irrespective of religion, and discouraging divisiveness and disloyalty. Even his virulent hostility to Spain, always thought to be a typically anti-Catholic stance, sprang largely from his opposition to Spain's record of religious persecution under men like the Count of Fuentes and the Duke of Alva. In Essex's eyes, and in the opinion of many others of his generation who had lived through the worst excesses of Philip II's reign, Spain was a religious tyranny bent on world domination. Essex promoted the formation of a joint European opposition to the Spanish superpower which included 'all Christian Princes', Catholic and Protestant alike. He viewed this as a moral crusade, very much as Philip Sidney, a national hero with whom he consciously identified, had done before him.[41] Essex's foreign policy and his domestic policy, then, had liberty of conscience as their starting point. Unlike the increasingly authoritarian regime under Lord Burghley, he offered England exactly what *The Rape of Lucrece*, *Venus and Adonis*, and other contemporary poems, plays, and pamphlets pleaded for—a release from the religious intolerance that had for the past sixty years been the hallmark of Tudor England.[42]

Many scholars see Essex's political manifesto—ecumenist, populist, anti-absolutist—as at best ahead of its time, at worst vague, idealistic, impractical, and coloured by outdated chivalric values. But it turns out that he was a down-to-earth, effective administrator: 'a man of great ability and dogged commitment', in the words of his biographer Paul Hammer.[43] Essex's writing style bears this out. Direct and succinct, written in a clear, flowing hand, his letters and treatises are the work of a man with something to say—not, as so often among his contemporaries, something to conceal. William Camden's famous comment that Essex was 'a man not made for the court' has always suggested a bluff, emotional character more suited to the battlefield than affairs of state. But Hammer pinpoints the real difference between Essex and others close to the centre of power under the ageing Elizabeth: 'If anything, he took politics too seriously because he framed his actions according to principle.'[44] Perhaps the most engaging of the many paintings of Essex is a miniature study by Isaac Oliver drawn at the height of his political career in 1596. It is the portrait of a man of integrity. Though even miniatures often had a propaganda purpose at that period, it is hard not to associate this open, reflective face with the enlightened human values of Shakespeare's plays and poems.

And here we come to the aspect of Essex's manifesto that aligns him most closely with the thrust of Shakespeare's poems and with other leading thinkers among the European intelligentsia of his day: his principled opposition to unlimited royal power, often billed as a new theory of republicanism, or anti-absolutism. But there was nothing novel in the view that the powers of a monarch were contractual. The traditional English Coronation Oath was specifically devised to limit the powers of the Crown. It asserted that English law derived from ancient tradition, 'which the folk and people have made', and stated that the monarch's role was to safeguard and preserve these laws. In 1534, aware that this wording contradicted the terms of the royal supremacy, Henry VIII took a pen to the oath and altered it, introducing a series of qualifications that reduced the monarch's obligations. Though Henry's amendments were in the end dropped, the new absolutist spirit continued. His son's coronation ceremony reduced the emphasis on the 'election' of an English monarch by the people, adding instead an element of enforcement—the people were to acclaim the new monarch 'as by your duties of allegiance ye be bound to do'.[45]

The result was a ballooning of 'resistance theory' literature from 1534 onwards, animatedly discussing the issues of election and deposition raised by the autocratic Tudor monarchy. Robert Persons's *Conference About the Next Succession* is just one of many treatises dedicated to Essex in the 1590s highlighting the historical powers of Parliament, the nobility, and the people to counsel the monarch, and even to intervene when monarchy begins to verge on tyranny—as many believed it had done, both in sixteenth-century England and in Europe under Spanish rule. Essex gave memorable voice to this spirit of individual liberty. In 1598, responding vigorously to a letter from a senior courtier who had reminded him of his sacred duty to obey the divinely appointed monarch, he wrote, 'Doth religion enforce me to serve? Doth God require it? Is it impiety not to do it? Why, cannot princes err, and cannot subjects receive wrong? Is earthly power and authority infinite? Pardon me, pardon me my good Lord, I can never subscribe to these principles.'[46] Though Essex acknowledged the duty he owed his sovereign, he viewed uncritical submission to the ruler as irreligious, because it overrode matters of conscience—hence the frequent charge by his supporters that Elizabeth's closest advisors were 'atheists'. Essex summed up his disapproval for their total subservience to the will of the monarch by concluding: 'Let them acknowledge an infinite absoluteness on earth that do not believe an infinite absoluteness in heaven.'[47]

This stance of the loyal but morally independent subject clearly struck a deep chord with the religious dissidents, the military, the nobility, and the whole range of Elizabeth's subjects who, as we've seen, might have responded to the image of tyrannical depredation in *Lucrece*, and of an oppressive female figure in *Venus and Adonis*. Essex would have known this. He had wider connections in the country and outside it than Elizabeth's court-centred inner circle, and they ranged from the European intelligentsia to the most deprived and marginalised in his own country.

He was also the leading cultural patron of his day; more publications were dedicated to him in the 1590s than to the queen herself.[48] His 'noble active mind' embraced art, music, theology, military history, sport, chivalry, and classical literature.[49] The pensive Oliver miniature suggests that Essex was at heart a scholar; he once wished he could have remained at Cambridge, and he continued to study and surround himself with men of learning throughout his life. The extensive library in his study at Essex House was used by friends and opponents alike, and there is a record of the queen herself borrowing his copy of Tacitus.[50]

At the same time, he was very far from bookish. He would talk to anyone, including, according to one friend, 'men of mean condition and place . . . in sports and sometimes in serious matters'.[51] He was famed for 'affable gestures, open doors, making his table and his bed . . . popularly places of audience to suitors'.[52] Essex House, formerly known as Leicester House when his stepfather lived there, was a complex of buildings and formal gardens extending from the Strand down to the River Thames. Under Essex and his family it became a social and cultural hub frequented by petitioners, scholars, clerics, and many foreigners, including the sons of friends he had made while abroad. Both Catholics and reformers found him a protective patron.

For England's leading exponent of the Catholic madrigal art-form, John Mundy, Essex was 'a religious sanctuary'.[53] His lib-erality was in striking contrast to the many at court who were busily investing in lucrative privateering ventures, real estate, jewellery, and plate. Essex, never a rich man, built nothing, and donated two magnificent books he acquired on his trip back from Cadiz to Thomas Bodley's new library at Oxford and to King's College, Cambridge.[54] The money he got from the lucra-tive monopoly of sweet wines, bestowed on him by the queen when he was a young favourite, went largely into funding her own cash-strapped army—an often ruinous expense which Es-sex thought essential.

As for soldiers, he wrote: 'I find sweetness in their conver-sation, strong assistance in their employment with me and hap-piness in their friendship. I love them for their virtues' sake, for their greatness of mind: for little minds, though never so full of virtue, can be but little virtuous.'[55] In return, soldiers loved him. As we shall see, many of his perceived military failures arose from the lack of logistical support and even from surreptitious sabotage from those back in England. He consistently pressed for reform of the military under Elizabeth, and despaired of its leadership. 'Princes that are at once in war, if they do too lit-tle must suffer much', he once wrote.[56] On campaign, his in-sistence on leading from the front, his refusal to wear armour under fire when his men had none, his flamboyant gestures in action, along with his meticulous planning and his concern for prisoners and unpaid men, have been described as exemplary by modern army officers.[57] Essex is often criticised for knighting his men on the field, in direct opposition to the queen's wishes—a typically foolish, ambitious, 'chivalric' gesture. His latest biogra-phers, however, argue that knighthoods were the only rewards

Essex could grant his followers, given his consistent inability to break into the charmed inner circle at court, with its crucial opportunities for patronage.

Limited though his influence was, Essex nonetheless attracted a wide range of political contacts which led to the formation of an effective intelligence service of his own, replacing Walsingham's after he died. Francis Bacon's brother Antony, an invaluable political analyst and information-gatherer, was one of the group who enabled him to conduct a long and covert diplomatic correspondence with James VI of Scotland, arguably the key to the Scottish king's eventual smooth accession to the English throne.

But Essex did have one major flaw. He may have been the closest England had, at that point, to a genuine statesman. But as his followers often reminded him, he was not a natural courtier, or a natural politician. He was explosive, emotional, dangerously uninhibited. He responded to the queen's mood swings with an unconcealed exasperation which at times bordered on the treasonous. He was quite unable to dissemble, and he repeatedly misread the motives of his opponents, expecting them to be as open as he was. This defect of character was frequently explored by Shakespeare, whose tragedies often dramatise the downfall of trusting, charismatic characters at the hands of Machiavellians like Richard III and Iago.

If this revised portrait is correct, then it is understandable that the young Earl of Southampton should have fallen under the spell of such a man, pinning on him all his hopes for the restoration of his own fortunes, and that of his country. And, given the new estimate of his character, it is probable that Shakespeare was captivated as well, dedicating his two great narrative poems to Essex's closest friend and supporter in order to advance what must indeed have seemed to their writer a noble cause. Evidence of how much the cause meant to him, and why, will emerge when we examine the impact of Essex's ultimate failure on Shakespeare's work. But first, we need to look at what actually precipitated the downfall of a man who may well have conformed, in many ways, to the Shakespearean concept of a hero.

CHAPTER TEN

THE DESTRUCTION OF THE EARL OF ESSEX

S IR EDWARD COKE, Elizabeth I's attorney general, was the outstanding lawyer of his day; he is still considered one of the greatest of English jurists. Nonetheless Coke's climactic denunciation of Essex's followers at their trial after his failed rebellion comes as a shock to modern ears: 'He that conspires to take London and surprise the Court, this doth merely concern the State; but this Catiline company to conspire against the queen herself, this concerns more! But the toleration of religion, this of all things, concerns most!'[1] For Coke and his audience, sedition and rebellion paled beside the dreadful spectre of religious toleration. The wide support that there was in the late 1590s for freedom of conscience in England, in sharp contrast with the stance of the government, voiced by Edward Coke, reminds us how different English history might have been had Essex played his cards another way. To what extent his political downfall was his own fault, and to what extent it was the work of his enemies, is still the subject of debate and ongoing research by historians, but a survey of what is known of his public career shows us that he was up against a powerful, devious, and experienced group of politicians whose survival depended on Essex's removal.

In the summer of 1593, when *Venus and Adonis* was published, Essex was still a rising star. At twenty-eight, he was a war hero who had fought with skill and bravery in several campaigns abroad; he had inherited the mantle both of his stepfather, the Earl of Leicester, who had been the queen's closest friend and greatest favourite, and of his stepbrother, Philip Sidney, the popular embodiment of chivalry, who had given Essex his sword as he lay dying in the Netherlands. He was also viewed as the coming man by a wide support base at home and among those he had met and impressed in France and the Low Countries: here, they believed, was the future chief advisor to the queen and the successor to Lord Burghley.

In that same year Essex became a privy councillor and devoted his considerable energy and organisational ability to defence and to building up a network of foreign policy and intelligence advisors. He backed the experienced diplomat William Davison for the key position of secretary of state, which had been left vacant since the death of Francis Walsingham in 1590. He became a model administrator, throwing himself into council business and working alongside the ageing Lord Burghley. There were differences between them. Essex was aware of the widespread corruption in the various departments under the authority of the Lord Treasurer. 'Burghley knew that the queen's finances were in a terrible mess', notes the historian Paul Hammer. 'But he could not reveal the full truth to his sovereign or colleagues without exposing his own inability, or unwillingness, to stem the massive corruption and waste.'[2] At the 1593 Parliament, Essex's supporters complained that at a moment when the poorest citizens of the country were being beggared by repeated tax demands to fund Elizabeth's wars, Burghley, as Lord Trea- surer, deliberately undervalued his own wealth for tax purposes, paying in some cases thirty times less than he should have done. Essex and his followers contrasted what they called the 'expence- ful vanities' of such men with the hardships endured by com- moners, struggling to earn a living in a decade of successively disastrous harvests and rampant inflation. Ireland was also Lord Burghley's responsibility, and there, too, modern historians have attacked him for the ruthlessness with which he pursued his own interests. Hiram Morgan accuses Burghley of conducting an 'ir- responsible, negligent and possibly corrupt policy towards Ire- land in the 1590s' when he 'destroyed good servitors and backed crooks in their place'. One case in particular, involving the un- just treatment and eventual death of a Lord Deputy of Ireland, Sir John Perrot, prompts Morgan to ask a wider question: 'What did Burghley himself get out of it? Was English policy in other areas where Burghley's influence was paramount similarly erratic and equally defective? Did English policy go completely hay- wire with the death of Secretary Walsingham in April 1590?'[3] The kind of 'subtle destruction' which characterised the treat- ment of Perrot, according to Paul Hammer, 'introduced a new brutality into high politics'.[4] Like recent research into Burghley's handling of the treasury, Morgan's disturbing questions about his activities in Ireland provide a counterbalance to the common assumption that Essex's accusations of systemic corruption in government were personally motivated. There was, too, a grow- ing rift between Lord Burghley and Essex over foreign policy. Essex continually argued for a concerted European campaign to reduce Spanish imperial ambition, while Burghley and the queen settled for piecemeal engagements abroad, which Essex maintained were expensive and self-defeating.

As Burghley lived on, keeping a tight grip on the levers of patronage, Essex's candidates were regularly passed over for high office, and a stealthy new contender for the office of secretary of state began to emerge. Burghley's son Robert had made it onto the Privy Council two years ahead of Essex. Now, to Essex's disbelief, he was being tipped by some as secretary of state. It was the first signal that Burghley's heir might not be Essex after all.

In 1596 Essex achieved his greatest military triumph: the sacking of Cadiz and the sinking of a considerable Spanish treasure fleet. This coup, accomplished along with the Lord Admiral, Charles Howard, dealt the kind of strategically accurate blow to Spain that Essex had been urging on the queen for years. Later that year, the usual picture of Essex as excitable and overbearing is belied by the description of him by a Venetian visitor as 'fair-skinned, tall, but wiry', sporting a beard, 'which he used not to wear', and 'right modest, courteous, and humane'.[5] But Cadiz proved to be the watershed of his career. Though he returned to loud popular acclaim, he found Burghley had been busy while he was away. The queen was enraged at the lack of plunder, which she blamed on Essex, and gave credit for the victory to Howard. And in Essex's absence, Robert Cecil had been made secretary of state.

Accepting at last that his powers to advance his following at court would always be blocked by the Cecils, who were already siphoning off those of his own supporters who valued their careers, Essex gambled on military methods of furthering his own fortunes. An expedition followed in 1597 known as the 'Islands Voyage' which attempted and failed to raid the Spanish coastline and intercept the Spanish fleet. Like all Essex's ventures, it attracted hundreds of volunteers among the gentry and nobility, including the poet John Donne, but the trip was dogged by storms, quarrels, and misfortunes and ended in failure and expensive losses. Essex returned to tempestuous scenes with the queen and with Howard, who had now been made Earl of Nottingham in a gesture that appeared to attribute the victory at Cadiz to him alone. In the end, the queen made a furious Essex Earl Marshal of England, but he realised he was being slowly marginalised. In August 1598, Lord Burghley died. His son Robert, whom Burghley had groomed as his successor, was now in a commanding position on the Privy Council and had become a key advisor to the queen. Before long, he had also taken over the post of Master of the Court of Wards, which had been widely expected to fall to Essex. Cecil's men now dominated all the areas which had previously been Lord Burghley's domain: the treasury, domestic politics, Ireland. And historians all agree on one point about the Cecils: if Burghley was corrupt, his son was doubly so.

There was no hope now of Essex implementing any of his agenda. As Master of the Ordnance he had done something towards ending corruption, but his scope was limited. His plans for an effective standing army, with regular pay and conditions, had got nowhere. Religious toleration was regarded as a nonstarter. But Essex did have one trump card left.

As early as 1589, when he was only twenty-four, Essex had already identified James VI of Scotland as the successor most likely to bring about a more enlightened regime in England. Believing Elizabeth had not long to live, he set up his first secret line of communication with the Scottish king ('Victor') in which he described himself as a 'Weary Knight' tired of the 'thrall' he was subjected to under Elizabeth (whose Essexian pseudonym, 'Venus', may have influenced Shakespeare's first narrative poem). His clumsy offer to assist the Stuart cause, a potentially treacherous move, was luckily intercepted by the government. Lord Burghley was at that point promoting Essex as a rival to Sir

Walter Ralegh, and the queen's young favourite escaped with a warning.[6]

Seven years later, however, in 1596, when Essex was an established military leader and privy councillor, he cautiously revived the link. As early as 1594, the word from Scotland was that 'all admired Essex', including King James, who compared him to Philip Sidney. A coded correspondence ensued which was kept secret for two reasons. The queen had forbidden speculation as to who would succeed her. And at this stage, the last candidate the Cecils could afford to consider was James VI. James correctly blamed the execution of his mother, Mary Queen of Scots, on Lord Burghley, who was described by a Scottish intermediary as 'bloody, cruel and conscienceless'.[7] James believed the Cecils were the driving force behind England's secret support of a Protestant Scottish faction led by his enemy, the Earl of Bothwell, and wrote to Essex in October 1595 saying, 'I am glad that he who rules all there is begun to be loathed at by the best and greatest sort there, since he is my enemy.'[8] There were other candidates, including Arabella Stuart and the Infanta, Isabella Clara of Spain, but James had the strongest claim. Leading Catholics, such as the Jesuit Robert Persons, as well as many of the reformers, including Peter Wentworth, grimly anticipated civil war: there would be 'rivers of blood' when Elizabeth died, in Wentworth's apocalyptic view.[9] James himself was making provision for armed support in the case of opposition and vigorously furthering his claim at every point, lobbying representatives of France, Spain, and even the papacy. His talk of toleration attracted a wave of Essexian support from England. James's reliance on Essex, and Essex's eagerness to assist James, intensified as the decade wore on.

From the Catholic point of view, there was a painful irony here. By 1599, while Catholics like Henry Constable were

attempting to get James to commit openly to Catholic toleration, the pragmatic Robert Cecil was making his own secret
overtures to the Spanish claimant most favoured by English
Catholics: Isabella Clara, a daughter of Philip II and sister to the
new Spanish king, Philip III. After decades of warfare, Spain
was cautiously exploring possible peace deals with England.
For Essex, this was the moment to attack. He viewed Spain as a
bloodthirsty Catholic tyranny which was ceasing hostilities only
in order to renew its persecution with greater intensity in the
Low Countries. But the privy councillors were as eager as Spain
to sign a truce. Robert Cecil opened tentative links with Robert
Persons, and even went so far as to commission portraits of Isabella and her husband, in great secrecy, and have them covertly
shipped to England.[10] One major incentive was the quiet transfer of backhanders from the Spanish government to influential
figures in England. It is known that from James's accession until
his own death in 1612, Robert Cecil, by now the all-powerful
secretary of state, received a secret pension of well over £1,000
(£175,000) a year from Spain. He was not the only one. From
1603 onwards, notes the historian Lawrence Stone, 'most of
the leading Jacobean statesmen were on the payroll of a foreign
power; a situation unique, as far as is known, in English history'.[11] It is therefore 'not unreasonable', as another scholar points
out, given Spain's anxiety with regard to the succession, to sup-
pose that these payments began earlier; indeed, as early as 1599,
Philip III was rumoured to be supporting the Infanta's claim by
bribing leading English statesmen.[12]

Ironically, the more hopeful James's cause began to look,
the more imperiled Essex himself became. As the Spanish claim
melted away (Isabella was against the idea), Cecil and his party
realised that their own hold on power—indeed, very probably their own survival—depended on a last-minute transfer of

allegiance to the Scottish king, and therefore, the removal of Essex, James's chief supporter and advisor, before Elizabeth died. A chilling letter from Ralegh to Cecil in 1600 strongly implies that Essex, who was already under house arrest, should be killed. He recommends boldness to Cecil, citing previous political deaths and murders that had gone unavenged, and warns that if Essex lives he will ruin the Cecils.[13]

By this time, Essex had already made what turned out to be a fatal move. In the crucial months of late 1598, as Robert Cecil put out feelers to Spain and consolidated his power base following the deaths of Lord Burghley at home and Philip II abroad, Essex left England, having accepted the command of an army mustered to defeat a major rebellion under the Earl of Tyrone in Ireland. Given the complete control now exerted by the Cecil faction at court, it looks as if Essex thought this was his one hope of regaining lost ground. But if he hoped he would defeat Tyrone, he was wrong. There is a strong argument that Robert Cecil sabotaged his attempts to do so. Desperate letters survive from Essex begging for the boats and carriage-horses required to establish the garrison to the very north of Tyrone's territory at Lough Foyle, which, as the Privy Council had already agreed, was indispensable to victory. Cecil consistently deflected his increasingly desperate requests for supplies, thereby wrecking Essex's multipronged strategy, which would be triumphantly implemented by his successor, Lord Mountjoy, three years later.[14] After four months of delay, his fellow privy councillor, William Knollys, wrote to Cecil in revealing terms: 'I beseech you not to look upon the person but the cause.'[15] In the words of John Guy, in his recent exposé of the last decade of Elizabeth's reign, 'the profound lack of support [Essex] received from Cecil and his allies invites the conclusion that they were setting him up to fail'.[16] If so, this reveals a great deal about Robert Cecil.

Essex was in command of the largest army ever to be dispatched to Ireland, yet Essex's failure mattered more to his political rival than the lives of soldiers and the defeat of Tyrone.

Essex's reaction as the summer months turned to autumn is also revealing. He met Tyrone to call a truce at a ford on the River Lagan, where the pair had a long private conversation together on horseback. Afterwards, Tyrone, whose agenda also included liberty of conscience and respect for the rights of the nobility, told a Spanish priest that Essex had reluctantly refused his offer of military support.[17] It seems Essex was contemplating the textbook option of using an invading force to topple a corrupt, unpopular regime at home. This was the option so frequently dramatised in Shakespeare's plays, most notably *Richard II*, and the option which, according to Philip Hughes, was the only effective form of rebellion. Essex knew he could rely on James VI, and also sounded out the possibility of military aid from Charles Mountjoy, who was in charge of the army in Wales. Armed invasion was a genuine possibility. But when it came to the crunch, Essex took a step back. At exactly this point, the autumn of 1599, Robert Cecil and Charles Howard mobilised London and the South Coast in response to an invasion scare that many at the time suspected of being a warning to Essex. Whether or not this was the reason, Essex, now suffering from an unspecified illness, returned alone to London to put his case to the queen in person. On the morning of 24 September, he surprised her in her bedchamber as he burst in unannounced. Initially she listened as he related his grievances, but by the end of the day he found himself under house arrest. Charges of treason were prepared. Essex was physically unwell and close to breakdown, and in the face of a huge wave of public support, a planned trial was cancelled. Essex nevertheless remained under house arrest for the next nine months. In the face of an increasing public outcry at his illegal detainment, he was charged again, this time with insubordination, at a hearing by his peers on 5 June 1600. With a self-command which impressed onlookers, Essex successfully rebutted the charges and was released—but he was suspended from all his offices: privy councillor, Master of the Ordnance, Master of the Queen's Horse, Lord Lieutenant of Ireland, and Earl Marshal of England. In October 1600, he suffered a crippling blow. His main source of income was cut off when the queen failed to renew his monopoly on sweet wines.

The privy councillors were well aware that a desperate move would follow: indeed, the technique of subtly goading adversaries into acts of folly had been the hallmark of the Cecil political strategy ever since Elizabeth's accession. Crowds of supporters converged over the winter months on Essex's London home. Essex knew that peace negotiations with Spain were under way. He also suspected that in the course of these talks, an inner group was stitching up the crucial succession question directly contrary, in his view, to the national interest.[18] That Christmas, aware that time was running out, Essex wrote an urgent appeal to James VI to send his ambassadors to secure the Scottish claim. 'A reigning faction', he wrote, 'is so potent in a state as they could suppress innocencie, cancel merit, justify conspiracy, make law, bury freedom, usurp sovereignty for the present, and prepare a way for an unjust succession hereafter.' Elizabeth was being 'led blindfold into her own extreme danger'. The faction suppressed 'all noble, virtuous and heroical spirits', and 'their juggling with our enemies' and 'practice for the Infanta of Spain' demanded instant action. For Essex, this was his 'Brutus' moment. 'Now am I summoned of all sides . . . to relieve my poor country that groans under her burden', he wrote to James.[19]

James's intelligence reports confirmed growing suspicions that Cecil was exploring the Spanish claim. He promised to send his ambassador, the Earl of Mar, to support Essex, and to back him up by force if need be.[20] By early February 1601, still under close surveillance, Essex had settled down at Essex House to wait for the Scottish ambassador. Close by, in the less conspicuous Drury House, his inner circle met under the leadership of the Earl of Southampton to work on their plan of campaign. As soon as support was in place, Essex and his party would detain the 'evil counsellors' and enter Whitehall under arms, accompanied by Scottish envoys. There, on their knees, they would put their case to the queen and persuade her to call upon Parliament to ratify a Stuart succession. The ultimate aim was to avoid civil unrest, prevent Spanish rule in England, ensure liberty of conscience, and secure Essex's own future and that of his party. So what went wrong? Why did this carefully planned initiative fizzle out into a so-called rebellion that was in fact nothing less than an embarrassing fiasco?

Years later, just before his own execution, Sir Walter Ralegh revealed that Essex had told him before he died that he had been 'fetched off by a trick'. Though Ralegh did not say any more, the consensus is that Essex's 'fetching off', or destruction, was a vintage piece of Cecilian provocation. On the evening of Saturday, 7 February, at least a week before the Scottish envoy was due to arrive, Essex received an unusual late-night summons to a meeting of the Privy Council. Ignoring such an order was a serious matter, but, suspecting a trap, Essex refused to go. A second summons followed, and almost simultaneously, an urgent warning that Ralegh's and Cobham's men were preparing to assassinate him: as we know, it was a course Ralegh had recommended earlier to Cecil. Essex believed the story. A few weeks earlier, Southampton, riding with a page, had been attacked in the street by a large group of armed men led by his enemy Lord Grey, an ally of Cecil's. Southampton successfully summoned support and fended off the attackers, but his page was severely injured, and Grey escaped with a token prison sentence. The government was evidently turning a blind eye to vendettas: it appeared to be open season on the Essex group.

Essex summoned his supporters, and a night of frenzied debate followed. In the end it was decided to bring forward the plan of entering Whitehall, even though Scottish support was not yet in place. They would rely instead on Essex's popularity in London. But would they go on foot or on horseback? And in what direction? Essex House lay halfway between Whitehall to the west and the ancient walls of the city to the east, just south of the spot where the church of St Clement Danes now stands. Should they go directly to Whitehall, or raise the city first, or even seize the Tower? In order to avoid the appearance of a coup d'état by a small, disaffected group, they decided to proceed east up the Strand the next morning, raise supporters in the city, then return to the Palace of Whitehall with the London crowds behind them. As Essex said afterwards, his aim was not to usurp the throne, but to secure the succession and to take on 'my great enemies, Secretary Cecil, the Lord Cobham and Sir Walter Ralegh, whom we had resolved to have removed from Her Majesty as altogether unfit to live so near her, being corrupt orators of the now corrupted state'.[21]

In the chaos and confusion, their plans were already being leaked by edgy followers, among them Ferdinando Gorges, who was spotted conferring with his half-brother, Walter Ralegh, on a boat on the Thames near Essex House.[22] However, Essex had received a guarantee from one of the city sheriffs, Thomas Smith, that he would supply him with a thousand armed men from the city militia. Partially armed, on foot, and having taken Communion, the group assembled in the forecourt and prepared to set off. But the Privy Council was ahead of them. Four senior ministers of state appeared at Essex's door, including the Lord Privy Seal and the Lord Chief Justice, John Popham, demanding they be told what was going on. There was a brief exchange amid cries from the crowd: 'They abuse you, my lord, they are undoing you. You lose your time!' Essex escorted them inside, initially for their protection from the crowd.

The mood can be gauged by an account of Essex's sister, Penelope Rich, one of the prime movers behind the rebellion, calling up for Popham's head to be tossed out the window. But once Essex had locked the library and set a guard on the door, the distinguished visitors became hostages. From this fateful moment onwards, Essex was committed. He drew his sword and ran out into the street followed by his closest allies, Rutland and Southampton. Around three hundred men followed him up the Strand towards the city, shouting that England had been sold to Spain, and that Essex's life was in danger. But by now the mayor had his orders, and the City of London was in lockdown. Essex talked the guards into letting him through Ludgate, but within the walls he found all doors shut, and no crowds to rally—the Sunday sermon at St Paul's Cross was over and the congregation had already dispersed. Worst of all, Thomas Smith vanished from his house, and there was no sign of any militia. Soaked with sweat—according to one report, he changed his shirt at this point—Essex halted at the sheriff's house in consternation before pressing on after an hour or so in search of the mayor.

Essex must have known by now that making directly for the court, as many of the crowd had urged him to do, would have been the better option, the one his enemies were dreading. The guards were largely loyal to him. The meticulous nineteenth-century historian John Lingard relays an account of the panic at that point within the corridors of Whitehall: 'At court the earl possessed so many friends', according to Lingard, 'that the ministers knew not whom to trust. . . . The queen alone had the boldness to talk of going in search of the insurgents. Not one of them would dare to meet a single glance of her eye; they would flee at the very notice of her approach.'[23]

At around two in the afternoon, government forces cautiously entered the city from various quarters, proclaiming Essex a traitor and offering a reward for his capture and pardon to anyone who left him. There were one or two brief skirmishes. Eventually Essex's disintegrating company turned for home, but the way back through Ludgate was blocked. Finally, taking their wounded with them, they returned to Essex House by boat. There, a bitter blow awaited them. Ferdinando Gorges had ordered the release of the hostages in a bid to secure his own pardon.

As darkness fell, the besieged occupants of Essex House threw up barricades of books, furniture, anything they could lay hands on, to block doors and windows. Meanwhile, the Lord Admiral drew up his troops and ordered cannon, powder, and shot from the Tower. At this point utter despair overwhelmed Owen Salusbury, one of Essex's many Catholic followers, who saw the whole event as a historic opportunity lost. If the enterprise had come off, he told his companions, they should have deserved public gratitude instead of anger, and a statue inscribed 'To the Reformers of the English Realm'.[24] He was killed after deliberately standing up within full view of a sniper on the roof of St Clement Danes.

Late that evening, a drum sounded for a parley and a negotiator stepped forward. He was Sir Robert Sidney, one of Essex's many early protégés, who had reluctantly chosen the Cecil path to advancement. The Earl of Southampton climbed out onto the rooftop of Essex House as spokesman for the rebels. Throughout, Southampton seems to have been one of the most determined and decisive of the group. Ferdinando Gorges recorded his burst of impatience at one of the many inconclusive sessions he chaired at Drury House: 'Shall we resolve upon nothing then?'[25] Given Southampton's leading role in the rebellion, the fact that he escaped the block is clear indication that throughout the whole affair, the overwhelming goal of the Cecil faction was the removal of Essex.

A vivid account survives of the torch-lit interchange between Sidney and Southampton. Throughout, pleading for a fair hearing from the queen herself, not the Privy Council, Southampton addressed Sidney as a brother, a cousin, one of their own. Refusing to yield without hostages, as that would be merely to 'put ourselves into the wolves' mouth', he asked Sidney, 'Good cousin, what would you do, if you were in our cases?' To Sidney's answer that they had no option but to yield, as the admiral was bringing up cannon, Southampton called down: 'If he blow us up we shall be the nearer heaven . . . for we have made choice rather to die like men with our swords in our hands, than some nine or ten days hence to end our lives on a scaffold.' This piece of rhetoric brought a more conciliatory Essex up to join him. Essex also addressed Sidney as a familiar friend, and the soldiers around him as his own men, 'for whose safety I have so often opposed myself to peril'; they were men who, to his grief, had been made 'agents against me', while 'those atheists, mine enemies', dare not approach. He asked Sidney how he would feel, had he been penned up for so long—'trodden under foot of every base upstart', his life now 'so narrowly sought by them': 'Would it not grieve you? Yes, yes, I am sure it would. Well, it is no matter: death will end all.'[26]

Sidney and the admiral offered a truce to permit the release of Essex's wife and sister. During the interval that followed, while the barricades were temporarily dismantled and the cannons primed, the whole group had time to reconsider. Finally, Essex and Southampton gave up. After securing the promise of a fair trial, 'they went down, and opened the doors; and each of them upon his knee surrendered his sword'.[27]

This was Robert Cecil's finest hour. The high-minded, idealistic Essexian enterprise, designed to rid the country of corruption and, in the words of one supporter, to bring about 'the settling of the succession by Act of Parliament on the king of Scotland', had been successfully transformed into a pathetic, and apparently treacherous, scramble for personal survival. London, it appeared, had remained inert in the face of their hero's feeble assault on the government. Thanks to Robert Cecil's manipulative skills, Essex's appeal for religious toleration, for a smooth succession, and for openness and honesty in public life would forever after be viewed as nothing more than a humiliating display of personal ambition.

The endgame was equally clinical. Within three weeks, and safely out of public view, Essex went to the block. Otherwise, with a small handful of exceptions, the Privy Council was merciful. Southampton's sentence was commuted to an indefinite period in the Tower. Key figures escaped with a brief imprisonment and a fine. Lingard's observation that 'at court the earl possessed so many friends, that the ministers knew not whom to trust' explains the virtual amnesty that followed the so-called rebellion. Machiavelli recommended that 'people should either be caressed or crushed'.[28] With the crushing of Essex, most of his erstwhile followers were all too eager to inform, recant, and adapt to the new order in exchange for official favour. Most important of all, James VI, his eyes fixed on the goal of the English throne, accepted Robert Cecil as his new contact in England, although, after his accession to the throne, he showered favours on the old associates of the Earl of Essex, releasing Southampton from prison and restoring Essex's son to his title and estates.

But the most impressive aspect of Robert Cecil's triumph was his success in ensuring that the reputation for honour which was central to Essex's character was comprehensively demolished. Between his conviction and his execution, Essex saw no one except his secretary, Henry Cuffe, four or five churchmen, and the powerful elite bent on destroying him. The story that he underwent a complete moral and emotional collapse in the Tower was widely disbelieved at the time.[29] Although he was particularly close to his mother and his sisters, he is said to have refused to see any of his family and friends between his conviction and his death. The official version is that Essex was broken by the reproaches of his chaplain, and that, overcome with remorse, he made a long, abject confession to four privy councillors, incriminating colleagues, heaping blame for the rebellion on his supporters, denouncing perfidious Londoners, attacking his sister, and lamenting his own crime. 'I am a burden to the commonwealth and should be spewed out. . . . [M]ine is a great sin, a crying sin, an infectious sin, infecting with a leprosy both far and near', he apparently wrote. His heartless sister, Penelope Rich, 'must be looked to, for she hath a proud spirit'.[30] The only fleeting witness to this 'broken' Essex was his timid, scholarly secretary, Henry Cuffe, who was also under sentence of death. The 'close-written' four-page confession—a crucial piece of pro-Cecil evidence—does not survive. At the time, none of the members of Essex's inner circle believed in its authenticity, and they denounced the chaplain who secured it as 'base, fearful and mercenary', and 'a hireling'. As for Essex's alleged longing for a private death to avoid rousing the people, his friend Henri IV of France laughed derisively when he heard it; Essex, he knew, had wanted his execution to be public.

One aspect of the tragedy takes us back to Shakespeare. Before returning to Essex House on the night before the rebellion, a group of Essex's supporters had been engaged in an activity which has ever since been the focus of intense interest among Shakespeare scholars as well as historians. They had been at the Globe Theatre watching Shakespeare's *Richard II*—the drama Jonathan Bate called Essex's 'signature play'.[31] The company had been paid a considerable sum to stage it, probably by Essex's friend Charles Percy, and managed to excuse themselves afterwards to the Privy Council on the grounds that it was an old play, and the large fee was irresistible. Scholars are divided as to whether or not the performance was intended to prepare the public mind for the Essex coup, theoretically due to take place within the coming month. Bate argues that it was no more than 'a bonding exercise' for the Essex group, 'a steeling of the will, a visible show of solidarity'.[32] Either way, it looks as if one aspect of the play was on Essex's mind the following evening, as he negotiated terms in the dark with Robert Sidney. Like many other plays of the period, *Richard II* attacks evil advisors who prey on a vulnerable monarch. Shakespeare dramatises their impact in a vivid piece of allegory in which Richard's royal gardeners, covertly talking politics, lament the effect of parasitical 'caterpillars' on their garden. Bolingbroke, the virtuous champion of the people, who, as Bate points out, has close similarities with Essex, uses the same phrase as he sets out to rescue the king from these men, calling them 'the caterpillars of the commonwealth / Which I have sworn to weed and pluck away' (2.3.166–167). The word was then a common synonym for parasites, but it is perhaps significant that Essex himself during his last stand seems to be quoting Bolingbroke in the play his supporters had watched the night before, when he says of the 'atheists' surrounding the queen, 'I would think my death most honourable, if by my death I might also end their lives, and that I had done to my prince and country good service by rooting out such caterpillars from the earth.'[33]

The first reaction of many after the Essex fiasco was profound disillusion, and, in many cases, shame. Scores of courtiers,
writers, scholars, noblemen, and dependents of all kinds raced to
disassociate themselves from their disgraced patron 'as it is the
custom for the English to betray each other', commented the
French ambassador sardonically in a letter about Essex's trial.[34]
He also observed that, judging by the expressions of the ranks
of nobility present, when Robert Cecil fell dramatically to his
knees, to deny Essex's charge that he had backed the Infanta's
claim, they were 'more afraid of this little man than they were of
their consciences or of their Queen'. Outside the court, the response was very different. The headsman was almost lynched by
furious crowds as he left the Tower, and ballads and pamphlets
circulated glorifying Essex and attacking Ralegh and Cecil. In
London and throughout the country there was an outpouring
of anger and indignation at Essex's downfall, which was widely
seen as the work of his enemies.

Impassioned argument about Essex, the nature of his rebellion, the reason for his failure, and the truth about his final
confession raged at the time and has continued ever since. One
aspect of the whole fiasco that clearly had a profound impact
on Shakespeare was the revelation that for almost everyone involved, self-interest turned out to be the primary motivation.
Francis Bacon became the symbol of those who abandoned Essex when he ceased to be of use to them. A close friend of Essex's
for many years, and the recipient of lavish gifts from him, Bacon
acted as prosecutor for the queen in Essex's informal trial after
his return from Ireland, spoke against him at his trial for treason,
and, after his execution, blackened his character still further in
his 'Apology', the penning of which he afterwards tried to blame
on pressure from the Privy Council.

Soon after Essex's death, Shakespeare wrote *Timon of Athens*, a sketchy, possibly unfinished play in which greedy parasites abandon a great man when he runs out of money. Timon dies cursing his followers. Foremost among them is his close friend Ventidius, whose betrayal of Timon has been seen as an allusion to Francis Bacon's betrayal of Essex.[35] Behind another, anonymous character there may lie a still more interesting defector. If this play really is about Essex, Shakespeare has included himself in the crowd of followers who abandoned him. Among the most repellent of Timon's hangers-on are a nameless poet and painter. Their vain, competitive exchanges open the play as they prepare to interest Timon in their latest dedications to him. Both are graciously received and handsomely rewarded. Later on, believing that Timon's fortunes have bounced back after his fall, the poet returns with another fawning proposal. This time, he says, the theme will be a satire on the 'infinite flatteries' that surround an unwary, wealthy young man: the very theme, in fact, of Timon. Timon's disgusted response suggests that the literary flatterer is indeed a self-portrait of Shakespeare: 'Must thou needs stand for a villain in thine own work?' (5.1.35).

If the play is a satire on the general desertion of Essex towards the end of his life, then Shakespeare was wise to include himself among the deserters, especially if it was written for a group who knew him well, and knew that his role was as ignominious, or as prudent, as that of almost everyone else. Unlike another implicated writer, John Hayward, Shakespeare was not interrogated or imprisoned in the wake of the Essex rising, and it was left to his business partner, Augustine Phillips, to defend the eve-of-rebellion performance of *Richard II* before the Privy Council. Casting himself as a villain in his own work was an act of atonement, perhaps, but also an expression of solidarity with the many others who felt they had betrayed a generous benefactor for reasons of self-preservation.

Betrayal and disillusion run through *Troilus and Cressida*, another play dated to this period. Like *Timon*, it could well have been written for the remnants of Essex's loyal supporters who called themselves 'Octavians' after the 8 February rising, and who were recorded as visiting Southampton while he was imprisoned in the Tower.[36] The setting of *Troilus and Cressida* is that Essexian favourite, the siege of Troy. But Shakespeare's bitter play demolishes the whole concept of honour embodied by Essex and promoted, at least outwardly, by his followers. Base, misguided, and foul-mouthed characters predominate. In a scene reminiscent of Essex's self-inflicted end, the chivalrous Hector, after rashly removing his armour, is cut down by Achilles' men. The idealistic lover, Troilus, is hopelessly deluded. The drama ends with a string of mirthless jokes about sexual disease.

If he thought Essex had completely failed in his aims, however, Shakespeare turned out to be wrong. On 24 March 1603, at the age of sixty-nine, after a long period of melancholy, Queen Elizabeth died. The event had been widely expected to trigger a period of social unrest, foreign invasion, even civil war. What actually happened appears to have taken the country by surprise. Posthumously, and against all the odds, Essex's years of unofficial diplomacy in England and Scotland appeared to have achieved the most ambitious of his goals. A major factor in the peaceful accession of the Scottish king to the English throne was the fact that James brought with him exactly what Essex and his followers had hoped for: the much-anticipated promise of toleration for both Catholics and Puritans. Son of the Catholic Mary, Queen of Scots, and married to the Catholic Ann of Denmark, yet Calvinist by upbringing, James professed himself 'averse from all severity of persecution against such as were of a different religion'.[37] Advised on all sides 'to give good hopes to the Catholics, that he might more easily come without impediment to the crown', James had agreed, confiding, in a letter to the Earl of Northumberland, that 'it were a pity to lose so good a kingdom for not tolerating mass in a corner, if upon that it resteth'.[38] He arrived in England genuinely committed to Christian unity, and vigorously promoted the concept of an ecumenical council under the authority of the papacy. He promised a debate to air Puritan grievances, and the penal laws against Catholics were barely enforced. In the last year of Elizabeth's reign, fines and forfeitures from Catholics had brought the treasury over £10,000 (equivalent to almost £3 million today).[39] In the first two years of James's reign, income from recusants fell to below £300.

The impact on the country of the year of limited toleration which inaugurated James I's reign is often passed over in later accounts of the period. Equally neglected is the importance of the English contribution to the growing argument for religious co-existence in Europe. A once-famous work, *A Relation of the State of Religion*, was a groundbreaking and highly influential survey of the various European religions written in 1599 by Edwin Sandys, an Essexian supporter and close friend and colleague of the Earl of Southampton.[40] After a two-year journey of enquiry across a fractured, post-Reformation Europe, Sandys concluded that Christian unity was no longer an option, but that coexistence between religions was a practical alternative. The thesis picks up and develops others written by Essex's followers, one of the most interesting being the anonymous *State of Christendom*, attributed by some scholars to Essex's advisor, Anthony Bacon. Sandys's seminal book was translated into several languages and was widely read throughout the seventeenth century. James I, who admired Sandys, knighted him in 1603, and the first royal speech to Parliament, which outlined plans for a General Council of Churches, shows his influence.

Shakespeare's Sonnet 107, dated by many scholars to the year 1603, reflects the way the new king's words and actions filled the realm, in Francis Bacon's words, 'as with a good perfume'. The tone of the sonnet is elated, and with good reason. Shakespeare's company was now 'The King's Men', personally appointed by James while he was still in Scotland to be the country's premier acting group. Sonnet 107 celebrates the momentous political events that accompanied his promotion: the peaceful passing of the old queen, the easing of persecution, and the dawn of a hopeful new era, all of it achieved without the bloodshed predicted by the doom-mongers.

Years later, the Catholic missionary priest John Gerard looked back in anguish on this brief interlude of peace, toleration, and royal goodwill. He compared its delusory promise to the way 'a flash of lightning, giving for a time a pale light unto those that sit in darkness, doth afterwards leave them in more desolation'.[41] With Robert Cecil as his chief advisor rather than the high-minded Essex, James rapidly woke up to the disadvantages of toleration. There were many more Catholics than he had anticipated, and far less money in the treasury. Ten thousand pounds a year was a sum he could ill afford to lose.[42] As for the Puritans, James had begun to appreciate the value of a national church with a divinely appointed monarch at its head. The church was an essential bulwark to his authority. 'No bishop, no king', as he famously put it.[43] He also discovered that in Cecil, now Earl of Salisbury, he had an experienced, assiduous, and competent deputy. After a lifetime of hard and perilous rule in Scotland he could at last afford to leave the day-to-day business of government to his 'little beagle' while he went hunting.

A year into James's reign, his government once again turned the full force of the law against Catholics. In a savage move, the fines of £20 per month for nonattendance at church services were reimposed retrospectively. Those who had taken advantage of the thirteen-month period of apparent remission were charged a crippling £260 (£74,000), or, failing that, the confiscation of two-thirds of their property. The ostensible reason for this sudden U-turn was that Catholics had taken liberties with the king's initial leniency towards them. In addition, the 1604 'Act for the Due Execution of Statutes Against Jesuits' revived and strengthened the stringent anti-Catholic statutes first enacted nineteen years earlier, in 1585. The new act rigorously reinforced all the old penalties, including confinement of Catholics without a travel permit to within five miles of their home, banishment from London, and a traitor's death for sheltering a priest. This time, there would be no prospect of diplomatic support or intervention from abroad. On 18 August 1604, after almost twenty years of war, a historic peace treaty was signed with Spain. It contained not a single clause safeguarding the rights of Catholics in England.

Shakespeare tackles the subject of the betrayal head-on in his first new drama for James, *Measure for Measure*, performed at court late in 1604, positioning the predicament of English Catholics at the heart of the plot, set safely in the city of Vienna. Using the well-established cover of romantic love, Shakespeare stages a sudden crackdown on extramarital sex in the city in the name of 'strict statutes and most biting laws' introduced nineteen years earlier, but rarely implemented (1.3.19). Nineteen is a curiously specific number. It was also a significant one. As we have just seen, it was exactly nineteen years earlier that England first introduced the statutes which James's government had revived a few months before.[44] The play dramatises the injustice of the 1604 act, its lethal implications, and the vindictive motivation behind it. Caught unawares, the innocent Claudio faces execution for taking 'too much liberty' with his pregnant fiancé.

His life hangs in the balance throughout the play, as Shakespeare appeals to the king through the action to relax the new laws, deploying in the process a chilling evocation of the horror of death. Claudio shrinks from what lies ahead of him:

> Ay, but to die, and go we know not where;
> To lie in cold obstruction, and to rot;
> This sensible warm motion to become
> A kneaded clod . . .
>
> (3.1.199–122)

The villain is the duke's hypocritical deputy, Angelo, who enacts the statutes with relish while the duke—recognised by most critics as a flattering portrait of King James—observes him in disguise.

Shakespeare knew his audience. Whatever his own private beliefs, his plea for an extension to the period of toleration would have had widespread support. Along with Queen Anne herself, a passionate play-goer, many of the leading figures in James's court were Catholics, exempted from the penalties by virtue of their rank, and tolerated so long as they did not make trouble. Shakespeare's play adroitly makes a case that many of the nobility supported, but could not afford to state openly, and it averts royal displeasure by casting James in his chosen role as the champion of justice and toleration.[45]

Appeals like these, which came from all quarters, fell on deaf ears, and the widely predicted cataclysm was only narrowly averted. On 5 November 1605, Catholic fury and despair erupted in the shocking form of the Gunpowder Plot—a scheme to blow up the Houses of Parliament devised by a small group of desperate men, some of whom had been followers of Essex. The plot was infiltrated and controlled by Robert Cecil from its

earliest stages, and its carefully stage-managed discovery deliv-
ered the decisive coup de grace to the English Catholic cause.
Among the multiple repercussions—the bloody executions, the
arrests, the demonization of Jesuits, the hellfire sermons, the
hurried conversions, the inauguration of annual bonfires celebrating the king's preservation—one small but significant event
has gone almost unnoticed. It marks the death-knell of something more than English Catholicism. In London in November
1605, all available copies of Edwin Sandys's book on peaceful
coexistence among religions were burned.

To 'a thoughtful person' like Sandys, himself a devout Protestant, religious toleration was, according to his biographer, 'the
most important issue of the day'.[46] In 1604, he, like many others,
gave up all hope of serious action from King James, and became instead one of his most formidable parliamentary opponents. Many others, including the Earl of Southampton, joined
him. Shakespeare, it seems, returned to the mood of deep disillusion which had set in after the death of Essex. From 1604
onwards the tone and style of his plays and poems alters. *Troilus*,
Measure for Measure, and *All's Well That Ends Well* are problem
plays, fraught with tragic material. Next come the great tragedies, *Othello*, *Lear*, *Macbeth*, succeeded by tragic dramas, *Cori-
olanus* and *Antony and Cleopatra*. The final romances—*Pericles*,
Cymbeline, *Winter's Tale*, and *The Tempest*—all have tragedy as
their starting point. Jacobean court taste in the early seventeenth
century was running to the spectacular, even the riotous; but
unlike his rivals, Shakespeare ignored the vogue for extravagant
masques and sharp city comedies. He continued instead with
plays that take for their material a world where, though it is redeemed by the rebirth of innocence in his last plays, 'humanity
must perforce prey on itself / Like monsters of the deep'.[47]

Grief and disillusion also begin to characterise the endings of his poetical works. Gone are the upbeat, confident conclusions of *The Rape of Lucrece* and the earlier sonnets. 'Truth and beauty buried be' is the last line of his beautiful but cryptic poem 'The Phoenix and the Turtle', written in 1601, just after the Essex rebellion. His collection of sonnets, published in 1609, ends with a sequence as misanthropic as the conclusions of *Timon* and *Troilus*. The same volume contains his final narrative poem, the brief, sketchy 'Lover's Complaint', a work so awkward and obscure that many Shakespeare scholars have argued that it must be the work of a different writer.[48] Viewed as a commentary on the events of 1604, however, the disturbing scenario of a fickle woman reluctantly returning to her abusive lover may carry a bitter topicality, and the odd intricacies of the narrative suggest the same level of political sophistication as Shakespeare's previous narrative poems. Here again, the twinned motifs of hypocrisy and sexual disease dominate the final few verses.

Biographers often attribute the change in Shakespeare's outlook to the death of his father in 1601, or to other unrecorded factors—illness, incipient blindness, an unhappy love affair, the onset of syphilis. His early narrative poems, however, indicate that Shakespeare saw himself as a public writer and that, certain sonnets apart, the affairs of England, rather than his own personal circumstances, are his fundamental concern. This book suggests that the change that overtook his writing at the turn of the seventeenth century has its roots in the early 1590s when he gave his allegiance to a cause which ultimately failed. The poems he wrote then gave eloquent and persuasive voice to the grievances Essex addressed. *Venus and Adonis* explored the immediate impact of the enforcement of conscience on Elizabeth's subjects towards the end of her reign: an enforcement which, as it turned out, was to be reimposed even more rigorously under James I. *The Rape of Lucrece* broadened the focus, tracing the religious policy of her regime back to its origin in the events of 1534, analysing the country's response, and urging action to remove an increasingly corrupt regime. Taken together, these poems provide a painful and searching portrait of what the late Tudor monarchy did to people of integrity. Hope of redress, of concerted resistance, of a national change of direction, evident in his dramatic work throughout the 1590s, died when Essex went to the block. The two great poems continued to be avidly read, but, after 1604, with the end of any prospect of a new age of tolerance, they became prophecies of social breakdown rather than calls to action. Looking back now, we can see that they provide us with Shakespeare's overlooked diagnosis of the English malaise that would lead the country into civil war.

EPILOGUE

T WENTY-EIGHT YEARS AFTER Shakespeare's death, the long-predicted blow fell. The English Civil War remains the most damaging conflict in the country's history, costing, as a proportion of the population, almost twice as many lives as the First World War.[1] Essex's fears, and those of his followers, were justified. The long fuse lit back in 1534, when Henry VIII rode roughshod over both church and Parliament as he extended the powers of the English monarch, finally ignited as Parliament, protesting at the spiritual and temporal 'tyranny' of the Church of England, rounded on the king. The bloodshed lasted a decade, culminating in the first and last judicial execution of an English monarch at Whitehall.

The savagery of the conflict, which affected every corner of the country, and the scars of which are still visible on monuments and public buildings today, arose from the prolonged repression of the religious rift created by the Act of Supremacy, to which Essex's derided proposals of toleration had provided the only possible solution. The former poet laureate Ted Hughes is one of the few modern writers to have caught the true nature

of the much-vaunted Elizabethan peace in terms Essex, Shakespeare, and Southampton would have understood. 'Those two
savage competitors for the English soul', he wrote, 'which were
the new Puritan spirit and the old, Catholic spirit, each intend-
ing to exterminate the other . . . were not openly deadlocked,
as on the Continent, with embattled cities and occasional massacre of populations. They were deadlocked out of sight, forcibly
disarmed, and forbidden any physical, direct expression whatsoever, inside Elizabeth's crucible.' He ends: 'The ghostly front
line of the deadlocked spirit armies of these two giant historical
forces was drawn through the solar plexus of each of Elizabeth's
subjects.'[2]

Ted Hughes rightly locates the hidden conflict within the
soul of the individual. Both Catholic and Puritan were required
to give public assent to the doctrines and liturgy of the other, as
both were enshrined in the obligatory services of the Church of
England. This requirement for what was, for many, a perjured
conformity created a continual crisis of conscience. Unlike most
other countries in Europe, where Protestant and Catholic were
either in direct opposition or coexisted relatively peacefully, England attempted to merge the two under the spiritual authority
of the Crown, creating a compromise intended to satisfy both.
Much of the Puritan loathing of papistry stemmed from disgust
at the popish practices Puritans were legally obliged to observe.
When these festering hatreds at last erupted in open warfare,
the result was bitter indeed, affecting not only the English but
Scotland, Wales, and Ireland as well, where brutal campaigns re-
sulted in mass killings, deportations, and famine. In Ireland, this
amounted to genocide.[3]

In the 1590s, Shakespeare was one of the many who shared
a common awareness of the frightening implications of the

religious problem, and it was this that led him to address the whole question of royal coercion in such detail and with such intensity. At the end of *Venus and Adonis*, after the long-detained Adonis escapes his captor, only to be gored to death by the boar, Shakespeare accurately predicts the bloody outcome of the state's inability to curb the Puritan extremism already at large, and shortly to ravage the country in a vicious conflict with similarly brutal Catholic and Royalist forces. Venus prophesies that the effect of the boar's murder of Adonis—a murder in which she herself was complicit—will be social disaster. Sorrow will from now on be part of love:

> The bottom poison and the top oe'r straw'd
> With sweets that shall the truest sights beguile:
>> The strongest body shall it make most weak,
>> Strike the wise dumb and teach the fool to speak.
>> (1141–1146)

> It shall suspect where is no cause of fear;
> It shall not fear where it should most mistrust
>> (1153–1154)

The prophecy ends with a prediction of civil war:

> It shall be cause of war and dire events,
> And set dissension twixt the son and sire;
> Subject and servile to all discontents,
> As dry combustious matter is to fire:
>> Sith in his prime death doth my love destroy,
>> They that love best their love shall not enjoy.
>> (1159–1164)

Shakespeare saw what was coming: there could scarcely be a better description of the state of the country fifty years on.

Much has been made of Puritan discontent in the House of Commons in the decades leading up to civil war, when anti-Catholic demands increasingly dominated the agenda. This was the reason the monarch, denied subsidies by a hostile Parliament, was driven to govern by direct rule, leading to accusations of outright tyranny. But there was a corollary to the Puritan resentment: the strength of equally angry but marginalised English Catholicism during those years. There are occasional indications of the perseverance of recusants. In 1616, four thousand Catholics are recorded as being imprisoned for their faith. In 1623, James I's income from Catholic fines was £36,000, well over £5 million in today's money. They were fitfully active in public life. Throughout the reign of the early Stuarts, though banned from secular office-holding, they remained a recognised presence among the nobility and upper gentry, all the more so when Charles I married a Catholic queen, Henrietta Maria of France.

When Charles raised his standard at Nottingham in 1642, English Catholics flocked to the Royalist cause, intent on proving their loyalty, and hoping for eventual toleration in return. According to one observer, more than a quarter of the gentry who fought for the king in the northern counties were Catholic; he knew none who had fought on the rebel side.[4] Michael Questier's study of high-ranking Catholic families under Elizabeth ends with a sobering body-count of the descendants of Southampton's extended family who fought as Royalists during the English Civil War.[5] This was not just a battle for power between king and Parliament—it was also a sectarian war, which the reformers were convinced 'had been originally provoked and was still continued by the papists for the sole purpose of the establishment of popery on the ruins of Protestantism'.[6]

At the end of the century, when the war was over, John Dryden, the poet laureate, took advantage of a brief period of religious toleration to publish a political poem analysing the causes of bloodshed. What is striking about 'The Hind and The Panther' is how close its language and imagery come to the neglected political subtexts this book has examined. The only difference is that Dryden, unlike Shakespeare and Spenser, can write openly about politics. His transparent beast fable begins with a royal rape by a lust-driven lion. Schism, sacrilege, and heresy follow, along with the trampling of divine and human laws. Like Shakespeare, Dryden attacks the opportunistic hypocrisy of those who 'By luxury reform'd incontinence, / By ruins, charity; by riots abstinence' (362–363). He also denounces the hybrid religion that emerged under Elizabeth, 'a creature of a double kind' (402), fundamentally Calvinist, but adorned with the trappings of the English state. Against her he sets the image of what he sees as the universal church: the spotless, innocent hind. Her attributes are those of the 'complaint' heroines before their fall, and of the early, guileless Lucrece. His reflection on the suffering endured by those forced to betray their consciences during this turbulent period sums up the message of Shakespeare's narrative poems: 'Of all the tyrannies of human kind / The worst is that which persecutes the mind' (239–240).

The assumption among many readers of sixteenth-century literature is that this tyranny did not exist. They maintain that all right-minded people in England, including Shakespeare and his fellow writers, welcomed the Elizabethan Settlement as the tolerant middle way offering all things to all men, a gentle, liberal, essentially English compromise, very like the modern Anglican church. This long-held assumption means that we miss the story that the censored and exiled writers of the time are attempting to tell us. Such is the power of the spin-doctors of the period that it is still difficult for us to view late Tudor and early Stuart England as a police state. If we do, we can begin to retrieve a neglected strand of English history which explains much that is puzzling about the times: the difficult, often inaccessible literature, the immense popularity of the Earl of Essex, James I's need to promise toleration to gain the throne, the sudden explosion of sectarian hatred that fuelled the Civil War.

Shakespeare's narrative poems belong to the huge corpus of poetry of the period that we tend to reject as dull and impenetrable. But as this book has argued, there was a reason for their original popularity, and a reason why, having read the new, expanded history of the period, we should re-enter the dark world they conjure up. In the two neglected poems *Venus and Adonis* and *Rape of Lucrece*, we find we are looking at a pair of masterpieces, while in Shakespeare we discover a man deeply engaged in the struggle to bring true tolerance and humanity to England.

ACKNOWLEDGEMENTS

My INITIAL THANKS must go to the scholar and biographer Gerard Kilroy, who helped to develop the concept of this book, and who has been a constant source of encouragement and advice throughout its long evolution. Without my agent, Kathy Robbins, it would never have reached publication: I owe a huge amount to her energy, wisdom, and insight. I have been privileged to have Clive Priddle as an editor; his clear guidance, informed interest in the subject, and timely sense of humour have been invaluable throughout. I must also thank Richard Cohen, Raymond Asquith, and Therese Sidmouth, who read early drafts of the first chapters and helped to set the general tone and direction of the narrative. I am especially grateful for the literary and editorial advice of the Shakespeare scholar Michael Scott, who took the time and trouble to read through the completed manuscript with such attention. Historians and literary scholars have responded generously to my requests for information and assistance, among them Jonathan Bate, James Carley, Lara Crowley, John Finnis, John Guy, Paul Hammer, Peter Lake, Graham Parry, and Emma Smith. Krystina Kujawinska-Courtney's own research on *The Rape of Lucrece*, and her encouragement of mine, was a particular stimulus. Alexandra Gajda, on whose work this book relies heavily, set aside a busy schedule for a long discussion of its historical context, while Natalie Mears was kind enough to give the book a thorough reading from a more critical angle. I am also grateful to Leah Veronese, who brought literary expertise to her reading of the book. Without the help of the London Library, the research necessary for this subject would have been beyond my reach; like many other independent scholars, I owe an enormous amount to the library's unique facilities and to the tolerance and expertise of its dedicated staff. I would also like to thank the assistant editor Athena Bryan, Stephanie Summerhays, the copy editor Kathy Streckfus, and the many others at Public Affairs who have been involved in the often thankless task of wrestling with the manuscript—they have been unfailingly painstaking, courteous, and patient. Finally, I would like to thank my family and friends, particularly Raymond, my mother, and my children and grandchildren, for enduring so much Tudor tyranny for so long.

Notes

Introduction

1. Quoted in Marion A. Taylor, *Bottom Thou Art Translated: Political Allegory in A Midsummer Night's Dream and Related Literature* (Amsterdam: Rodopi, 1973), 3.

2. Peter Ackroyd, *William Shakespeare: The Biography* (New York: Vintage, 2006), 20, 64, 104, 151, 173, 226.

3. Stephen Greenblatt, *Shakespearean Negotiations* (Berkeley: University of California Press, 1989).

4. Curtis Breight, *Surveillance, Militarism and Drama in the Elizabethan Era* (London: Macmillan, 1996), 27.

5. Paul E. J. Hammer's major work appeared in 1999, *The Polarisation of Elizabethan Politics: The Political Career of Robert Devereux, 2nd Earl of Essex, 1585–1597* (Cambridge: Cambridge University Press), and Alexandra Gajda's in 2012, *The Earl of Essex and Late Elizabethan Political Culture* (Oxford: Oxford University Press).

6. Breight, *Surveillance*, 51.

7. Peter Lake, *How Shakespeare Put Politics on the Stage: Power and Succession in the History Plays* (New Haven, CT: Yale University Press, 2016), 172.

8. Breight, *Surveillance*, 3. Christopher Haigh, author of numerous works on the English Reformation, is an influential 'revisionist' historian of the period.

9. Lake, *How Shakespeare Put Politics on the Stage*, x.

10. I first read Michael Questier's major work in manuscript, which he kindly showed me; it was published in 2006 as *Catholicism and Community in Early Modern England* (Cambridge: Cambridge University Press). Patrick Collinson's *Elizabethan Puritan Movement* (London: Methuen, 1967) is one of his many works on the English reformers.

11. Clare Asquith, 'A Phoenix for Palm Sunday: Was Shakespeare's Poem a Requiem for Catholic Martyrs?', *Times Literary Supplement*, no. 5115 (13 April 2001): 14.

12. John Finnis and Patrick Martin, 'Another Turn for the Turtle', *Times Literary Supplement*, no. 5220 (13 April 2003): 14.

13. David Scott Kastan, *A Will to Believe: Shakespeare and Religion* (Oxford: Oxford University Press, 2014), 38–40.

14. Alison Shell, *Shakespeare and Religion*, The Arden Shakespeare (London: Bloomsbury, 2010), 3. G. Wilson Knight (1897–1985) is best known for his collections of essays on Shakespeare, such as *The Wheel of Fire* (Oxford: Oxford University Press, 1930) and *The Crown of Life* (Oxford: Oxford University Press, 1947), which focus on what he saw as the organic, mystical 'core' of each play.

CHAPTER ONE: THE PRISONER

1. Charlotte Carmichael Stopes, *The Life of Henry, Third Earl of Southampton, Shakespeare's Patron* (Cambridge: Cambridge University Press, 1922), 65.

2. The picture, which hangs at Welbeck Abbey, is in the Royal Collection. It belonged to the Dukes of Portland, who married into the Wriothesley family.

3. 'To Henry Wriothesly, Erle of Sovthampton', in Samuel Daniel, *Poems and A Defence of Ryme*, edited by Arthur Colby Sprague (Chicago: University of Chicago Press, 1965), 29–30.

4. There is another concealed cross in the 1594 miniature of the twenty-year-old Southampton by Nicholas Hilliard in the Fitzwilliam Museum, Cambridge. The cross is formed by the folds of red fabric behind him. There are similar crosses composed of folded material in Hans Eworth's two portraits of Mary I painted in 1554, one also against red cloth. Hilliard's picture gives the best impression of Southampton's youthful beauty.

5. See Nicola Shulman, *Graven with Diamonds* (London: Short Books, 2012), 20–22. Henry Wyatt was later imprisoned in Scotland for two years, making it likely that his story was also known north of the border. A later family painting of the incident, dated to the eighteenth century, depicts a large cat dragging a pigeon through the bars of the cell window for the woeful occupant.

6. Sonnet 20, *Shakespeare's Sonnets*, edited by Katherine Duncan-Jones, The Arden Shakespeare (London: Bloomsbury, 1997), 151.

7. 'Non fert ullum ictum illaesa foelicitas' (Happiness does not sustain any blow uninjured). This epigraph to Daniel's poem is taken from Seneca's *De Providentia* and links Southampton's ordeal with the Stoic attitude to suffering; it also connects him with Seneca's list of good men who resist tyranny and oppression.

8. William Dunn Macray, ed., *The Pilgrimage to Parnassus with the Two Parts of The Return from Parnassus* (Oxford: Clarendon Press, 1886), 1.1.304.

9. Gabriel Harvey, 1598, quoted in E. K. Chambers, *William Shakespeare: A Study of Facts and Problems*, vol. 2 (Oxford: Clarendon Press, 1930), 197.

10. Colin Burrow, 'Introduction,' in *The Oxford Shakespeare: The Complete Sonnets and Poems*, edited by Colin Burrow (Oxford: Oxford University Press, 2008), 58.

CHAPTER TWO: SUICIDE OR MURDER?

1. Livy, *History of Rome*, Book 1, parts 57–59; Ovid, *Fasti*, Book 2, ll. 721–852.

2. Geoffrey Chaucer, *A Legend of Good Women*, ll. 1871; John Gower, *Confessio Amantis*, Book 7, ll. 4754–5130.

3. Philip Sidney, *A Defence of Poesie*, written around 1579. See *English Essays: Sidney to Macaulay*, Harvard Classics, vol. 27 (New York: P. F. Collier and Son, 1909–1914), available on Bartleby.com, 2001, www.bartleby.com/27.

4. Martin Luther, 'Against the Robbing and Murdering Hordes of Peasants', in *A Reformation Sourcebook*, edited by Michael W. Bruening (Toronto: University of Toronto Press, 2017 [1525]), 85.

5. Heinrich Bullinger, *Lucretia und Brutus* (1526).

6. Pia F. Cuneo, 'Jorg Breu the Elder's Death of Lucrece: History, Sexuality and the State', in *Saints, Sinners and Sisters: Gender and Northern Art in Medieval and Early Modern Europe*, edited by Jane L. Carroll and Alison G. Stewart (Farnham, UK: Ashgate, 2003); Kristin Zapalac, *In His Image and Likeness: Political Iconography and Religious Change in Regensburg, 1500–1600* (Ithaca, NY: Cornell University Press, 1990), 119–120.

7. Hubert Languet, *Vindiciae contra Tyrannos, Concerning the Legitimate Power of a Prince over the People, and of the People over the Prince* (1579).

8. See Ian Donaldson's study both of Shakespeare's poem and of the many political identities of Lucrece, *The Rapes of Lucretia: A Myth and Its Transformations* (Oxford: Oxford University Press, 1982).

CHAPTER THREE: A PROBLEM POEM

1. Linda Woodbridge, quoted in *The Oxford Shakespeare: The Complete Sonnets and Poems*, edited by Colin Burrow (Oxford: Oxford University Press, 2008), 333.

2. James Morice, in a letter from prison in 1593 addressed to Lord Burghley. The letter is published in full in the *Gentleman's Magazine* 133 (1823): 518.

3. Elizabeth knew that she was identified with Richard II by the

Essex circle, as she revealed in a famous exchange with William Lambarde, the Keeper of the Records in the Tower of London, shortly after Essex's execution in 1601: 'I am Richard II, know ye not that?'

4. White conveyed the plain, unornamented walls and glass, the black-and-white printed page, the direct, unmediated link between the divine and inner light; red conjured up the marks of the 'Scarlet Woman'—ornamentation, the old calendar filled with red letters, and the red robes of the Roman clergy.

CHAPTER FOUR: RAPE

1. William Cobbett, *A History of the Protestant Reformation in England and Ireland* (London: Burns and Oates, 1925 [1824–1827]), 39–40.

2. William Cobbett is better known to later readers for his description of the English countryside on the eve of the Industrial Revolution in his much-loved classic *Rural Rides* than for his political writings.

3. William Cobbett, *Protestant Reformation*, 52–53, 111.

4. G. W. Bernard, 'The Dissolution of the Monasteries', *History* 96, no. 4 (2011): 390.

5. Many of the church bells removed from monasteries were turned into munitions. After Elizabeth's excommunication by the papacy, scrap metal from buildings destroyed after the Reformation was shipped by English merchants to the Ottoman Turks, potentially for use against Spain and the Christian armies in the eastern Mediterranean. S. A. Skilliter, *William Harborne and the Trade with Turkey, 1578-1582* (Oxford: Oxford University Press, 1977), 23.

6. Philip Hughes, *The Reformation in England*, vol. 1 (London: Hollis and Carter, 1950), 237.

7. Peter Clery, *The Monastic Estate* (London: Phillimore, 2015), chap. 1.

8. Thomas Fuller, *The Church History of Britain,* Book 6 (London: John Williams, 1655).

9. Michael Sherbrook, 'The Fall of Religious Houses', in *Tudor Treatises,* edited by A. G. Dickens (Leeds, UK: Yorkshire Archeological Society, 1959 [c. 1591]), 124–125.

10. Alec Ryrie, 'Reformations', in *A Social History of England, 1500–1750*, edited by Keith Wrightson (Cambridge: Cambridge University Press, 2017), 110.

11. Margaret Aston, 'English Ruins and English History: The Dissolution and the Sense of the Past', *Journal of the Warburg and Courtauld Institute* 36 (1973): 231–255.

12. Greg Walker, *Plays of Persuasion: Drama and Politics at the Court of Henry VIII* (Cambridge: Cambridge University Press, 1991), 108.

13. Roger E. Moore, 'The Hidden History of Northanger Abbey: Jane Austen and the Dissolution of the Monasteries', *Religion & Literature* 43, no. 1 (2011): 62.

14. William Dugdale, *Monasticon Anglicanum*, vol. 1 (London: R. Harbin, 1718 [1655–1673]), 123.

15. R. W. Hoyle, 'Origins of the Dissolution of the Monasteries', *Historical Journal* 38, no. 2 (1995): 278.

16. Thomas Nashe, *Christ's Tears over Jerusalem* (London, 1815 [1593]), 100–101.

17. Aston, 'English Ruins and English History', 236.

18. Ibid., 252. Cobbett's visualization of what his own currently 'devastated' county of Surrey might once have looked like, 'ornamented and benefited by the establishments which grew out of the Catholic Church', is in his *Protestant Reformation*, 137–138. 'All is wholly changed', he ends, 'and all is changed for the worse. There is now no hospitality in England. Words have changed their meaning. We now give entertainment to those who entertain us in return.'

19. Moore, 'Hidden History', 64, 73.

20. Fuller, *Church History*, Book 6, 335.

21. Ibid., 335.

22. Graham Parry, *The Trophies of Time: English Antiquarians of the Seventeenth Century* (Oxford: Oxford University Press, 1995), 162.

23. Ibid., 165.

24. John Donne, 'A Hymne to the Saints, and to Marquess Hamilton', *Complete Poetry and Selected Prose*, edited by John Haywood (London: Nonesuch Press, 1967), 249. Donne's concept of the dissolved abbeys as soulless bodies pinpoints the sense of spiritual loss that animates so many other writers:

All former comeliness
Fled, in a minute, when the soul was gone
And having lost that beauty, would have none;
So fell our Monasteries, in one instant growne
Not to less houses, but to heaps of stone.

Shakespeare echoes the concept in his early play *Edward III*, when the Countess of Salisbury refuses to commit adultery with the king. Here again is the idea that sacred buildings die when they are given over to secular use. The king later compares her steadfastness favourably to the wavering Lucrece:

As easy may my intellectual soul
Be lent away, and yet my body live,
As lend my body, palace to my soul,
Away from her, and yet retain my soul.
My body is her bower, her Court, her abbey,
And she an Angel, pure, divine, unspotted:
If I should leave her house, my Lord, to thee,
I kill my poor soul and my poor soul me.

William Shakespeare, *King Edward III*, edited by Giorgio Melchiorio (Cambridge University Press, 1998), 2.1.234–243.

25. Sherbrook, 'Fall of Religious Houses', 124–125.

26. Aston, 'English Ruins and English History', passim.

27. Fuller, *Church History*, 335.

28. Sherbrook, 'Fall of Religious Houses', 125.

29. William Camden, *Britannia*, vol. 1, edited by Richard Gough (London: Hutchinson, 1789), cxxxiv.

30. William Dugdale, *The Antiquities of Warwickshire* (London: Thomas Warren, 1656), 797–803.

31. Cobbett, *Protestant Reformation*, 128.

32. Aston, 'English Ruins and English History', 235.

33. Herbert of Cherbury, *The Life and Reign of Henry the Eighth* (London, Printed by E.G. for T. Whitaker, 1649), ii: 'I am not yet ignorant that the king whose history I write is subject to more obloquies than any since the worst Roman times,' and 444: 'All which being by some openly called rapine and sacrilege, I will no way excuse.'

34. Derek Beales, 'Edmund Burke and the Monasteries of France', *Historical Journal* 48, no. 2 (2005): 427–428.

35. Moore, 'Hidden History', 55.

36. In *The Protestant Reformation*, Cobbett wrote: 'The tyrant's passions were now in motion, and he resolved to gratify them, cost what it might in reputation, in treasure, and in blood' (36), and, 'The tyrant was, of course, the great pocketer of this species of plunder' (131).

37. Cobbett, *Protestant Reformation*, 136.

38. Dugdale is quoting Luther's version of the line here, as Juvenal's original version starts with the word 'Hoc', not 'Sic'.

39. George Cavendish, *The Life and Death of Cardinal Wolsey* (Boston: Houghton Mifflin, 1905 [printed at London: Riverside Press]). This work was widely circulated in manuscript from 1558. 'Is it not a world', Cavendish begins, 'to consider the desire of willful princes, when they fully be bent and inclined to fulfill their voluptuous appetites, against the which no reasonable persuasions will suffice; little or nothing weighing or regarding the dangerous sequel that doth ensue as well to themselves as to their realm and subjects' (69–70).

40. Cavendish, *Life and Death of Cardinal Wolsey*, 69–70.

41. Thomas Nashe, *The Unfortunate Traveller and Other Works*, edited by J. B. Steane (London: Penguin, 1972), 283.

42. John Harington, *The Epigrams of Sir John Harington*, edited by Gerard Kilroy (Farnham, UK: Ashgate, 2009), 196 (Book 3, Epigram 70).

43. Gerard Kilroy, *Edmund Campion: A Scholarly Life* (Farnham, UK: Ashgate, 2015), 31.

CHAPTER FIVE: THE POETRY WAR

1. Patrick Fraser Tytler, *Life of Walter Raleigh* (Edinburgh: Oliver and Boyd; London: Simpkin and Marshall, 1833), 335.

2. The subject is fully covered in Greg Walker's *Writing Under Tyranny* (Oxford: Oxford University Press, 2005). Elsewhere a small detail noted by James Carley illustrates the general fear of opposing Henry

VIII's policies. In 1533, the historian John Leland described Richard Whiting, the abbot of Glastonbury, as 'a truly splendid man and my special friend'; 'my greatest friend'; 'always to be counted among gentlemen'. When Whiting was hanged, drawn and quartered in 1539 after refusing to surrender the abbey to the Crown, Leland deleted these references: the deletions, which still survive, are faint and tremulous. *De uiris illustribus*, edited and translated by James P. Carley, with the assistance of Caroline Brett (Toronto: Pontifical Institute of Mediaeval Studies, 2010), lviii n. 176.

3. Annabel M. Patterson, *Censorship and Interpretation: The Conditions of Writing and Reading in Early Modern England* (Madison: University of Wisconsin Press, 1991), 52, 63. As well as this groundbreaking study of censorship and coded communication in sixteenth-century England, see Richard Dutton, *Mastering the Revels: The Regulation and Censorship of English Renaissance Drama* (Iowa City: University of Iowa Press, 1991), and Andrew Hadfield, ed., *Literature and Censorship in Renaissance England* (London: Palgrave Macmillan, 2001).

4. Douglas Gray, 'John Lydgate', in Oxford Dictionary of National Biography, 2004, www.oxforddnb.com/view/10.1093/ref:odnb/9780 198614128.001.0001/odnb-9780198614128-e-17238?rskey=CEbrkm &result=2. The remark was made in 1802 by the Victorian scholar Joseph Ritson.

5. Jim Ellis, 'Embodying Dislocation: *A Mirror for Magistrates* and Property Relations', *Renaissance Quarterly* 53, no. 4 (2000): 1032–1053.

6. Scott C. Lucas, *A Mirror for Magistrates and the Politics of the English Reformation* (Amherst: University of Massachusetts Press, 2009).

7. 'The Life of Lady Ebbe', in *The Mirror for Magistrates*, vol. 1, edited by Joseph Haslewood (London: Lackington, Allen, and Longman, Hurst, Rees, Orme, and Brown, 1815), 446.

8. Ibid., 444.

9. Ibid., 445.

10. William Baldwin, *The Mirror for Magistrates*, edited by Lily Campbell (Baltimore: Johns Hopkins University Press, 1970), 370, 374.

11. Philip Sidney, *Defence of Poesie*, edited by William Ponsonby, Renascence Editions Online, transcribed by Risa S. Bear (Eugene: University of Oregon, 1992 [1595]), l. 152.

12. 'The personification of the different churches as distinct types of women became a common feature of debates about the identity of the Church of England.' Emma Major, *Madam Britannia* (Oxford: Oxford University Press, 2011), 32.

13. Suzanne Conklin Akbari, *Idols in the East: European Representations of Islam and the Orient, 1100–1450* (Ithaca, NY: Cornell University Press, 2012), 122.

14. Southampton's grandfather, the 1st Viscount Montague, made a bold speech against the changes in religion in the House of Lords in

1559, defending the Catholic Church 'as the spouse and only beloved of Christ'. Michael Questier, *Catholicism and Community in Early Modern England* (Cambridge: Cambridge University Press, 2006), 121.

15. John Donne, *Complete Poetry and Selected Prose*, edited by John Hayward (London, Nonesuch Press, 1967), 128–129, 287.

16. George Herbert, 'The British Church', *The Temple* (London: S. Roycroft for R.S., 1679), 102.

17. E. K. Chambers, *William Shakespeare: A Study of Facts and Problems* (Oxford: Clarendon Press, 1930), 195.

18. Jim Ellis, 'Embodying Dislocation: A Mirror for Magistrates and Property Relations', *Renaissance Quarterly* 53, no. 4 (December 2000): 1032–1053.

19. Thomas Nashe, 'Strange News', quoted in *Encyclopaedia Britannica*, 14th ed., vol. 5 (London: Encyclopaedia Britannica, 1929).

20. *The Mirror for Magistrates*, vol. 1, edited by Joseph Haslewood (London: Lackington, Allen, and Longman, Hurst, Rees, Orme, and Brown, 1815), 466, 465.

21. Ibid., 465.

22. Ibid., 469.

23. Edmund Spenser, *Complaints*, in *Spenser, Poetical Works*, edited by J. C. Smith and E. de Selincourt (Oxford: Oxford University Press, 1912 [1591]).

24. Edmund Spenser, 'The Teares of the Muses', in Spenser, *Complaints*, 480–486.

25. Edmund Spenser, 'The Ruines of Time', in Spenser, *Complaints*, 471–478.

26. William Camden, *Britannia*, vol. 2, edited by Richard Gough (London: Hutchinson, 1789), 73.

27. Spenser's *Faerie Queene* also covertly criticizes England's Reformation. The figure who sows the poem's initial seeds of discord is disguised as a hermit. Like *Mother Hubberd's* fox, he can be read as William Cecil, the architect of the Elizabethan settlement, who outwardly conformed under Mary I and liked to be known from 1594 as 'the hermit of Theobalds'.

28. Samuel Daniel, 'The Complaint of Rosamond', in *Poems and A Defence of Ryme*, edited by Arthur Colby Sprague (Chicago: University of Chicago Press, 1965), 39–63.

29. Michael Drayton, *Matilda*, in *The Works of Michael Drayton*, vol. 1, edited by J. William Hebel (Oxford: Basil Blackwell, 1931), l. 48. It is uncertain whether Drayton is referring to Shakespeare's poem here, as he seems to allude to a staged version of the story. Nonetheless, this poem echoes Shakespeare's at several points. Curiously, he drops Lucrece from his list of loose women in later editions of 'Matilda'. He may have realised that Shakespeare's Lucrece, in the end, is not one of the group of looser wantons.

30. The priory is at Dunmow, which belonged to the Fitzwalters and where Matilda is buried. Drayton describes its charitable foundation by Lady Juga Baynard in the twelfth century, 'a holy vestal maid / At whose great charge this monument was done'. He invents the fact that Matilda 'vowed to live a holy nun' (736–740).

31. Epigram 40, 'Of Christs Cote', in John Harington, *The Epigrams of Sir John Harington*, edited by Gerard Kilroy (Farnham, UK: Ashgate, 2009), 225.

CHAPTER SIX: *LUCRECE*: THE ACT

1. Gordon J. Spykman, *Reformational Theology* (Grand Rapids, MI: William B. Eerdmans, 1992), 451.

2. William Dugdale, *Antiquities of Warwickshire* (London: Thomas Warren, 1656), 803.

3. George Cavendish, *The Life and Death of Cardinal Wolsey* (Boston: Houghton Mifflin, 1905 [printed at London: Riverside Press]), 148.

4. Gavin E. Schwartz-Leeper, *From Princes to Pages: The Literary Lives of Cardinal Wolsey, Tudor England's 'Other King'* (Leiden: Brill, 2016), 232. The characteristic phrase is also quoted by Shakespeare as one of the charges against Wolsey, indicating his ambition, in *Henry VIII*, 3.2.331.

5. Praemunire was a charge Wolsey could technically have resisted—but not now, at the end of his life, confronted by a vindictive court and king. Though it did him no good, Wolsey humbly acknowledged the offence, apologised, and forfeited all his treasures—one of the first of a rapid and increasingly sweeping series of capitulations by the English church to the English Crown.

6. Sybil M. Jack, 'Thomas Wolsey', in Oxford Dictionary of National Biography, 2004, www.oxforddnb.com/view/10.1093/ref:odnb /9780198614128.001.0001/odnb-9780198614128-e-29854?rskey=YJ 8cIZ&result=1. For a study of the relationship between sexual assault and theft, see Nazife Bashar, 'Rape in England Between 1550 and 1700', in *The Sexual Dynamics of History: Men's Power, Women's Resistance*, edited by the London Feminist History Group (London: Pluto Press, 1983).

7. Michael Drayton, 'The Legend of Cromwell', 369, in *The Works of Michael Drayton*, vol. 2, edited by J. William Hebel (Oxford: Basil Blackwell, 1932), 451–475.

8. To encourage the bishops to resist the king, More quoted a story from Tacitus in which a Roman emperor is unable to execute the daughter of his rival because of a law forbidding the execution of virgins. One of his advisors proposes raping her, so that she can be legally executed. More sees the same process at work, metaphorically, in 1533. Urged to demonstrate public assent to Henry VIII's divorce and remarriage, and well aware that this consent will shortly be enforced, More maintains his 'virginity' by refusing to be coerced into accepting what he believes are illegal demands on English subjects. The passage

demonstrates the connection readily made at the time between virginity and integrity:

> Your lordships have in the matter of matrimony hitherto kept yourselves pure virgins, yet take good heed my lords that you keep your virginity still. For some there be that by procuring your lordships first at the coronation to be present and next to preach for the setting forth of it, and finally to write books to all the world in defence thereof, are desirous to deflower you; and when they have deflowered you, then will they not fail soon after to devour you. Now my lords . . . it lieth not in my power but that they may devour me; but God being my good lord, I will provide that they shall never deflower me.

Cresacre More, *The Life of Thomas More* (London: W. Pickering, 1828), 217.

9. Edward Hall, *Chronicle* (London: Longman, 1809 [1547]), 755–756.

10. By an extraordinary quirk of fate, Shakespeare's company later acquired part of the Blackfriars Priory, a sprawling monastic complex near the Thames used for state occasions after the dissolution. They staged the play *Henry VIII*, including a dramatised version of this exchange, in the very same room some eighty years later. Though much of the play is ahistorical, details about Wolsey, in particular, come straight from the chroniclers.

11. There is a possible pun in this opening sentence which announces the theme of the poem, the momentous break with Rome. By leaving the Roman host, Tarquin leaves the Roman army. But the phrase 'Roman host' may also have carried overtones of papal Rome, and of the Catholic Eucharist. The round wafer of bread held up at Mass for adoring worshippers, often caricatured by reformers, is still known as a 'host'.

12. The second verse of the poem, which includes the word 'peculiar', a legal term implying a particular ecclesiastical privilege, also hints at Wolsey's controversial dominance of the Star Chamber.

13. Tarquin was also a third child and a younger son, as Henry VIII was.

14. *The Oxford Shakespeare: The Complete Sonnets and Poems*, edited by Colin Burrow (Oxford: Oxford University Press, 2008), 52.

15. One of the most perceptive studies of Shakespeare's narrative poems draws attention to the fact that Tarquin is paradoxically both an idolator and an iconoclast: he begins by adoring beauty as something sacred, and ends by destroying it. Anna Swärdh, *Rape and Religion in English Renaissance Literature: A Topical Study of Four Texts by Shakespeare, Drayton and Middleton* (Uppsala, Sweden: Acta Universitatis Upsaliensis, 2003), 124.

16. The vivid image of the soul as a vulnerable princess in a temple may derive partly from Robert Southwell's widely disseminated spiritual

imagery. In his 'Epistle Unto His Father', Southwell describes the soul as 'the temple, the paradise, and spouse of Almighty God'; after sins have been committed, the temple is 'profaned', and God's 'spouse deflowered and become an adultress to his utter enemies'. Southwell asks: 'Durst we offer such usage to our prince's, yea, or to our farmer's daughter?' Like Shakespeare, Southwell portrays the soul as the rightful governor of the body, vulnerable, however, to rebellion by the passions: 'And whereas the soul should have the sovereignty and the body follow the sway of her direction, servile senses and lawless appetites do rule her as superiors, and she is made a vassal in her own dominions.' Shakespeare, too, personifies the rebellious senses and faculties as well as the fallen princess in *Lucrece*. See Robert Southwell, *Two Letters and Short Rules of a Good Life*, edited by Nancy Pollard Brown (Charlottesville: University Press of Virginia, 1973), 15–17.

17. See David Knowles, *Bare Ruined Choirs* (Cambridge: Cambridge University Press, 1959), 165. The visitations began in 1535. Ostensibly these were normal visitations by the church authorities, involving the leisurely completion of a standard questionnaire about the holdings and conduct of the monastery. Cromwell, however, as vicar-general of the new church, had selected hardened civil servants ('grasping, worldly and without a trace of spiritual feeling', p. 159), who replaced the usual process with sessions of 'relentless questioning' of individuals using the interrogation techniques in which they were expert. Accounts, libraries, plate, and jewels were closely scrutinised. Their commission was to assess the wealth and secure the surrender of the monastery to the king through bribery, threats, or persuasion. For one of the best accounts of the process, see John Lingard, *A History of England*, vol. 5 (London: Charles Dolman, 1849).

18. Burrow, *Oxford Shakespeare*, 64.

19. William Claxton, *Rites of Durham*, edited by J. T. Fowler, Publications of the Surtees Society, vol. 107 (Durham, UK: Andrews and Company, 1903 [1593]), 102. Claxton includes a graphic account of the destruction of the tomb of St Cuthbert by the king's commissioners. Their methods, as they destroy a rich tabernacle, are reminiscent of Tarquin trampling on the light in Lucrece's chamber: 'The said Dr Harvie . . . did tread upon it with his feet and did break it all in pieces' (108–109).

20. Cowslips are still known as St Peter's Keys, a medieval name which gives them a particular link with Catholicism.

21. Richard Morison, quoted by Michael R. Graves in 'Thomas Wriothesley, First Earl of Southampton', Oxford Dictionary of National Biography, 2004,www.oxforddnb.com/view/10.1093/ref:odnb/9780198614128.001.0001/odnb-9780198614128-e-30076?rskey=yRTAcZ&result=1.

22. Graves, 'Thomas Wriothesley'.

23. Ibid.

24. For a family tree showing the connection between Robert Southwell and Henry Wriothesley, see Christopher Devlin, *The Life of Robert Southwell* (London: Longmans, 1956), 15. Southwell's brother and sister both married direct descendants of Thomas Wriothesley.

25. See Curtis Breight, *Surveillance, Militarism and Drama in the Elizabethan Era* (London: Macmillan, 1996), 40–41, and Alan H. Nelson, *Monstrous Adversary: The Life of Edward de Vere, 17th Earl of Oxford* (Liverpool: Liverpool University Press, 2003), 312–319.

26. Roger Emerson Moore, *Jane Austen and the Reformation: Remembering the Sacred Landscape* (London: Taylor and Francis, 2016), 22. Discussing the widespread superstition that there was a curse on those who appropriated monastic lands, Moore quotes Spelman and others who believed the curse gradually spread like a 'Leprosie' throughout the kingdom, as the monastic lands were continually broken up until almost everyone owned a piece. The curse took many forms, including barrenness, as we have seen, but there was also the common belief that monastic buildings acted consciously after the dissolution, throwing out the owners who had appropriated them. Moore quotes Alison Shell, who discusses the presence of the curse in the gothic novel: 'A belief in the malefic consequence of sacrilege was a familiar superstition in England for a very long time after the Reformation' (22).

Chapter Seven: *Lucrece*: The Aftermath

1. 'Master Sackville's Induction', in *The Mirror for Magistrates*, vol. 2, edited by Joseph Haslewood (London: Lackington, Allen, and Longman, Hurst, Rees, Orme, and Brown, 1815), 318.

2. For Lord Buckhurst's 'outward conformity' and his protection of Catholics, including the construction of a priest's hole in his great house at Knole, see Michael Questier, *Catholicism and Community in Early Modern England* (Cambridge: Cambridge University Press, 2006), 59–60, 85–86.

3. One of the most compelling of the many studies of this subject is by Eamon Duffy, *Voices of Morebath: Reformation and Rebellion in an English Village* (New Haven, CT: Yale University Press, 2001).

4. The plan proposed that 'You shall, under cover of education, have them as hostages for their parent's fidelities'. James Arthur, *The Ebbing Tide: Policy and Principles of Catholic Education* (Leominster, England: Gracewing, 1995), 9.

5. For the building of prisons to contain the large numbers of recusants, see Philip Hughes, *The Reformation in England*, vol. 2 (London: Hollis and Carter, 1954), 367. Also Richard Challoner, *Memoirs of the Missionary Priests*, vol. 1 (London: John T. Green, 1839), 107.

6. Katherine Duncan-Jones, *Sir Philip Sidney: Courtier Poet* (London: Hamish Hamilton, 1991), 126–127.

7. Questier, *Catholicism and Community*, 123.

8. Ibid., passim.

9. Ibid., 63.

10. Robert Southwell, 'Epistle unto his Father', in *Two Letters and Short Rules of a Good Life*, edited by Nancy Pollard Brown (Charlottesville: University Press of Virginia, 1973), 9.

11. Questier, *Catholicism and Community*.

12. This image clearly resonated with early readers. 'Revealing day through every cranny peeps' is scribbled on a sheet of Elizabethan doodles known as the Northumberland manuscript. E. K. Chambers, *William Shakespeare: A Study of Facts and Problems*, vol. 2 (Oxford: Clarendon Press, 1930), plate xxv. John Donne also picks up the idea in his poem 'The Sun Rising'. John Donne, *Complete Poetry and Selected Prose*, edited by John Hayward (London: Nonesuch Press, 1967), 6.

13. Paul E. J. Hammer notes that a sign of 'Essex's good will towards Catholics' was his crucial role in encouraging 'the new form of madrigals composed in English, which attained considerable vogue during the 1590s. Many of the composers of these madrigals were Catholic, while the Italian origins of the genre helped to ensure that a Catholic association adhered to those written in English'. Paul E. J. Hammer, *The Polarisation of Elizabethan Politics: The Political Career of Robert Devereux, 2nd Earl of Essex, 1585–1597* (Cambridge: Cambridge University Press, 2005), 175–176.

14. Lucrece's inability to tell Collatine what happens in a letter (1296–1331) allows Shakespeare to give us a first hint of the superiority of speech and action to the written word or even to images, a theme he goes on to develop in the next few pages. Lucrece's words and phrases, as she sits with her quill at the ready, 'Much like a press of people at a door / Throng her inventions which shall go before' (1301–1302). This is a perfect description of writer's block. The written word is too static, too limited to convey the full story. 'To see sad sights moves more than hear them told' (1324), Lucrece tells us in the end, deciding to send a brief note, and wait until she can tell her tale with groans, tears, and 'action'. Here there may well be an indication of why this was to be Shakespeare's last narrative poem, in spite of its popularity. He had already recast the theme of the rape of a virtuous woman for the stage—it was published in *Titus Andronicus* that same year—and seven years later, he revisits the poem's main political theme in his greatest play, *Hamlet*. In his own lifetime, the stage had become a new and magnetic medium for political debate.

15. See David Bevington, *Tudor Drama and Politics* (Cambridge, MA: Harvard University Press, 1968), and Annabel M. Patterson, *Censorship and Interpretation: The Conditions of Writing and Reading in Early Modern England* (Madison: University of Wisconsin Press, 1991). The Queen's Men were formed by the queen's spymaster, Francis Walsingham, in 1583 on behalf of the government. They travelled the country gathering intelligence and promoting the state agenda, employing twelve of the finest

actors of the day. By the 1590s, other, more oppositional acting compa-
nies, notably Lord Strange's Men, had replaced them; the formation of
the Lord Chamberlain's Men in the mid-1590s was intended to redress
the balance.

16. Charlotte Carmichael Stopes, *The Life of Henry, Third Earl of
Southampton, Shakespeare's Patron* (Cambridge: Cambridge University
Press, 1922), 173.

17. *Hamlet*, 2.2.518–519.

18. See George Cavendish, *The Life and Death of Cardinal Wolsey*
(Boston: Houghton Mifflin, 1905 [printed at London: Riverside Press]),
who, in detailing the consequences of the Reformation, writes, 'whereof
[the plague] has not ceased' (80); also Philip Caraman, *The Other Face:
Catholic Life Under Elizabeth I* (London: Longmans, 1960), 31, and Alexandra Walsham, *Catholic Reformation in Protestant Britain* (London: Routledge, 2016), 99. In the second two extracts, Catholics are blamed for the
plague.

19. John Leslie, preface to *A Treatise of Treasons* [1572] (Ann Arbor,
MI: Early English Books Online, 2003), xx–xxiii, http://name.umdl
.umich.edu/A21247.0001.001.

20. The repetition of 'he' and the suggestion that Lucrece cannot
finish the word hint at the name Henry, rather than Tarquin.

21. Capital letters are used inconsistently at the beginning of words
in the first editions of Shakespeare's *Venus and Adonis* and *Rape of Lucrece*.
As Katherine Duncan-Jones points out, they deserve closer study, as they
are among the very few works we can be sure were printed directly from
Shakespeare's manuscript, and whose publication Shakespeare authorised
himself. *Shakespeare's Poems*, edited by Katherine Duncan-Jones and H.
R. Woodhuysen, The Arden Shakespeare (London: Bloomsbury, 2007),
471.

22. W. B. Yeats, *Collected Poems of W. B. Yeats*, edited by Richard J.
Finneran (New York: Simon and Schuster, 2008), 345.

CHAPTER EIGHT: THE GUARDIAN

1. Richard Morison, quoted by Michael R. Graves in 'Thomas
Wriothesley, First Earl of Southampton', Oxford Dictionary of National Biography, 2004, www.oxforddnb.com/view/10.1093/ref:odnb
/9780198614128.001.0001/odnb-9780198614128-e-30076?rskey=yRTAc
Z&result=1First Earl of Southampton.

2. G. P. V. Akrigg, *Shakespeare and the Earl of Southampton* (London: Hamish Hamilton, 1968), 177. Akrigg is as concerned to exonerate
Southampton of Catholicism as he is of the other 'problematic area in his
life', homosexuality (181). He records, but does not accept, evidence that
he abandoned his religion in 1603, speculating that he must have done
so much earlier. Both he and Michael Questier (*Catholicism and Community in Early Modern England* [Cambridge: Cambridge University Press,

2006], 63–65) record Southampton's continuing protectiveness towards Catholics and recusants throughout his later life, Akrigg saying he acted as 'a useful middleman between Catholics and the Protestant government, trusted by both' (181). Questier notes that the circle of Catholics in Hampshire and Sussex to which he belonged included political activists (63). Charged with being a papist at his trial, Southampton answered equivocally, saying he was 'never conversant with any of that sort', and was not pressed further. See *Trials of the Earls of Essex and Southampton*, edited by Margaret Pierce Secara for Renaissance: The Elizabethan World, 1999, www.elizabethan.org/trial/trial-toc.html.

3. Joel Hurstfield, 'Lord Burghley as Master of the Court of Wards, 1561–98', *Transactions of the Royal Historical Society* 31 (1949), passim.

4. Ibid., 108.

5. Ibid., 101–102.

6. Gregory Kneidel, 'Coscos, Queen Elizabeth I and John Donne's "Satyr II"', *Renaissance Quarterly* 61, no. 1 (2008): 92–121.

7. Jill Husselby and Paula Henderson, 'Location, Location, Location! Cecil House in the Strand', *Architectural History* 45 (2002): 159–193.

8. The following description is based on Martin Andrews, 'Theobalds Palace: The Gardens and Park', *Garden History* 21, no. 2 (1993): 129–145.

9. Alan Nelson, *Monstrous Adversary: The Life of Edward de Vere, 17th Earl of Oxford* (Liverpool: Liverpool University Press, 2003), 36.

10. Lawrence Stone, *Family and Fortune: Studies in Aristocratic Finance in the Sixteenth and Seventeenth Centuries* (Oxford: Oxford University Press, 1973), 35.

11. Nelson, *Monstrous Adversary*, 47–48.

12. Ibid., 70.

13. *The Compleat Statesman*, in Francis Peck, *Desiderata Curiosa*, vol. 1 (London, 1732), 1–66.

14. Ibid., 58.

15. Ibid., 59.

16. Ibid., 60–65.

17. *Hamlet*, 1.3.55–81. This is Polonius's first long speech in the play, and it would readily have identified the character from the start with the Burghley of *The Compleat Statesman*. Polonius's later amorality and fondness for deception would have publicly contradicted the eulogy.

18. *Compleat Statesman*, 60–62.

19. Richard Dutton, '*Volpone* and Beast Fable: Early Modern Analogic Reading', *Huntington Library Quarterly* 67, no. 3 (2004): 347–370.

20. A. G. Dickens, *The English Reformation* (London: Fontana, 1967), 401.

21. Philip Hughes, *The Reformation in England*, vol. 3 (London: Hollis and Carter, 1954), chapter 2. The way the bishops were removed and deprived of their sees is described on p. 37, and pp. 245–247 detail their

subsequent imprisonment, eight of them for life. See also John Lingard, *A History of England*, vol. 6 (London: Dolman, 1849), 13–20.

22. Lingard, *History of England*, 6:13–20.

23. Hughes, *Reformation in England*, 3:4.

24. Peter Milward, *Elizabethan Controversialists* (Campbell, CA: Fastpencil, 2012), 112–113.

25. Ibid., 118–119.

26. Ibid., 120.

27. A. F. Pollard, 'Burghley, William Cecil, Baron', in *Encyclopaedia Britannica*, 11th ed., vol. 4, edited by Hugh Chisolm (Cambridge: Cambridge University Press, 1911), 816, online at https://archive.org/stream/encyclopaediabri04chisrich.

28. Edmund Spenser, *Mother Hubberd's Tale*, ll. 1050–1052.

29. Ibid., 1145–1146.

30. Questier, *Catholicism and Community*, 123.

31. In his 'Apologie', Essex uses an extended image of the siege of Troy and the fraudulent role of Sinon to denounce the Spanish peace overtures to England, which were welcomed by the Cecils. *An Apologie of the Earle of Essex* (1600), Early English Books Online, quod.lib.umich.edu, 16.

32. Earlier, less flattering portraits include Nicholas Hilliard's likeness in the Burrell Collection and the anonymous 1560s portrait in the National Portrait Gallery, London.

33. Questier, *Catholicism and Community*, 59.

34. *Compleat Statesman*, 65.

35. Ibid.

36. Questier, *Catholicism and Community*, 37.

37. It is notoriously difficult to give modern equivalents to sixteenth- and early seventeenth-century currency, partly because this was a period of intermittent inflation. In 1560, the average wage of a labourer was 7 pence a day; the annual salary of a surgeon was £30. The estate of the Earl of Leicester at his death was worth £8,000, and the queen's annual expenditure on her wardrobe was £9,535: Lisa Picard, *Elizabethan London* (London: Weidenfeld and Nicholson, 2003), 322–324. Lawrence Stone calculates that Southampton had an annual income from his lands of well over £3,000 a year, on which 'a young man of the 1590s could live in considerable style'. Stone, *Family and Fortune*, 216. This book uses the National Archive website to establish the purchasing power of a pound sterling in 1590 at somewhere around £175 in today's currency; in 1600 it dropped to £137, and by 1620 it was £131. See National Archives, Currency Converter, www.nationalarchives.gov.uk/currency-converter.

38. Nelson, *Monstrous Adversary*, 315.

39. Ibid., 316.

40. Akrigg, *Shakespeare and the Earl of Southampton*, 32.

41. Ibid.

42. Clara Longworth de Chambrun, *Shakespeare: A Portrait Restored* (London: Hollis and Carter, 1957), 160.

43. Akrigg, *Shakespeare and the Earl of Southampton*, 32.

CHAPTER NINE: RALLYING THE OPPOSITION:
VENUS AND ADONIS

1. Charles Martindale and Colin Burrow, 'Clapham's *Narcissus*: A Pre-Text for Shakespeare's *Venus and Adonis?*', *English Literary Renaissance* 22, no. 2 (1992): 147–176.

2. Ibid., 159.

3. Ibid., 163.

4. Ibid., 163.

5. Richard Wilson, *Secret Shakespeare: Studies in Theatre, Religion and Resistance* (Manchester: Manchester University Press, 2004), 135.

6. In November 1594, the underground head of the Jesuits in England, Henry Garnet, wrote to Robert Persons: 'The young Earl of Southampton, refusing the Lady Vere, payeth 5000 of present payment.' Henry Foley, *Records of the English Province of the Society of Jesus: Historic Facts Illustrative of the Labours and Sufferings of Its Members in the Sixteenth and Seventeenth Centuries* (London: Burns and Oats, 1877), available at Internet Archive, https://archive.org/stream/recordsofenglish04fole /recordsofenglish04fole_djvu.txt. Southampton's situation was evidently public knowledge.

7. *The Mirror for Magistrates*, vol. 1, edited by Joseph Haslewood (London: Lackington, Allen, and Longman, Hurst, Rees, Orme, and Brown, 1815), 274.

8. 'He has left nothing to say about nothing or anything.' John Keats, *The Letters of John Keats*, vol. 1, edited by Hyder Edward Rollins (Cambridge: Cambridge University Press, 2012).

9. William Reynolds, the first recorded reader of the poem, interpreted this disclaimer as a direct portrait of Elizabeth. Katherine Duncan-Jones, 'Much Ado with Red and White', *Review of English Studies* 44, no. 176 (1993): 479–454.

10. Richard Wilson, 'A Bloody Question: The Politics of Venus and Adonis', in *Secret Shakespeare, Studies in Theatre, Religion and Resistance* (Manchester: Manchester University Press, 2004), 126–143.

11. Philip Hughes, *The Reformation in England*, vol. 3 (London: Hollis and Carter, 1954), 245.

12. The story of Venus and Adonis appears in Ovid, *Metamorphoses*, Book 10, ll. 503–559. The account of the Calydonian boar hunt is in Book 8, ll. 329–375.

13. Letter from James Morice to Lord Burghley, 1593, Cecil Papers, quoted in *The Gentleman's Magazine*, edited by F. Jefferies, vol. 133 (1823): 373.

14. Rosemary Sgroi, '1593: 8th Parliament of Queen Elizabeth, 35 Eliz. I', History of Parliament Online, www.historyofparliamentonline .org/volume/1558-1603/parliament/1593.

15. Lord Burghley himself had protested at their methods, especially the use of a self-incriminating *ex officio* oath, saying that 'the Inquisitors of Spain use not so many questions to comprehend and to trap their preys'. J. R. Tanner, *Tudor Constitutional Documents, AD 1485–1603* (Cambridge: Cambridge University Press, 1930), 173.

16. Letter from James Morice to Lord Burghley, 1593, Cecil Papers, quoted in *The Gentleman's Magazine*, edited by F. Jefferies, vol. 133 (1823): 373.

17. Duncan-Jones, 'Much Ado with Red and White', 480.

18. Ibid., 488

19. For an illuminating study of this subject, see Curtis Breight, *Surveillance, Militarism and Drama in the Elizabethan Era* (London: Macmillan, 1996).

20. Sir William Stanley and Rowland Yorke were the two defectors. Stanley was about to be made viceroy of Ireland. In a plea to the Privy Council just before he changed sides, Yorke wrote that 'the poor miserable subjects of her majesty . . . now are dying of cold, yea more than two hundred since my comying'. Sarah Clayton, 'Yorke [York], Rowland', Oxford Dictionary of National Biography, www.oxforddnb.com.ezproxy2 .londonlibrary.co.uk/view/10.1093/ref:odnb/9780198614128.001.0001 /odnb-9780198614128-e-30236.

21. Mark Charles Fissell, *English Warfare, 1511–1642* (London: Routledge, 2016), 164.

22. Curtis Breight, 'Caressing the Great: Viscount Montague's Entertainment of Elizabeth at Cowdray, 1591', *Sussex Archeological Collections* 127 (1989): 147–166.

23. Breight, *Surveillance*, 149, 157.

24. Hughes, *Reformation in England*, 244.

25. Andrew Hiscock, 'Achilles Alter: The Heroic Lives and Afterlives of the Earl of Essex', in *Essex: The Cultural Impact of an Elizabethan Courtier*, edited by Annaliese Connolly and Lisa Hopkins (Manchester: Manchester University Press, 2013), 103.

26. Paul E. J. Hammer, *The Polarisation of Elizabethan Politics: The Political Career of Robert Devereux, 2nd Earl of Essex, 1585–1597* (Cambridge: Cambridge University Press, 2005), 22. Though biographies continue to repeat the story that Elizabeth liked to call Essex her wild horse, there is no evidence for this—it appears that unlike her other favourites, he did not receive a nickname from her.

27. Shakespeare, *Henry V*, Prologue, 28–34.

28. Jonathan Bate, *Soul of the Age: The Life, Mind and World of William Shakespeare* (London: Penguin, 2009), 249–286. Bate gives one of the best

and most readable accounts of the dramatic events of the Essex Rebellion and its relationship to the literature on the reign of Richard II.

29. For a full discussion of the connection between Cobham and Falstaff, see Peter Lake, 'Oldcastle/Falstaff. Cobham/Essex', In *How Shakespeare Put Politics on the Stage: Power and Succession in the History Plays* (New Haven, CT: Yale University Press, 2016), chap. 16.

30. Ibid., 3.

31. John Harington, *The Metamorphosis of Ajax: A Cloacinean Satire* (London: Chiswick, C. Whittingham, 1814), 60.

32. Alexandra Gajda, *The Earl of Essex and Late Elizabethan Political Culture* (Oxford: Oxford University Press, 2012), 126.

33. Ibid., 78.

34. Ibid., 123.

35. Ibid., 108.

36. Andrew Graham-Dixon, 'Start the Week', BBC Radio 4, 22 January 2018.

37. From 'Musophilus', ll. 289–290, in Samuel Daniel, *Poems and A Defence of Ryme*, edited by Arthur Colby Sprague (Chicago: University of Chicago Press, 1965), 76.

38. From 'Cleopatra', in Samuel Daniel, *Poetical Works of Mr. Samuel Daniel*, vol. 1 (R. Gosling, 1743), 264. 'Cleopatra', a 'closet drama' written in 1594, has so many close similarities to *The Rape of Lucrece*, particularly on the political, allegorical level, that the two poems may have been written to complement each other. Daniel, an admirer and imitator of Shakespeare, was also patronised by supporters of the Earl of Essex, such as Lord Mountjoy.

39. Gajda, *Earl of Essex*, 108.

40. Ibid., 119.

41. Ibid., 129.

42. Ibid. In Chapter 3, 'Profane Policy? Religion, Toleration and the Politics of Succession', Gajda gives new insight into the widespread support for religious toleration among Essex's supporters, and on the part of Essex himself.

43. Hammer, *Polarisation*, 404.

44. Ibid., 403.

45. Thea Cervone, *Sworn Bond in Tudor England: Oaths, Vows and Covenants in Civil Life and Literature* (Jefferson, NC: McFarland and Company, 2011), 23–25. After Henry's alterations, the king was bound to preserve merely those things which were in conformity with 'his conscience' and 'his jurisdiction and dignity royal', a change for the first time setting the will of the monarch above the law.

46. Gajda, *Earl of Essex*, 161.

47. Ibid., 161–162. The Privy Council made the mistake of circulating this letter to discredit Essex after his return from Ireland, but from

Elizabeth's impatient reaction to their efforts, it seems to have merely increased his popularity.

48. Paul E. J. Hammer, 'Devereux, Robert, Second Earl of Essex', in Oxford Dictionary of National Biography, 2004, www.oxforddnb .com/view/10.1093/ref:odnb/9780198614128.001.0001/odnb-97801 98614128-e-7565.

49. Gajda, *Earl of Essex*, 161.

50. Hiscock, 'Achilles Alter', 110.

51. Ibid., 108.

52. Gajda, *Earl of Essex*, 168.

53. Hammer, *Polarisation*, 175.

54. The great psalter, given on the Queen's Accession Day in 1597 as a mark of his disillusion with the court, is still on display there.

55. Hammer, *Polarisation*, 229.

56. Ibid., 250.

57. I am grateful to Major Alexander Baring and Lieutenant Colonel Robert Hanscomb for this information.

CHAPTER TEN:
THE DESTRUCTION OF THE EARL OF ESSEX

1. 'The Trial of Sir Christopher Blount and Others for High Treason', *Cobbett's State Trials*, vol. 1 (London: R. Bagshaw, 1809), 1421.

2. Paul E. J. Hammer, *The Polarisation of Elizabethan Politics: The Political Career of Robert Devereux, 2nd Earl of Essex, 1585–1597* (Cambridge: Cambridge University Press, 2005), 354–355.

3. Hiram Morgan, 'The Fall of Sir John Perrot', in *The Reign of Elizabeth I: Court and Culture in the Last Decade*, edited by John Guy (Cambridge: Cambridge University Press, 1995), 125.

4. Hammer, *Polarisation*, 398.

5. Calendar of State Papers, Venice, 1592–1603, 9.238, quoted by Paul E. J. Hammer in 'Devereux, Robert, Second Earl of Essex', in Oxford Dictionary of National Biography, 2004, www.oxforddnb .com/view/10.1093/ref:odnb/9780198614128.001.0001/odnb-978019 8614128-e-7565.

6. Guy, *Reign of Elizabeth I*, 138.

7. Ibid., 128.

8. Alexandra Gajda, *The Earl of Essex and Late Elizabethan Political Culture* (Oxford: Oxford University Press, 2012), 185. Gajda stresses that James's hostility to the Cecils was independent of his links with Essex.

9. Ibid., 106.

10. Ibid.

11. Lawrence Stone, *Family and Fortune: Studies in Aristocratic Finance in the Sixteenth and Seventeenth Centuries* (Oxford: Oxford University Press, 1973), 15.

12. Robert Cecil, Earl of Salisbury, and George Carew, Earl of Totnes, *Letters from Sir Robert Cecil to Sir George Carew*, edited by John Maclean (London: Camden Society, 1864), 68.

13. Charlotte Carmichael Stopes, *The Life of Henry, Third Earl of Southampton, Shakespeare's Patron* (Cambridge: Cambridge University Press, 1922), 205. Stopes transcribes the whole letter. See also Gajda, *Earl of Essex*, 212, who confirms the date as 1600, before the rebellion.

14. John Guy, *Elizabeth, The Forgotten Years* (London: Penguin, 2016), 309–310.

15. Chris Butler and Willy Maley, '"Bringing Rebellion Broached on His Sword": Essex and Ireland', in *Essex: The Cultural Impact of an Elizabethan Courtier*, edited by Annaliese Connolly and Lisa Hopkins (Manchester: Manchester University Press, 2013).

16. Guy, *Forgotten Years*, 308. See also Gajda, *Earl of Essex*, 149–151, for an analysis of Essex's lack of logistical support in Ireland and the rapid growth in Cecil's dominance at court during his absence.

17. Paul E. J. Hammer, *Elizabeth's Wars: War, Government and Society in Tudor England, 1544–1604* (London: Palgrave Macmillan, 2003), 215.

18. Gajda, *Earl of Essex*, 104–107.

19. Ibid., 38–39.

20. Ibid., 187.

21. Paul E. J. Hammer, 'Shakespeare's *Richard II*, the Play of 7 February 1601 and the Essex Rising', *Shakespeare Quarterly* 59, no. 1 (2008): 15, 31.

22. Mark Nicholls and Penry Williams, 'Ralegh, Sir Walter', *Oxford Dictionary of National Biography*, 2015, www.oxforddnb.com/view/10.1093/ref:odnb/9780198614128.001.0001/odnb-9780198614128-e-23039.

23. John Lingard, *A History of England*, vol. 6 (London: Dolman, 1849), 611.

24. Hammer, 'Shakespeare's *Richard II*', 30.

25. Stopes, *Life of Henry, Third Earl*, 201.

26. Lingard, *History of England*, 6:715–718.

27. Ibid., 6:717.

28. Machiavelli, *The Prince*, edited by Quentin Skinner and Russell Price (Cambridge: Cambridge University Press 1988), 9.

29. Stopes, *Life of Henry, Third Earl*, 219.

30. 'The Trial of Sir Christopher Blount and Others for High Treason', *Cobbett's State Trials*, vol. 1 (London: R. Bagshaw, 1809), 1431.

31. Jonathan Bate, *Soul of the Age: The Life, Mind and World of William Shakespeare* (London: Penguin, 2009), 275.

32. Ibid.

33. Lingard, *History of England*, 6:716.

34. Stopes, *Life of Henry, Third Earl*, 215.

35. Dixon Wecter, 'Shakespeare's Purpose in *Timon of Athens*', *PMLA* 43, no. 3 (1928): 701–721.

36. Kristen Dieter, *The Tower of London in English Renaissance Drama: Icon of Opposition* (London: Routledge, 2008), 105.

37. Philip Caraman, *Henry Garnet and the Gunpowder Plot* (London: Longmans, 1964), 307.

38. Robert Vaughan, *History of England Under the House of Stuart*, vol. 1 (London: Baldwin and Cradock, 1840), 51.

39. Ibid.

40. Theodore K. Rabb, *Jacobean Gentleman: Sir Edwin Sandys, 1561–1629* (Princeton, NJ: Princeton University Press, 1998).

41. Caraman, *Henry Garnet*, 307

42. Ibid., 307–308. 'His Majesty did suffer himself to be guided and as it were governed by those that had so long time inured their hands and hardened their hearts with so violent a persecution.' In these pages, Caraman gives a full description of the grounds Catholics were given to expect toleration from James.

43. A conference at Hampton Court in January 1604 saw the first clash between James and the Puritans. Most of their long list of requests, ranging from the abolition of bishops to the eradication of 'outward badges of popish error', were comprehensively shot down by the king, though he announced a project for a new, authorised translation of the Bible, welcomed by Puritans. Crown and Parliament now embarked on a century-long battle over the identity of the state church and the nature of its governance as Puritans, who, unlike Catholics, had no problem with the anti-papal Oath of Allegiance required of Members of Parliament, used the House of Commons as a platform to air their grievances. '05 July 1604', in *Journal of the House of Commons*, vol. 1, *1547–1629* (London: His Majesty's Stationery Office, 1802), 252–253, available at British History Online, www.british-history.ac.uk/commons-jrnl/vol1/pp252-253.

44. Act Against Recusants of 1585. The play stresses that the statutes, like the 1585 act, had been only fitfully enforced. The editors of the state documents note: 'The present act was stringently enforced . . . in 1604, 1606 and 1625.' See Henry Gee and William John Hardy, eds., *Documents Illustrative of English Church History* (New York: Macmillan, 1896), 485–492.

45. There is a strong possibility that the Court would also have seen a series of references in *Measure for Measure* to the betrayal of the Catholic cause by Spain. Claudio's sister, Isabella, a Poor Clare nun, pleads for his life with Angelo, but piously refuses to trade her virtue for it, which is what Angelo demands. There is a shadowy parallel here with the Infanta, Isabella Clara of Spain, a lay member of the Poor Clare order who declined involvement in the English succession issue; Spain argued that it had no moral obligation to assist English Catholics.

46. Rabb, *Jacobean Gentleman*.

47. *King Lear*, 4.2.48–49.

48. See Brian Vickers, 'A rum "do"', *Times Literary Supplement*, 5 December 2003, 13.

EPILOGUE

1. Four per cent of the population died in the English Civil War, as opposed to 2.4 per cent in the First World War.

2. Ted Hughes, *Shakespeare and the Goddess of Complete Being* (London: Faber and Faber, 1992), 74.

3. Robin Clifton, '"An Indiscriminate Blackness"? Massacre, Counter-Massacre and Ethnic Cleansing in Ireland, 1640–1660', in *The Massacre in History*, edited by Mark Levene and Penny Roberts (New York: Berghahn Books, 1999), 108.

4. John Lingard, *A History of England*, vol. 8 (London: Dolman, 1849), 70.

5. Michael Questier, *Catholicism and Community in Early Modern England* (Cambridge: Cambridge University Press, 2006), 506.

6. Ibid., 501.

BIBLIOGRAPHY

QUOTED EDITIONS

QUOTATIONS FROM SHAKESPEARE'S plays are taken from *The Complete Works of Shakespeare*, edited by Peter Alexander (London: Collins, 1958). Quotations from the poems are from *The Oxford Shakespeare: The Complete Sonnets and Poems*, edited by Colin Burrow (Oxford: Oxford University Press, 2008). In most cases, early modern spellings have been modernized.

THE RAPE OF LUCRECE: THE CRITICS

This reading relies on the insights of the many outstanding scholars who have written on *The Rape of Lucrece*. An indispensable introduction to the poem is Ian Donaldson's *The Rapes of Lucretia: A Myth and Its Transformations*. Donaldson's wide-ranging study of the relevance of the political identities of Lucrece to the poem is combined with a detailed and perceptive analysis of the many reasons why it fails on the literary level. He stresses its political adroitness, however, noting the poem's support for kingship alongside the attack on tyranny. In the preface to his edition of the poems, *The Oxford Shakespeare: The Complete Sonnets and Poems*, Colin Burrow has written a similarly searching and informative study. While highlighting its qualities, he finds much of the poem unsatisfactory, citing the incoherent imagery, the political uncertainties, the confusing perspectives, the unanswered questions, the sententious utterance. In *Shakespeare on Love and Lust*, Maurice Charney also points out the apparent faults and almost comic incongruities of the poem—its 'maddeningly' slow pace, its distancing techniques, its ingeniously far-fetched but inapposite images. John Roe, in his edition of Shakespeare's poems, is one of the many critics who attribute these drawbacks to the conventions of the times; for him, the rhetoric is an end in itself. In *Shakespeare's Poems*, Katherine Duncan-Jones and Henry Woodhuysen provide one of the fullest discussions of the social and literary contexts of the two narrative poems, again encouraging an awareness of Renaissance literary convention.

For some critics, the political interest of the poem eclipses the human story and even the poem's literary qualities. These writers generally focus on the debate between Tarquin and Lucrece before the rape and situate the poem among the treatises on governance circulating in the mid-1590s. In *Shakespeare and Renaissance Politics*, Andrew Hadfield, one of the few to note that the poem foreshadows the aims of the Essex Rebellion, uses Lucrece's arguments with Tarquin to connect Shakespeare to the republican debate which he detects among the intellectual circles of the 1590s. Melissa Sanchez, in *Erotic Subjects: The Sexuality of Politics in Early Modern English Literature*, sees Shakespeare discussing the 'crisis of counsel' at the end of Elizabeth's reign in a country which traditionally combined monarchical rule with the subjects' consent. Both Collatine and Lucrece represent the failure of counsel in the face of tyranny. Sanchez links Shakespeare's position with Essex's aristocratic opposition to court corruption, but sees Shakespeare discouraging revolt.

Instead, the poem is 'a melancholic look at the situation of the early modern subject who . . . lived lives defined by vulnerability and compromise' (p. 92). Peter Smith, in 'Rome's Disgrace: The Politics of Rape in Shakespeare's "Lucrece,"' discusses the 'geopolitical' aspects of both Lucrece and the rape, interpreting the poem as the analysis of the fall of Rome rather than of the downfall of a woman.

For others, religious themes predominate. Anna Swärdh, in *Rape and Religion in English Renaissance Literature*, highlights the fusion of idolatry and iconoclasm in the first half of the poem, and the relevance to Elizabethans of the pervading theme of misuse of power. She relates the poem to the more openly Catholic motifs which she sees in Shakespeare's contemporary play *Titus Andronicus*. For John Klause, the poem is heavily influenced by the writings of the Jesuit poet Robert Southwell. In Klause's view, argued in *Shakespeare, the Earl, and the Jesuit*, Lucrece represents the compromised and persecuted English Catholic Church, opting for martyrdom as a form of resistance. In spite of Lucrece's heroism, the poem warns of the price to be paid by what is portrayed as a suicidal policy.

Feminist criticism frequently connects Lucrece to the tradition of female complaint. Most of these works highlight the link with the political theme of the powerless subject, contrasting other fallen women with the more effective Lucrece. One of the finest feminist essays on the poem is by Nancy Vickers, whose article 'This Heraldry in Lucrece' Face' highlights the extent and importance of Collatine's possessive attitude to his wife.

Finally, a succession of excellent critics, among them Heather Dubrow, continue to illuminate new aspects of the psychological, rhetorical, and social aspects of the poem, but avoid relating their conclusions to contemporary Elizabethan politics: for them, the issues of rape, male possessiveness, theft, and a divided and corrupt society relate to Rome, and the Roman Lucrece, not to England.

SOURCES

Ackroyd, Peter. *William Shakespeare: The Biography*. New York: Vintage, 2006.

Akbari, Suzanne Conklin. *Idols in the East: European Representations of Islam and the Orient, 1100–1450*. Ithaca, NY: Cornell University Press, 2012.

Akrigg, G. P. V. *Shakespeare and the Earl of Southampton*. London: Hamish Hamilton, 1968.

Alford, Stephen. *Burghley: William Cecil at the Court of Elizabeth I*. New Haven, CT: Yale University Press, 2008.

Andrews, M. C. 'Michael Drayton, Shakespeare's Shadow'. *Shakespeare Quarterly* 65, no. 3 (2014): 273–306.

Andrews, Martin. 'Theobalds Palace: The Gardens and Park'. *Garden History* 21, no. 2 (1993): 129–145.

Armstrong, W. A. 'The Influence of Seneca and Machiavelli on the Elizabethan Tyrant'. *Review of English Studies* 24, no. 93 (1948): 19–35.

Arnold, Oliver. *The Third Citizen: Shakespeare's Theatre and the Early Modern House of Commons*. Baltimore: Johns Hopkins University Press, 2007.

Arthur, James. *The Ebbing Tide: Policy and Principles of Catholic Education*. Leominster, England: Gracewing, 1995.

Asquith, Clare. 'A Phoenix for Palm Sunday: Was Shakespeare's Poem a Requiem for Catholic Martyrs?' *Times Literary Supplement*, no. 5115 (13 April 2001), 14–15.

Aston, Margaret. 'English Ruins and English History: The Dissolution and the Sense of the Past'. *Journal of the Warburg and Courtauld Institutes* 36 (1973): 231–255.

Baldwin, William. *The Mirror for Magistrates*. Edited by Lily Campbell. Baltimore: Johns Hopkins University Press, 1970.

Bale, John. *The Image of Both Churches* (c. 1545). Edited by Gretchen Minton. New York: Springer Science and Business Media, 2014.

Bashar, Nazife. 'Rape in England Between 1550 and 1700'. In *The Sexual Dynamics of History: Men's Power, Women's Resistance*, edited by the London Feminist History Group. London: Pluto Press, 1983.

Bate, Jonathan. 'Sexual Perversity in "Venus and Adonis"'. *Yearbook of English Studies* 23 (1993): 80–92.

———. *Soul of the Age: The Life, Mind and World of William Shakespeare*. London: Penguin, 2009.

Beales, Derek. 'Edmund Burke and the Monasteries of France'. *Historical Journal* 48, no. 2 (2005): 415–436.

Bernard, G. W. 'The Dissolution of the Monasteries'. *History* 96, no. 4 (2011): 390–409.

————. *The King's Reformation.* New Haven, CT: Yale University Press, 2007.

Bevington, David. *Tudor Drama and Politics.* Cambridge, MA: Harvard University Press, 1968.

Bossy, John. *The English Catholic Community, 1570–1650.* London: Darton, Longman and Todd, 1975.

Breight, Curtis. 'Caressing the Great: Viscount Montague's Entertainment of Elizabeth at Cowdray, 1591'. *Sussex Archaeological Collections* 127 (1989): 147–166.

————. *Surveillance, Militarism and Drama in the Elizabethan Era.* London: Macmillan, 1996.

Bromley, Laura. 'Lucrece's Re-Creation'. *Shakespeare Quarterly* 34, no. 2 (1983): 200–211.

Brown, Barbara. 'Sir Thomas More and Thomas Churchyard's "Shore's Wife"'. *Yearbook of English Studies* 2 (1972): 41–48.

Bruce, John, ed. *Correspondence of King James VI. of Scotland with Sir Robert Cecil and Others in England.* London: Longmans, 1861.

Bruening, Michael W., ed. *A Reformation Sourcebook.* Toronto: University of Toronto Press, 2017.

Burke, E., and L. Mitchell. *Reflections on the Revolution in France.* Oxford: Oxford University Press, 2009.

Butler, C., and W. Maley. '"Bringing Rebellion Broached on His Sword": Essex and Ireland'. In *Essex: The Cultural Impact of an Elizabethan Courtier,* edited by Annaliese Connolly and Lisa Hopkins. Manchester: Manchester University Press, 2013.

Camden, William. *Britannia.* Edited by Richard Gough. London: Hutchinson, 1789.

Caraman, Philip. *Henry Garnet and the Gunpowder Plot.* London: Longmans, 1964.

————. *The Other Face: Catholic Life Under Elizabeth I.* London: Longmans, 1960.

Carleton, Dudley, and John Chamberlain. *Dudley Carleton to John Chamberlain, 1603–1624.* New Brunswick, NJ: Rutgers University Press, 1972.

Cavendish, George. *The Life and Death of Cardinal Wolsey.* Boston: Houghton Mifflin, 1905; printed at London: Riverside Press, 1905.

Cecil, David. *The Cecils of Hatfield House.* London: Houghton Mifflin, 1973.

Cecil, Robert, Earl of Salisbury, and George Carew, Earl of Totnes. *Letters from Sir Robert Cecil to Sir G. Carew.* Edited by John Maclean. London: Camden Society, 1864.

Cervone, Thea. *Sworn Bond in Tudor England: Oaths, Vows and Covenants in Civil Life and Literature.* Jefferson, NC: McFarland and Company, 2011.

Challoner, Richard. *Memoirs of the Missionary Priests,* vol. 1. London: John T. Green, 1839.

Chambers, E. K. *William Shakespeare: A Study of Facts and Problems*, vol. 2. Oxford: Clarendon Press, 1930.

Charney, Maurice. *Shakespeare on Love and Lust*. New York: Columbia University Press, 2000.

Claxton, William. *The Rites of Durham*. Edited by J. T. Fowler. Publications of the Surtees Society, vol. 107. Durham, UK: Andrews and Company, 1903 [1593].

Clery, Peter. *The Monastic Estate*. London: Phillimore, 2015.

Clifton, Robin. '"An Indiscriminate Blackness"? Massacre, Counter-Massacre and Ethnic Cleansing in Ireland, 1640–1660'. In *The Massacre in History*, edited by Mark Levene and Penny Roberts. New York: Berghahn Books, 1999.

Cobbett, William. *A History of the Protestant Reformation in England and Ireland*. London: Burns and Oates, 1925 [1824–1827].

Collinson, Patrick. *The Birthpangs of Protestant England*. London: Macmillan, 1988.

———. *The Elizabethan Puritan Movement*. London: Methuen, 1967.

———. *Elizabethans*. London: Hambledon Continuum, 2003.

Connolly, Annaliese, and Lisa Hopkins. *Essex: The Cultural Impact of an Elizabethan Courtier*. Manchester: Manchester University Press, 2013.

Corbett, Margery. 'The Title-Page and Illustrations to the Monasticon Anglicanum, 1655–1673'. *Antiquaries Journal* 67, no. 1 (1987): 102–110.

Croft, Pauline. *Patronage, Culture and Power: The Early Cecils*. New Haven, CT: Yale University Press, 2002.

———. 'The Reputation of Robert Cecil: Libels, Political Opinion and Popular Awareness in the Early Seventeenth Century'. *Transactions of the Royal Historical Society* 1 (1991): 43–69.

Crowley, Laura. 'Was Southampton a Poet? A Verse Letter to Queen Elizabeth [with text]'. *English Literary Renaissance* 41, no. 1 (2011): 111–145.

Cuneo, Pia F. 'Jorg Breu the Elder's Death of Lucrece: History, Sexuality and the State'. In *Saints, Sinners and Sisters: Gender and Northern Art in Medieval and Early Modern Europe*, edited by Jane L. Carroll and Alison G. Stewart. Farnham, UK: Ashgate, 2003.

Daniel, Samuel. *Poems and a Defence of Ryme*. Edited by Arthur Colby Sprague. Chicago: University of Chicago Press, 1965.

Danson Brown, R. '"A Talkative Wench (Whose Words a World Hath Delighted In)": Mistress Shore and Elizabethan Complaint'. *Review of English Studies* 49, no. 196 (1998): 395–415.

Dawson, Lesel. 'The Earl of Essex and the Trials of History: Gervase Markham's "The Dumbe Knight"'. *Review of English Studies* 53, no. 211 (2002): 344–364.

Deiter, Kristen. *The Tower of London in English Renaissance Drama: Icon of Opposition*. London: Routledge, 2008.

Devereux, Robert, Earl of Essex. *An Apologie of the Earle of Essex*. London: Imprinted by Richard Bradocke, 1603.

Devlin, Christopher. *The Life of Robert Southwell*. London: Longmans, 1956.

Dickens, A. G. *The English Reformation*. London: Fontana, 1967.

Dobski, Bernard J. *Shakespeare and the Body Politic*. New York: Lexington Books, 2015.

Donaldson, Ian. *The Rapes of Lucretia: A Myth and Its Transformations*. Oxford: Oxford University Press, 1982.

Donne, John. *Complete Poetry and Selected Prose*. Edited by John Haywood. London: Nonesuch Press, 1967.

Drayton, Michael. *Matilda the Fair*. In *The Works of Michael Drayton*, vol. 1, edited by J. William Hebel. Oxford: Basil Blackwell, 1931.

Dryden, John. *The Poems and Fables of John Dryden*. Edited by J. Kinsley. Oxford: Oxford University Press, 1970.

Dubrow, Heather. 'Captive Victors: Shakespeare Narrative Poems and Sonnets'. *Renaissance Quarterly* 41, no. 4 (1988): 752–754.

Duffy, Eamon. *Reformation Divided: Catholics, Protestants and the Conversion of England*. London: Bloomsbury Continuum, 2017.

———. *Voices of Morebath: Reformation and Rebellion in an English Village*. New Haven, CT: Yale University Press, 2001.

Dugdale, William. *The Antiquities of Warwickshire*. London: Thomas Warren, 1656.

———. *Monasticon Anglicanum*. Translated by John Stevens. London: R. Harbin, 1718 [1655–1673].

———. *A Short View of the Late Troubles in England*. London, 1685.

Duncan-Jones, Katherine. '"Much Ado with Red and White": The Earliest Readers of Shakespeare's *Venus and Adonis*'. *Review of English Studies* 44, no. 176 (1993): 479–501.

———. 'Ravished and Revised: The 1616 Lucrece'. *Review of English Studies*, n.s., 52, no. 208 (2001): 516–523.

———. *Sir Philip Sidney: Courtier Poet*. London: Hamish Hamilton, 1991.

Dutton, Richard. *Mastering the Revels: The Regulation and Censorship of English Renaissance Drama*. Iowa City: University of Iowa Press, 1991.

———. '*Volpone* and Beast Fable: Early Modern Analogic Reading'. *Huntington Library Quarterly* 67, no. 3 (2004): 347–370.

Elizabeth I. *Collected Works*. Edited by L. S. Marcus, J. Mueller, and M. B. Rose. Chicago: University of Chicago Press, 2000.

Ellis, Jim. 'Embodying Dislocation: *A Mirror for Magistrates* and Property Relations'. *Renaissance Quarterly* 53, no. 4 (2000): 1032–1053.

Elyot, Sir Thomas. *The Book Named the Governor*. Edited by John Major. New York: Teacher's College Press, 1970.

Erickson, Carolly. *The First Elizabeth*. London: Macmillan, 1983.

Finnis, John, and Patrick Martin. 'Another Turn for the Turtle'. *Times Literary Supplement*, no. 5220 (13 April 2003).

Fissell, Mark Charles. *English Warfare, 1511–1642*. London: Routledge, 2016.

Foley, Henry. *Records of the English Province of the Society of Jesus: Historic Facts Illustrative of the Labours and Sufferings of Its Members in the Sixteenth and Seventeenth Centuries*. London: Burns and Oats, 1877.

Fuller, Thomas. *The Church History of Britain*. London: John Williams, 1655.

Gajda, Alexandra. *The Earl of Essex and Late Elizabethan Political Culture*. Oxford: Oxford University Press, 2012.

———. 'The Earl of Essex and "Politic History"'. In *Essex: The Cultural Impact of an Elizabethan Courtier*, edited by Annaliese Connolly and Lisa Hopkins. Manchester: Manchester University Press, 2013.

———. '*The State of Christendom*: History, Political Thought and the Essex Circle'. *Historical Research* 81, no. 213 (2008): 423–446.

Garrison, J., and K. Pivetti. *Sexuality and Memory in Early Modern England*. London: Routledge, 2015.

Gazzard, H. '"Those Graue Presentments of Antiquitie": Samuel Daniel's *Philotas* and the Earl of Essex'. *Review of English Studies* 51, no. 203 (2000): 423–450.

Gee, Henry, and William John Hardy, eds. *Documents Illustrative of English Church History*. New York: Macmillan, 1896.

Gerson, Armand J. 'The English Recusants and the Spanish Armada'. *American Historical Review* 22, no. 3 (1917): 589–594.

Go, Kenji. 'The Bawdy "Talent" to "Occupy" in *Cymbeline*, the "Complaint of Rosamond", and the Elizabethan Homily for Rogation Week'. *Review of English Studies* 54, no. 213 (2003): 27–51.

Greenblatt, Stephen. *Shakespearean Negotiations*. Oxford: Oxford University Press, 1989.

Gurr, A., and F. Karim-Cooper, *Moving Shakespeare Indoors*. Cambridge: Cambridge University Press, 2014.

Guy, John. *Elizabeth: The Forgotten Years*. London: Penguin, 2016.

Hadfield, Andrew, ed. *Literature and Censorship in Renaissance England*. London: Palgrave Macmillan, 2001.

———. *Shakespeare and Renaissance Politics*. Arden Critical Companions. London: Bloomsbury, 2014.

Hall, Edward. *Chronicle*. London: Longman, 1809 [1547].

Hammer, Paul E. J. 'The Accession Day Celebrations of 1595'. In *The Politics of the Stuart Court Masque*, edited by David Bevington and Peter Holbrook. Cambridge, 1998.

———. 'The Earl of Essex'. In *The Oxford Handbook of the Age of Shakespeare*, edited by R. Smuts. Oxford: Oxford University Press, 2016.

———. 'The Earl of Essex and Elizabethan Parliaments'. *Parliamentary History* 34, no. 1 (2015): 90–110.

———. *Elizabeth's Wars: War, Government and Society in Tudor England, 1544–1604*. London: Palgrave Macmillan, 2003.

————. *The Polarisation of Elizabethan Politics: The Political Career of Robert Devereux, 2nd Earl of Essex, 1585–1597*. Cambridge: Cambridge University Press, 2005.

————. 'Shakespeare's *Richard II*, the Play of 7 February 1601, and the Essex Rising'. *Shakespeare Quarterly* 59, no. 1 (2008): 1–35.

Harington, John. *The Epigrams of Sir John Harington*. Edited by Gerard Kilroy. Farnham: Ashgate, 2009.

————. *The Metamorphosis of Ajax: A Cloacinean Satire*. London: Chiswick, C. Whittingham, 1814.

————. *A New Discourse of a Stale Subject, Called The Metamorphosis of Ajax*. Edited by Elizabeth Donno. London: Routledge, 1962.

Harris, Brice. 'The Ape in "Mother Hubberd's Tale"'. *Huntington Library Quarterly* 4, no. 2 (1941): 191–203.

Hayne, Victoria. '"All Language Then Is Vile": The Theatrical Critique of Political Rhetoric in Nathaniel Lee's Lucius Junius Brutus'. *ELH* 63, no. 2 (1996): 337–365.

Heinemann, Margot. 'Rebel Lords, Popular Playwrights, and Political Culture: Notes on the Jacobean Patronage of the Earl of Southampton'. *Yearbook of English Studies* 21 (1991): 63–86.

Herbert, George. *The Temple*. London: S. Roycroft for R.S., 1679.

Higgins, John, Thomas Blenerhasset, and Lily Bess Campbell. *Mirror for Magistrates*. Cambridge: Cambridge University Press, 1946.

Hill, Christopher. *The Century of Revolution*. London: Routledge, 1980.

Hiscock, Andrew. 'Achilles Alter'. In *Essex: The Cultural Impact of an Elizabethan Courtier*, edited by Annaliese Connolly and Lisa Hopkins. Manchester: Manchester University Press, 2013.

Holaday, Allan. *Thomas Heywood's* The Rape of Lucrece. Urbana: University of Illinois Press, 1950.

Howell, T. *Cobbett's Complete Collection of State Trials and Proceedings for High Treason and Other Crimes and Misdemeanours from the Earliest Period to the Year 1783, with Notes and Other Illustrations*. London: Longman, 1822.

Hoyle, R. 'The Origins of the Dissolution of the Monasteries. *Historical Journal* 38, no. 2 (1995): 275–305.

Hughes, Philip. *The Reformation in England*. Vol. 1, London: Hollis and Carter, 1950; vol. 2, London: Hollis and Carter, 1954; vol. 3, London: Hollis and Carter, 1954.

Hughes, Ted. *Shakespeare and the Goddess of Complete Being*. London: Faber and Faber, 1992.

Hurstfield, Joel. 'Lord Burghley as Master of the Court of Wards, 1561–98'. *Transactions of the Royal Historical Society* 31 (1949): 95–114.

Husselby, J., and P. Henderson. 'Location, Location, Location! Cecil House in the Strand'. *Architectural History* 45 (2002): 159–193.

James, Mervyn. *Society, Politics and Culture*. Cambridge: Cambridge University Press, 1988.

Joseph, Miriam. *Shakespeare's Use of the Arts of Language*. Philadelphia: Dry Books, 2005.

Kastan, David Scott. *A Will to Believe: Shakespeare and Religion*. Oxford: Oxford University Press, 2014.

Keats, John. *The Letters of John Keats*, vol. 1. Edited by Hyder Edward Rollins. Cambridge: Cambridge University Press, 2012.

Kerrigan, John, ed. *Motives of Woe: Shakespeare and 'Female Complaint'. A Critical Anthology*. Oxford: Oxford University Press, 2002.

Kerrigan, John. *On Shakespeare and Early Modern Literature: Essays*. Oxford: Oxford University Press, 2001.

Kietzman, Mary Jo. "'What Is Hecuba to Him or [S]he to Hecuba?' Lucrece's Complaint and Shakespearean Poetic Agency'. *Modern Philology* 97, no. 1 (1999): 21–45.

Kilroy, Gerard. *Edmund Campion: A Scholarly Life*. Farnham, UK: Ashgate, 2015.

Klause, John. *Shakespeare, the Earl, and the Jesuit*. Oxford: Oxquarry Boks Online, 2008.

Kneidel, Gregory. 'Coscus, Queen Elizabeth, and Law in John Donne's "Satyre II"'. *Renaissance Quarterly* 61, no. 1 (2008): 92–121.

Knight, G. Wilson. *The Crown of Life*. Oxford: Oxford University Press, 1947.

———. *The Wheel of Fire*. Oxford: Oxford University Press, 1930.

Knowles, David. *Bare Ruined Choirs*. Cambridge: Cambridge University Press, 1959.

Kolin, Philip C., ed. *Venus and Adonis: Critical Essays*. London: Psychology Press, 1997.

Lacey, Robert. *Robert, Earl of Essex: An Elizabethan Courtier*. London: Weidenfeldt, 1971.

Lake, Peter. *How Shakespeare Put Politics on the Stage: Power and Succession in the History Plays*. New Haven, CT: Yale University Press, 2016.

Languet, Hubert. *Vindiciae contra tyrannos: A Defence of Liberty Against Tyrants*. Edited by Richard Baldwin. London, 1689 [1579].

Lee, Nathaniel. *Lucius Junius Brutus*. Dublin, 1763.

Lingard, John. *A History of England*. London: Dolman, 1849.

Loades, David. *The Cecils*. London: Bloomsbury, 2013.

Longworth de Chambrun, Clara. *Shakespeare: A Portrait Restored*. London: Hollis and Carter, 1957.

Lucas, Scott C. *A Mirror for Magistrates and the Politics of the English Reformation*. Amherst: University of Massachusetts Press, 2009.

MacCulloch, Diarmaid. *Reformation: Europe's House Divided, 1490–1700*. London: Penguin, 2003.

Macray, William Dunn, ed. *The Pilgrimage to Parnassus with the Two Parts of The Return from Parnassus*. Oxford: Clarendon Press, 1886.

Major, Emma. *Madam Britannia*. Oxford: Oxford University Press, 2011.

Manning, Peter J. 'The History of Cobbett's "A History of the Protestant 'Reformation'"', *Huntington Library Quarterly* 64, no. 3/4 (2001): 429–443.

Martindale, Charles, and Colin Burrow. 'Clapham's *Narcissus*: A Pre-Text for Shakespeare's *Venus and Adonis*?' *English Literary Renaissance* 22, no. 2 (1992): 147–176.

McCoy, Richard C. *The Rites of Knighthood*. Berkeley: University of California Press, 1989.

Mears, Natalie. 'Regnum Cecilianum? A Cecilian Perspective of the Court'. In *The Reign of Elizabeth I: Court and Culture in the Last Decade*, edited by John Guy. Cambridge: Cambridge University Press, 1995.

Milward, Peter. *Elizabethan Controversialists*. Campbell, CA: Fastpencil, 2012.

The Mirror for Magistrates, vol. 1. Edited by Joseph Haslewood. London: Lackington, Allen, and Longman, Hurst, Rees, Orme, and Brown, 1815.

Moore, Roger E. 'The Hidden History of *Northanger Abbey*: Jane Austen and the Dissolution of the Monasteries'. *Religion & Literature* 43, no. 1 (2011): 55–80.

———. *Jane Austen and the Reformation: Remembering the Sacred Landscape*. London: Taylor and Francis, 2016.

More, Cresacre. *The Life of Thomas More*. London: W. Pickering, 1828.

More, Thomas. *The Complete Works of St. Thomas More*. Edited by Clarence H. Miller and Stephen M. Foley. New Haven, CT: Yale University Press, 1984.

Morgan, Hiram. 'The Fall of Sir John Perrot'. In *The Reign of Elizabeth I: Court and Culture in the Last Decade*, edited by John Guy. Cambridge: Cambridge University Press, 1995.

Nashe, Thomas. *The Unfortunate Traveller and Other Works*. Edited by J. B. Steane. London: Penguin, 1972.

Nelson, Alan H. *Monstrous Adversary: The Life of Edward de Vere, 17th Earl of Oxford*. Liverpool: Liverpool University Press, 2003.

Parry, Graham. *The Trophies of Time: English Antiquarians of the Seventeenth Century*. Oxford: Oxford University Press, 1995.

Parsons, Robert (pseudonym Doleman). *A Conference About the Next Succession to the Crowne of Ingland*. [Amsterdam?], 1594.

Patterson, Annabel M. *Censorship and Interpretation: The Conditions of Writing and Reading in Early Modern England*. Madison: University of Wisconsin Press, 1991.

Peck, Francis. *Desiderata Curiosa*. London, 1732.

Phillips, Joshua. *English Fictions of Communal Identity, 1485–1603*. London: Routledge, 2016.

Picard, Lisa. *Elizabethan London*. London: Weidenfeld and Nicholson, 2003.

Platt, Michael. "'The Rape of Lucrece" and the Republic for Which It Stands'. *Centennial Review* 19, no. 2 (1975): 59–79.

Primeau, Ronald. 'Daniel and the Mirror Tradition: Dramatic Irony in "The Complaint of Rosamond"'. *Studies in English Literature, 1500–1900* 15, no. 1 (1975): 21–36.

Questier, Michael. *Catholicism and Community in Early Modern England*. Cambridge: Cambridge University Press, 2008.

Quintrell, B. W. 'The Practice and Problems of Recusant Disarming, 1585–1641'. *Recusant History* 17, no. 2 (1985): 208–222.

Raath, A., and S. De Freitas. 'Rebellion, Resistance and a Swiss Brutus?' *Historical Journal* 48, no. 1 (2005): 1–26.

Rabb, Theodore K. *Jacobean Gentleman: Sir Edwin Sandys, 1561–1629*. Princeton, NJ: Princeton University Press, 1998.

Rhodes, Neil. 'Shakespeare's Popularity and the Origins of the Canon'. In *The Elizabethan Top Ten: Defining Print Popularity in Early Modern England*, edited by Andy Kesson and Emma Smith. Farnham, UK: Ashgate, 2013.

Roper, Lyndal. *Martin Luther, Renegade and Prophet*. London: Penguin, 2016.

Ryrie, Alec. 'Reformations'. In *A Social History of England, 1500–1750*, edited by Keith Wrightson. Cambridge: Cambridge University Press, 2017.

Sanchez, Melissa E. *Erotic Subjects: The Sexuality of Politics in Early Modern English Literature*. Oxford: Oxford University Press, 2011.

Schilling, Heinz. *Martin Luther: Rebel in an Age of Upheaval*. Oxford: Oxford University Press, 2017.

Schwartz-Leeper, Gavin E. *From Princes to Pages: The Literary Lives of Cardinal Wolsey, Tudor England's 'Other King'*. Leiden: Brill, 2016.

Shakespeare, William. *The Oxford Shakespeare: The Complete Sonnets and Poems*. Edited by Colin Burrow. Oxford: Oxford University Press, 2008.

———. *The Poems: Venus and Adonis, The Rape of Lucrece, The Phoenix and the Turtle, The Passionate Pilgrim, A Lover's Complaint*. Edited by John Roe. Cambridge, 1992.

———. *Shakespeare's Poems*. Edited by Katherine Duncan-Jones and H. R. Woudhuysen. The Arden Shakespeare. London: Bloomsbury, 2007.

———. *Shakespeare's Sonnets*. Edited by Katherine Duncan-Jones. The Arden Shakespeare. London: Bloomsbury, 1997.

———. *The Sonnets and A Lover's Complaint*. Edited by John Kerrigan. London: Penguin, 1986.

Sharon-Zisser, Shirley. *Critical Essays on Shakespeare's A Lover's Complaint: Suffering Ecstasy*. London: Routledge, 2006.

Shell, Alison. *Shakespeare and Religion*. The Arden Shakespeare. London: Bloomsbury, 2010.

Sherbrook, Michael. 'The Fall of Religious Houses' (c. 1591). In *Tudor Treatises*, edited by A. G. Dickens. Leeds, UK: Yorkshire Archeological Society, 1959.

Shulman, Nicola. *Graven with Diamonds: The Many Lives of Thomas Wyatt.* London: Short Books, 2012.

Sidney, Sir Philip, Ben Jonson, Abraham Cowley, et al. *English Essays: Sidney to Macaulay.* Harvard Classics, vol. 27. New York: P. F. Collier and Son, 1909–1914.

Skilliter, S. A. *William Harborne and the Trade with Turkey, 1578–1582.* Oxford: Oxford University Press, 1977.

Smith, Peter J. 'Rome's Disgrace: The Politics of Rape in Shakespeare's "Lucrece"'. *Critical Survey* 17, no. 3 (2005): 15–26.

Snow, Vernon F. 'New Light on the Last Days and Death of Henry Wriothesley, Earl of Southampton'. *Huntington Library Quarterly* 37, no. 1 (1973): 59–69.

Southwell, Robert. *Two Letters and Short Rules of a Good Life.* Edited by Nancy Pollard Brown. Charlottesville: University Press of Virginia, 1973.

Spelman, Henry. *The History and Fate of Sacrilege Discover'd by Example . . . Wrote in the Year 1632.* Edited by R. Twisden. London, 1853.

Spenser, Edmund. *Complaints.* In *Spenser, Poetical Works*, edited by J. C. Smith and E. de Selincourt. Oxford: Oxford University Press, 1912 [1591].

Spykman, Gordon J. *Reformational Theology.* Grand Rapids, MI: William B. Eerdmans, 1992.

Stone, Lawrence. *Family and Fortune: Studies in Aristocratic Finance in the Sixteenth and Seventeenth Centuries.* Oxford: Oxford University Press, 1973.

Stopes, Charlotte Carmichael. *The Life of Henry, Third Earl of Southampton, Shakespeare's Patron.* Cambridge: Cambridge University Press, 1922.

Swärdh, Anna. *Rape and Religion in English Renaissance Literature.* Uppsala, Sweden: Acta Universitatis Upsaliensis, 2003.

Tanner, J. R. *Constitutional Documents of the Reign of James I.* Cambridge: Cambridge University Press, 1930.

Taylor, Marion A. *Bottom Thou Art Translated: Political Allegory in A Midsummer Night's Dream and Related Literature.* Amsterdam: Rodopi, 1973.

Thompson, J. A. K. *Shakespeare and the Classics.* London: Allen and Unwin, 1952.

Tillotson, Kathleen. 'Michael Drayton as a "Historian" in the "Legend of Cromwell"'. *Modern Language Review* 34, no. 2 (1939): 186–200.

Tytler, Patrick Fraser. *Life of Walter Raleigh.* Edinburgh: Oliver and Boyd; London: Simpkin and Marshall, 1833.

Valbuena Olga L. *Subjects to the King's Divorce: Equivocation, Infidelity, and*

Resistance in Early Modern England. Bloomington: Indiana University Press, 2003.

Vaughan, Robert. *History of England Under the House of Stuart*, vol. 1. London: Baldwin and Cradock, 1840.

Vickers, Nancy. 'This Heraldry in Lucrece' Face'. *Poetics Today* 6, no. 1/2 (1985): 171–184.

Walker, Greg. *Plays of Persuasion: Drama and Politics at the Court of Henry VIII.* Cambridge: Cambridge University Press, 1991.

———. *Writing Under Tyranny.* Oxford: Oxford University Press, 2005.

Walsham, Alexandra. *Catholic Reformation in Protestant Britain.* London: Routledge, 2016.

———. *The Reformation of the Landscape.* Oxford: Oxford University Press, 2011.

Warner, J. C. *Henry VIII's Divorce: Literature and the Politics of the Printing Press.* New York: Boydell, 1999.

Wecter, Dixon. 'Shakespeare's Purpose in *Timon of Athens*'. *PMLA* 43, no. 3 (1928): 701–721.

Weston, William. *William Weston: The Autobiography of an Elizabethan.* Translated by Philip Caraman. London: Longmans, 1955.

Williams, C. H. 'In Search of the Queen'. In *Elizabethan Government and Society*, edited by S. T. Bindoff, J. Hurstfield, and C. H. Williams. London: Athlone Press, 1961.

Wilson, Ian. *Shakespeare: The Evidence.* London: Headline, 1993.

Wilson, R. Rawdon. *Shakespearean Narrative.* Newark: University of Delaware Press, 1995.

Wilson, Richard. *Secret Shakespeare: Studies in Theatre, Religion and Resistance.* Manchester: Manchester University Press, 2004.

Winston-Allen, Anne. *Stories of the Rose.* Philadelphia: Penn State University Press, 1997.

Yeats, W. B. *Collected Poems of W. B. Yeats.* Edited by Richard J. Finneran. New York: Simon and Schuster, 2008.

Young, Francis. *A Medieval Book of Magical Stones: The Peterborough Lapidary.* Cambridge, 2016.

Zapalac, Kristin. *In His Image and Likeness.* Ithaca, NY: Cornell University Press, 1990.

ILLUSTRATION CREDITS

Lucretia, **Rembrandt:** Wikimedia Commons, revision as of 5 July 2017, 02:09 UTC, 11 December 2017, 18:08, https://commons.wikimedia .org/w/index.php?title=File:Rembrandt_van_Rijn_-_Lucretia_-_Google _Art_Project.jpg&oldid=250330089.

Frontispiece to Dugdale's *Monasticon*, engraving, Hollar: William Dugdale, *Monasticon Anglicanum*, vol. 1, 2nd ed. (London: Printed by Christopher Wilkinson, 1682). From the frontispiece by Wenceslaus Hollar.

Pegasus and Apollo, engraving: Artokoloro Quint Lox Limited / Alamy Stock Photo.

Southampton in the Tower, John de Critz: Wikimedia Commons, revision as of 17 September 2017, 09:02 UTC, 11 December 2017, 18:12, https://commons.wikimedia.org/w/index.php?title=File :Wriothesley_southampton.jpg&oldid=258840779.

View of Troy Burning, **Johann Georg Trautmann:** Johann Georg Trautmann, *Blick auf das brennende Troja*, Wikimedia Commons, revision as of 5 December 2017, 15:22 UTC, 11 December 2017, 18:17, https:// commons.wikimedia.org/w/index.php?title=File:J_G_Trautmann_Das _brennende_Troja.jpg&oldid=270735285.

England Divided, woodcut: 'The Kingdomes Monster Uncloaked from Heaven', from a Puritan broadside of 1643, British Museum Library, 669, f. 8/24, and C.20, f. 'Luttrell Collection', vol. 3, p. 118. Described in the *Catalogue of Prints and Drawings in the British Museum*, vol. 1, p. 268.

William Cecil: William Cecil, 1st Baron Burghley (1520–1598), attributed to Marcus Gheeraerts the Younger, 1598. National Portrait Gallery, London.

Robert Cecil: Robert Cecil, Lord Salisbury (1563–1612), by unknown artist, after John de Critz the Elder, oil on panel, 1602, National Portrait Gallery, London.

Robert Devereux: Robert Devereux, 2nd Earl of Essex, K.G. (1566–1601) (gouache and ink on vellum laid down on card), Isaac Oliver (c. 1565–1617), Yale Center for British Art, Paul Mellon Collection, USA / Bridgeman Images.

Map of Elizabethan London, Georg Braun and Franz Hogenberg: *Folgerpedia*, Folger Shakespeare Library, accessed 8 December 2017, http://folgerpedia.folger.edu.

Plan of Essex House: Artokoloro Quint Lox Limited / Alamy Stock Photo.

INDEX

Magdalen Howard

CLARE ASQUITH, the Countess of Oxford and Asquith, is an independent scholar and the author of *Shadowplay: The Hidden Beliefs and Coded Politics of William Shakespeare*. She studied English literature at St Anne's College Oxford, where she gained a congratulatory First, and spent the early part of her married life in Eastern Europe, where her husband was posted as a diplomat. Her ideas about Shakespeare's political and religious standpoint were first raised in the *Shakespeare Newsletter* in 1999 and the *Times Literary Supplement* in 2001. Since then she has written numerous reviews and articles and has lectured on Shakespeare in England, Europe, Russia, and America.

PublicAffairs is a publishing house founded in 1997. It is a tribute to the standards, values, and flair of three persons who have served as mentors to countless reporters, writers, editors, and book people of all kinds, including me.

I. F. STONE, proprietor of *I. F. Stone's Weekly*, combined a commitment to the First Amendment with entrepreneurial zeal and reporting skill and became one of the great independent journalists in American history. At the age of eighty, Izzy published *The Trial of Socrates*, which was a national bestseller. He wrote the book after he taught himself ancient Greek.

BENJAMIN C. BRADLEE was for nearly thirty years the charismatic editorial leader of *The Washington Post*. It was Ben who gave the *Post* the range and courage to pursue such historic issues as Watergate. He supported his reporters with a tenacity that made them fearless and it is no accident that so many became authors of influential, best-selling books.

ROBERT L. BERNSTEIN, the chief executive of Random House for more than a quarter century, guided one of the nation's premier publishing houses. Bob was personally responsible for many books of political dissent and argument that challenged tyranny around the globe. He is also the founder and longtime chair of Human Rights Watch, one of the most respected human rights organizations in the world.

· · ·

For fifty years, the banner of Public Affairs Press was carried by its owner Morris B. Schnapper, who published Gandhi, Nasser, Toynbee, Truman, and about 1,500 other authors. In 1983, Schnapper was described by *The Washington Post* as "a redoubtable gadfly." His legacy will endure in the books to come.

Peter Osnos, *Founder*